minority canadians 1

Native Peoples

EDITED BY

Jean Leonard Elliott

Department of Sociology and Anthropology
Dalhousie University

PRENTICE-HALL P OF CANADA LTD.

Scarborough h Ontario

For Katherine Dupré Lumpkin

© 1971 by Prentice-Hall of Canada, Ltd.
Scarborough, Ontario

PRENTICE-HALL, INC., ENGLEWOOD CLIFFS, NEW JERSEY
PRENTICE-HALL INTERNATIONAL, INC., LONDON
PRENTICE-HALL OF AUSTRALIA, PTY., LTD., SYDNEY
PRENTICE-HALL OF INDIA PVT., LTD., NEW DELHI
PRENTICE-HALL OF JAPAN, INC., TOKYO

Library of Congress Catalog Card No. 71 - 155710

13-584623-4 (pa)
13-584631-5 (cl)

PRINTED IN CANADA   3 4 5   75 74 73 72

Table of Contents

INTRODUCTION

ESKIMO

INDIAN

METIS

CONTENTS OF VOLUME 2

Preface

Canada's history has left a legacy of social inequality to various disadvantaged ethnic groups. In fact, minority Canadians such as the Metis are uniquely a product of the Canadian experience. The articles included in this reader attempt to analyze the status of minority groups within the framework of modern Canadian society. The contributing authors try to go beyond the usual descriptive accounts of ethnic life and inter-group relations in order to explain the social processes responsible for creating and perpetuating minority groups, and forecast their future standing in Canadian society.

The minority group studies selected illustrate the dynamics of prejudice and discrimination and analyse the institutional structures responsible for the continuance of minority groups in our complex society. In addition the studies chosen present a geographic cross-section of Canada's minorities. Indians, Eskimos and Metis are discussed in Volume 1., *Native Peoples,* and racial, religious and national origin ethnic groups in Volume 2., *Immigrant Groups.* It is hoped that *Minority Canadians* will provide valuable material for students of minority groups, social change, Canadian society and Canadian social problems.

I wish to thank the contributers to *Minority Canadians* for their patience with my editorial style, and the publishers and editors who have allowed previously published articles to be reprinted here.

I gratefully acknowledge by indebtedness and my wholehearted appreciation to Bridget Trim and Maree Leung for typing this manuscript, and to Janet Ross for her assistance with the French translations.

Minority Canadians benefited from the financial assistance granted by the Committee for the Development of Research in the Humanities and Social Sciences, Dalhousie University, Halifax, Nova Scotia.

J.L.E.

1
Minority Groups:
A Canadian Perspective

Jean Leonard Elliott

All Canadians at birth belong to either a majority or a minority group. Membership in the majority group is heavily dependent upon such physical and social attributes as white skin, English-speaking parents, and Christian ancestors who emigrated to Canada from a Western European industrial nation. All other Canadians belong to a variety of minority groups because they occupy a relatively disadvantaged power position in the Canadian social structure.

At first glance, it may not be apparent that minority groups are disadvantaged relative to the majority. It is commonly accepted by Canadians that their society is egalitarian. Immigrants have been drawn by this ideology to Canada's shores, seeking a higher standard of living as well as political and personal freedom. In spite of society's beliefs in fair play and the inherent worth and dignity of man, our society suffers from ethnic and social class prejudice and discrimination. Therefore, if we are to sense the meaning of a minority group as a disadvantaged group *vis à vis* the majority, it is necessary to develop an analytical definition of the terms *majority* and *minority*.

1. THE MAJORITY GROUP

The majority group in any society may or may not constitute a numerical majority. A majority group is termed *majority* because it exerts influence and possesses or controls the bulk of the power within a given society. Moreover, the *establishment* staffs its ranks primarily from the majority group. The establishment consists of the upper social classes, in general, and specifically, those individuals who act in a decision-making capacity in such spheres as government and Big Business, and belong to prestigious occupational groups.

Since the establishment tends to be drawn from the majority group, it follows that the culture of the majority is the one which tends to be transmitted *via* the public school and the mass media.[1] Consequently, the values, beliefs, and dreams of the majority group are synonymous with mainstream Canadian culture. Groups outside the mainstream, i.e., *minority groups,* may be either passively neglected or actively discriminated against by the larger society.

2. MINORITY GROUPS

One element in the definition of a minority group is a shared physical, social, or cultural characteristic that sets the group apart from the larger society. The distinguishing characteristic responsible for the group's subjection to unequal and differential treatment is usually an "ascribed" rather than an "achieved" characteristic. Examples of ascribed statuses important in Canada are skin colour, mother tongue, religious heritage, and national origin. That is to say, a person literally is born a minority Canadian. A final element in the definition of a minority group concerns the group's awareness of itself as possessors of a depressed status relative to other groups in society. A minority group usually senses the fact that it does not fully participate in the life of the larger society.

A broader definition of a minority group is needed, however, to include those minorities which are not the collective targets of discrimination by the host society, but are minorities because they are cultural "drop-outs". These minorities have an identity which sets them apart from other groups and limits their participation in the larger society. For example, the Hutterite minority does not participate fully in all institutions of the larger society because of the communal nature of their religious life. Thus the Hutterites may be considered to be a voluntary minority group in comparison with the involuntary minority status of for example, native people.

In short, a group is a minority group if (a) its culture is not the one transmitted by agents of socialization controlled by the larger society and (b) its members are under-represented in decision-making bodies. In addition, the minority tends to be subjectively aware of its "differentness" and makes we/they distinctions concerning its own members and members of the dominant society.

3. ETHNIC GROUPS

"Minority" and "ethnic" are adjectives that tend to be used interchangeably to describe groups which share a common language, race, religion, or national origin other than that of the dominant or core group. If "minority" and "ethnic" are treated as synonyms, the particular reference to *power* in the term "minority group" is lost. The obfuscation takes place because an ethnic group need not be in a disadvantaged position *vis à vis* other ethnic groups. (In fact, a majority group may be composed of numerous ethnic groups.) A minority group, by definition, is disadvantaged with respect to the power it has to control its own destiny.

Whether an ethnic group is a minority group may vary from one region of the country to another, may change over time, and may reflect individual differences in sensitivity and experience. For these reasons in Canada it is impossible to specify with any accuracy all ethnic groups which are minority groups and all ethnic groups which are subsumed under the heading of the majority. The blatant exception to this statement is the British ethnic group. The British as a *charter group*[2] in Canada consistently have enjoyed higher status in the larger Canadian society than any other ethnic group. In some instances the French, also a charter group, have attained positions of privilege and power equal to those of the British. Nevertheless, it could be argued that all ethnic groups which have not completely assimilated the British model are potentially minority groups because the prevailing cultural, economic, and political winds tend to blow against them.

4. MINORITIES OTHER THAN ETHNIC MINORITIES

There are minority groups in Canada which cross cut ethnic groups, e.g., women and the poor. Women constitute an oppressed social category because they tend to be exploited in the market place and in the home. Differential sex role socialization places most women in an inferior position to men. Moreover, economically disadvantaged females suffer from the double burden of poverty and minority sex status.[3] Being poor involves more than not having an adequate share of society's resources; the poor often bear the additional burden of being morally stigmatized. Status inequality in Canada is perpetuated by the social class system.

Although women and the poor are not included in the framework of this reader, it is necessary to point out that while many minority groups are ethnic groups, minorities may also be conceptualized as disadvantaged social categories and classes.[4]

[1] For a discussion of this phenomenon see Howard S. Becker, "Schools and Systems of Stratification," in A.H. Halsey, J. Floud, and C.A. Anderson (eds.), *Education, Economy, and Society* (New York: Free Press of Glencoe, 1961).

[2] The charter group concept is developed by John Porter in *The Vertical Mosaic*, (Toronto: University of Toronto Press, 1965), especially pp. 60-61.

[3] The minority position of women is thoroughly documented in the *Report of the Royal Commission on the Status of Women in Canada*, (Ottawa: Queen's Printer, 1970).

[4] The theme of women and the poor as minority groups is developed in H. Gamberg, "An Introduction to the Sociology of Oppression" (unpublished manuscript, Halifax: Dalhousie University, 1970).

5. WHY ARE THERE MINORITY CANADIANS?

Minorities in Canada have tended to form as the result of three basic processes — culture-contact, conflict, and migration. Each process may be illustrated by reference to a Canadian minority.

Culture-contact

Aboriginal groups — Indian and Eskimo — became minorities by virtue of a prolonged period of culture-contact with Eurocanadians. As so often is the case when western culture is superimposed upon a "primitive" one, the latter succumbs. The preliterate Stone Age culture of the Eskimos, for example, was no match for the white man's technological expertise. Culture-contact tends to result in the dislocation of the more vulnerable culture and the dominant culture's incorporation of bits and pieces from the culture with which it has come in contact. Thus majority Canadians may esteem the art of native people, but their appreciation of it is from their own vantage point, removed from the total cultural pattern in which it had its origins.

The native people, on the other hand, are becoming increasingly *acculturated*; they are taking on the dress, language, customs and values of the dominant society. In time, there will be few cultural reminders of the pre-culture-contact era which are not in some way eclectic, reflecting the unequal influence of both cultures.

Conflict

Those of French origin in Canada bear different labels — Acadian, Québecois, French Canadian, and even Metis — depending upon date of arrival, region of settlement, and intermarriage patterns. The statuses of those of French origin in Canada relate to periods of conflict followed by accommodation.

ACADIANS

The Acadians settled in Nova Scotia in the 1630's. In the eighteenth century when Britain and France struggled for control of what is now Canada, the Acadians adopted a neutral position. Their neutrality was not recognized by the British who forcibly dispersed them *en masse* in the mid 1700's. Many Acadians made their way to Louisiana; however, when the French threat was removed in the early 1760's, the British permitted some Acadians to return. Today it is estimated that one-sixth to one-fifth of the total population of Nova Scotia, New Brunswick, and Prince Edward Island are of Acadian origin; roughly two-thirds of all Acadians live in New Brunswick. Moncton is the Acadian nerve centre.[5]

The Acadians were pawns in the warfare between the British and the French, expelled as a result of religious and political conflict.

Such expulsion is one of the most severe forms discrimination may take, and is similar in ruthlessness to apartheid or even genocide.

Today Canadians, especially those outside the Maritimes, tend to lump *Acadien* and *Canadien* together. The blurring of the boundaries between the two groups may in some respects be justified, since the future of the Acadians tends to be bound up with the future of Quebec within a bilingual and bicultural Canada.

QUEBECOIS

While French Quebeckers are not a numerical minority in their "homeland", they are in a minority position with respect to the ownership and control of their economy. The bulk of Quebec's mineral resources and industry is Anglo-owned — American, British, or English-Canadian. This neo-colonial motif, an undercurrent in French-English relationships, has been brought to the surface by Quebec separatists in their bid for Quebec self-determination.

Although *les Québecois* and other Canadians are divided in their viewpoints regarding Quebec's special status in the Canadian Confederation, the fact of her special status has never been disputed. Quebec is officially recognized as a charter member group in the Canadian experiment, not a "conquered people". The institutional basis of Canadian dualism was reinforced when the 1968 Federal-Provincial Conference endorsed the recommendations of the Royal Commission on Bilingualism and Biculturalism regarding the language rights of French speakers in all provinces.[6] Some of the discrimination against French Canadians will be removed if these recommendations are implemented. In short, Anglo-conformity has never been a deliberate policy advanced by the Federal Government *vis à vis les Québecois* in spite of the British military conquest in the eighteenth century. Mutual accommodation by *les deux nations* following episodes of conflict has characterized Canadian history from its beginning.

METIS

Metis, primarily the descendants of French- and Scottish-Canadian trappers and Indians, formed the Red River Colony in territory which was to become Manitoba. The Manitoba Act of 1870 provided for the continuance of Metis self-government and language rights.

---

[5] This historical sketch of the Acadians is based upon Andrew Hill Clark, *Acadia: The Geography of Early Nova Scotia to 1760* (Madison: The University of Wisconsin Press, 1968), especially p. viii.

[6] Report of the Royal Commission on Bilingualism and Biculturalism," Book I Ottawa: Queen's Printer, 1967). **Book IV** (1970) Part 3 "The Maintenance of Language and Culture", pp. 113-136, considers the status of ethnic groups other than the French.

Momentarily the West was heralded as the new Quebec. However, Canada did not keep her promises. The Northwest Rebellion of 1885 was a brief last-ditch attempt on the part of the Metis Nation to gain recognition. When the Rebellion was quashed, the Metis minority group status was solidified once and for all.[7]

Migration

Some immigrant groups were minorities in the Old World. Religious persecution, for example, was responsible for the communal Christian sects' emigration to Canada. The immigration of the Hutterites and Mennonites involved the transplanting of a minority group from a hostile to a tolerant host society.

The "push/pull" concept has been used to explain in part why groups or individuals emigrate. The Ukrainians, for example, were *pushed* by adverse political and religious conditions and *pulled* by the promise of a stable and peaceful future in Canada. The Italian and Chinese immigrants may be pictured as being *pulled* to Canada by the lure of a higher standard of living, employment and educational opportunities.

Whatever the reasons for emigration, however, upon arriving in Canada, the non-British immigrant often assumes an "entrance status" lower than that which he occupied in his native land.[8] Language difficulties, job certification problems, "culture shock", the absence of primary group support from friends and relatives may be factors contributing to the initially depressed status of the newcomer. In time, though, some immigrants achieve upward social mobility and perhaps are assimilated into the majority group while others retain their entrance status. Why are there differences in the assimilation rates of immigrant groups?

Immigrants may differ in their desire to assimilate or retain their ethnic identity. If they wish to assimilate, their success is often directly related to their *visibility*. Race, religion, language, name, cultural customs such as dress and diet, are visible factors identifying the newcomer. Race, however, is often the one insurmountable barrier to complete assimilation. Cultural assimilation (change of language, dress, etc.) may take place, but structural assimilation (entry into professions, primary groups, etc.) may be impeded by racial visibility.[9]

6. MINORITY GROUP REACTION TO SUBORDINATE STATUS

Viewed in the extreme, ethnic minorities in Canada attempt to achieve one of two incompatible goals — survival as a distinct ethnic group or admittance into the mainstream of Canadian life. The belief in *cultural pluralism* in Canada permits ethnic groups to make this choice.[10] Conflict occurs, however, when the minority group's self-definition does not correspond with the definition of the minority group held by the wider society. The reaction of minority groups to subordinate status is varied depending upon the nature of the minority, its goals, and its tendency to accept or reject the norms of the larger society.

Acceptance

A passive acceptance of the *status quo* of the dominant society and a willingness to become acculturated often leads to assimilation. If discrimination is institutionalized in the larger society, however, only cultural assimiliation may occur, with structural assimilation curtailed.

If an active acceptance of the *status quo* and an eagerness to become Canadian is characteristic of a minority, the minority may exhibit *anglo-conformity*. Anglo-conformity demands "the complete renunciation of the immigrant's ancestral culture in favor of the behaviour and values of the Anglo-Saxon core group."[11] Although the minority group member may try repeatedly to be accepted as a Canadian, his success is often dependent upon the number of structural obstacles blocking his path. If society permits, the individual who conforms to dominant Anglo-Saxon norms and values tends to be absorbed relatively quickly even though it may take generations for the minority group as a whole. Failure and frustration, however, may be the fate of racial minorities if they evidence anglo-conformity and are barred admittance to the majority group.

Minorities wishing to retain their ethnic identity must resist social pressures favouring anglo-conformity. If they passively accept

---

[7] For a detailed account of the Metis struggle (1818-1897) see Mason Wade, *The French Canadians (1760-1967)*, Vol. 1 (Toronto: Macmillan of Canada, 1968), pp. 393-446.

[8] The phenomenon of the depressed "entrance status" is empirically documented in Anthony Richmond, *Postwar Immigrants in Canada* (Toronto: University of Toronto Press, 1967), p. 119.

[9] This distinction between cultural and structural assimilation is made by Milton Gordon, *Assimilations in American Life*, Oxford University Press, 1964.

[10] The constitutional basis of French/English dualism has also had the effect of other ethnic groups maintaining "a pluralistic form of integration with the wider society." Anthony Richmond, "Immigration and Pluralism in Canada," *The International Migration Review*, 4, 1 (Fall, 1969), p. 22.

[11] *Assimilations*, p. 85. Gordon provides an analytical discussion of the various dimensions of assimilation.

TABLE 1

Minority Reaction to Subordinate Status

| | MINORITY STRATEGY | | | |
| MINORITY GOAL | Acceptance of the status quo of the dominant society | | Rejection of the status quo of the dominant society | |
	passive	active	passive	active
Entry into majority group	assimilation	anglo-conformity	involuntary segregation	militant integration
Survival as an ethnic group	accommodation	ethnocentrism	voluntary segregation	militant separation

the *status quo* and have come to terms with the dominant group, the adjustment to minority status is termed *accommodation*. Before accommodation is reached, there is often a period of minority/majority conflict.

If a minority group member is a vocal and active advocate of ethnic survival, his adjustment to minority status may be characterized by *ethnocentrism*. Ethnocentrism is the firm conviction that one's culture is superior to that of any other ethnic group. An ethnocentric minority would believe that "one's own group is the center of everything and all others are scaled with reference to it ... [12] An ethnocentric minority may tend to be immune to assimilative forces and have a high group morale.

Table 1 presents a typology of minority group reaction to subordinate status. The minority's goal is cross-classified with a behavioural strategy compatible with the goal. Minorities are classified with respect to their acceptance or rejection of the dominant society and their wish to forfeit or retain their ethnic identity. The resulting minority action may take a relatively active or passive form and may occur on an individual or a group level.

Rejection

A minority group may be dissatisfied with the rate at which assimiliation is taking place. Although actively rejecting the *status quo,* they need not reject the core value premises underlying Canadian society. In fact, they want to be accepted as full-fledged Canadians, not hyphenated Canadians (e.g., Chinese-Canadians), or second class citizens. Such is the goal of *militant integration*. This strategy attempts to tear down those barriers which prevent the minority group from partaking of the good life of the Canadian majority.

A passive rejection of the *status quo* and a willingness to adopt a Canadian identity results in *involuntary segregation*. Subjectively, the minority group defines itself as being held back. Its members want to enjoy the full benefits of Canadian life, but are not organized in a militant way. This type of minority reaction means that the minority group is discontent with "its place" in the larger social structure, but is ineffective with respect to changing it.

Minorities concerned with cultural maintenance or ethnic survival may reject the *status quo* of the dominant society in order to achieve their desired goal. If the rejection is active, the minority's strategy may be militant separation.

In Quebec, the *Parti Québecois* may be a case in point. This legitimate political party has as its basis the self-determination of the minority. This goal may ultimately lead to the political secession of Quebec, determined by the ballot box. The goal of militant separation, however, can also lead to revolution. This result could be expected if the ascendency of the outlawed *Front de Libération du Québec* occurred.

An alternate strategy a minority group may adopt if it rejects the *status quo* of the dominant society and has a survival ideology, is *voluntary segregation*. Voluntary segregationists physically and culturally withdraw from the larger society and establish their own (often utopian) community. This self-segregated minority group co-exists within the larger society, but systematically avoids contact with the dominant group. Thus many self-segregated minorities live in communities which are institutionally complete. When all the needs of the minority are met within the community, contact outside the group is minimized. The Hutterite religious sect is illustrative of a minority practicing voluntary segregation.

7. PREJUDICE AND DISCRIMINATION

It is important to distinguish analytically between *prejudice* and *discrimination*. Prejudice usually refers to an attitude or predisposition to judge negatively members of the minority group. Discrimination is the behaviour which results in minorities being maltreated or

---

[12] William Graham Sumner, *Folkways* (Boston: Ginn and Co., 1906), p. 13. A majority group by definition is characterized by ethnocentrism.

excluded. Most frequently there is a high correlation between prejudiced attitudes and discriminatory behaviour, but the two need not be correlated. For example, social institutions may prohibit prejudiced individuals from engaging in discriminatory acts.[13] And conversely, racist institutions may negate the behaviour of well-intentioned individuals. *That is, prejudice and discrimination may be seen as properties of group structure as well as attributes of individuals.*[14]

Causes

No one theory of the causes of prejudice and discrimination can explain completely every occurrence of these phenomena. However, when taken in combination, economic and psychological theories make some of the causes of prejudice and discrimination clearer.

The economic theory presupposes conditions of scarcity. The valued resources of a society are either inadequate in an absolute sense or adequate but distributed inequitably. In the case of the latter, the poor are in competition with each other for the necessities of life — food, shelter, and employment. Consequently, if an ethnic minority is poor, it may be the subject of attack by members of an ethnic majority who also happen to be poor. An ethnic minority may serve as a scapegoat for the majority. A scapegoat is a target for collective hostility, a symbol for the majority which explains why it is poor or generally ill-fated.[15] More commonly, however, the majority is the ruling or relatively affluent class and it may morally stigmatize the minority to rationalize the oppression of an obvious underdog.[16]

Prejudice and discrimination are perhaps most severe when the poor tend to belong to one ethnic group and the rich tend to belong to a different ethnic group. This has been the case in Quebec. The French Canadians have been members of the working class, and the English Canadians have traditionally been in higher positions of authority. Consequently, tension, instead of erupting along class lines has sometimes been manifest along ethnic lines.

A psychological theory of prejudice and discrimination has as its focal point the personality structure of the individual. For example, an individual with an *authoritarian personality* tends to view the world as being populated by *the weak* and *the strong*.[17] Authoritarians by definition side with the strong and support traditional power figures. Thus the authoritarian personality, unconsciously perhaps, is prone to making prejudicial statements and discriminating against powerless minority group underdogs.

An alternative psychological explanation views the intolerant individual as one who compensates for his own insecurities by affirming the inferiority of an out-group. His self-worth is dependent upon his being superior by definition to all members of the out-group. In psychoanalytic terms, a person's fears and self-doubts may be *projected* on to the minority group. The minority group, in turn, is rejected because it allegedly possesses undesirable qualities which are actually attributes of the majority[18]

A synthesis of the economic and psychological theories of prejudice and discrimination would produce the conclusion that individual insecurities and frustrations are heightened under conditions of economic scarcity and deprivation. When minority and majority groups compete for scarce resources, the minority group becomes the unwitting target against which the majority group may direct its anger.

Consequences

Prejudice and discrimination clearly have deleterious effects both on the individual and on society. On the individual level, prejudice and discrimination often result in personality disorganization or what is commonly referred to as mental illness.[19] Minority group status is a heavy burden under which some minority members may collapse. A minority individual may not be able to function effectively or cope with a social system that is systematically designed to exclude or frustrate him. Understandably he "breaks down" or becomes personally disorganized as a result of day-to-day stresses and strains.

[13] The effects of anti-discrimination legislation on the racist beliefs of individuals is discussed by Robert K. Merton, "Discrimination and the American Creed," in R. M. McIver (ed.), Discrimination and National Welfare (New York: Harper, 1949). Also, Arnold M. Rose, "The Influence of Legislation on Prejudice," in A. M. Rose (ed.), Race Prejudice and Discrimination (New York: Knopf, 1951).

[14] For a description of the ways in which social institutions — legal, educational, and medical — discriminate against the Black in White America, see Louis L. Knowles and Kenneth Prewitt, Institutional Racism in America (Englewood Cliffs: Prentice-Hall, 1969).

[15] The classic example of a scapegoat is the tragic history of the Jew in Hitler's Germany. German Christians attributed their adverse economic plight to the Jewish presence.

[16] Whites, for example, have labelled Blacks "inferior" and Indians "childlike" in order to justify patterns of prejudice and discrimination.

[17] T. W. Adorno, et. al., The Authoritarian Personality (New York: Harper, 1950).

[18] Psychological theories of prejudice and discrimination have been elaborated by John Dollard and associates. Cf. John Dollard, Caste and Class in a Southern Town (New York: Harper and Row, 1949); John Dollard, et. al., Frustration and Aggression (New Haven: Yale University Press, 1939).

[19] William H. Grier and P. M. Cobbs, Black Rage (New York: Basic Books, 1968). Case studies of mental illness among Black people are interpreted by two Black psychiatrists.

The counterpart to personality disorganization on the societal level, of course, is social disorganization. Some indices of social disorganization are crime, unemployment, drug addiction, poverty, broken homes, and ill health. All of the above social conditions are abetted by prejudice and discrimination. Elimination of the conditions responsible for prejudice and discrimination would tend to reduce the number of "social problems" in a society.

It should be emphasized that Canada as a nation suffers if minority Canadians are not fully encouraged to participate in or contribute to Canadian society. An ethnic mosaic as a societal symbol is qualitatively different from a vertical mosaic, however, in that implicitly contained in the latter concept are ethnic groups stratified in a hierarchical order — the British and French "charter" member groups on or close to the top with power and prestige, and native peoples and other immigrant groups on the bottom. A vertical mosaic, in other words, contains minority and majority group structures. Such is not the case with an ethnic mosaic. An ethnic mosaic does not have the insidious rank-ordered ethnic stratification patterns inherent in the vertical mosaic concept. Thus an ethnic mosaic is perhaps a more accurate statement of Canada's purpose than the vertical mosaic imagery. The vertical mosaic, though, persists as a current description of the Canadian social structure.

If Canada is to bring into being a vibrant "Just Society", it cannot afford to neglect, waste, and fail to recognize minority Canadian talent. A society which draws from a talent pool limited to one group of ethnic elites and does not provide the conditions under which a national identity and involvement characterize all ethnic groups is *unjust* and quickly stagnates.

Change

A strategy for change which will reduce the level of prejudice and discrimination in a society should be linked to a theory of why prejudice and discrimination exist in the first instance. For example, according to the economic theory, prejudice and discrimination exist because minority and majority members are forced to compete for scarce resources. Canada has not provided adequate housing, employment, education and income for all its members. If the economic theory is credible, it follows that the way to reduce prejudice and discrimination is by either redistributing the valued resources of the country so that minority and majority have an equitable share, or by integrating minority Canadians into a Canadian society where economic conditions of plenty and cooperation rather than scarcity and competition prevail. A guaranteed annual income would be an important step in this direction.

Attempts to reduce prejudice and discrimination often fail because a thorough understanding of the causal factors is lacking.

Informational efforts such as "Brotherhood Weeks" are often ineffective, especially in terms of permanent social change. Educational campaigns attempting to change in-group attitudes concerning out-group members are irrelevant *if the institutional structure of society remains unchanged.* Majority Canadians may like Metis, Indians, Eskimos, and Blacks, but attitudes alone do not alter the high rate of infant mortality, substandard housing, and poor quality of life which these minority Canadians face. Social consciousness on the part of majority Canadians is of the utmost importance, of course, if it leads to concrete social action.

The most effective type of education related to the reduction of prejudice and discrimination is not formal didactic instruction. Effective education is that which involves majority and minority in *cooperative equal-status contact.*[20] Equal status contact is interaction that takes place between occupants of the same position in the social structure, e.g., soldiers of the same rank, hockey players on the same team, housewives of the same social class, students in the same program of studies, etc. As the result of prejudice and discrimination, however, few minority and majority group members have the opportunity to interact on an equal status basis. Therefore a society intent upon reducing prejudice and discrimination cannot rely upon equal status contact as a major strategy for social change.

A strategy for change used increasingly by minority groups in North America in recent years is *confrontation.* Non-violent confrontation is often an attempt on the part of the minority group to educate the general public directly, inform the power structure of their demands, solicit support from the mass media, and build morale among their own ranks which will sustain them in future action. Violent confrontation is seen as the next step; this strategy attempts to institute immediate social change either by reform from the existing social structure or revolutionary action establishing a new social system.[21]

Regardless of various social change efforts, however, the relative status positions of minority and majority groups in any social system tend to persist over time. Change is especially difficult to bring about in Canada because ethnic group membership and social class position

---

[20] *Cf.* Morton Deutsch and Mary E. Collins, *Interracial Housing* (University of Minnesota Press, 1951); Samuel A. Stouffer, *et. al., The American Soldier,* Vol. I (Princeton: Princeton University Press, 1949); Allison Davis, "Acculturation in Schools," in M. L. Barron, ed., *American Minorities* (New York: Knopf, 1957).

[21] For an assessment of this strategy for radical social change in the United States, see Lewis M. Killian, *The Impossible Revolution?* (New York: Random House, 1968).

tend to be strongly correlated. Nothing short of a radical transformation of the social class structure would change the distribution of power and prestige currently associated with the various Canadian ethnic groups.

Efforts to replace the vertical mosaic with the ethnic mosaic are often labelled *token* attempts. Such token attempts range from the hiring of a few minority Canadians by Big Business to the establishment of a scholarship program for minority students. Is there an alternative to token or piecemeal social change, given the fact that the culture of Canada may also tend to perpetuate minority and majority group status? Values, attitudes, and beliefs which are held in common by most Canadians — majority and minority alike — function to maintain the institutional arrangements of the larger society.[22]

---

[22] This statement is especially important if the shared values, attitudes, and beliefs are prejudicial to a minority group. For example, derogatory ethnic stereotypes may be believed in by all ethnic groups — even the stereotyped group. See, for example, John Harding, *et. al.*, "Prejudice and Ethnic Relations" in Gardner Lindzey, ed., *Handbook of Social Psychology*, Vol. II (New York: Addison-Wesley, 1954), pp. 1021-1061.

2

Eskimos in a Satellite Society*

Jack Ferguson

The situation in the western Arctic in the mid-sixties, if allowed to continue unabated, would transform the Eskimo into an Arctic variety of the "hill-billy." Sporadic and minimal opportunities for wage labour have partially integrated the Eskimo into a cash economy. The traditional living-off-the-land life style is no longer feasible, but a modern alternative has not been satisfactorily developed.

Although the Eskimo must adapt to a changing socio-cultural environment, the gravest problem facing him may well be symbolized by the presence of his Southern caretakers. Ferguson coins the term "satellite society" to convey the new colonialism engulfing the Eskimo. Viewed within the context of paternalism, the plight of the Eskimo as a powerless minority is clear. In the Arctic town-sites, the Eskimo tends to be physically segregated and has poorer housing than the Eurocanadian, but more important, "the government is not indigenous to the population." The Eskimo, therefore, is subtly exploited and his culture systematically "debased and pauperized."

The Eskimos of Canada's Western Arctic have had a long history of contact with white men, and their aboriginal culture is now being altered by the larger society to the south. They undoubtedly will be forced to take their place alongside other minority groups in the Canadian hegemony and in this process the unique Eskimo culture will certainly be altered if not eliminated. This process, which is changing primitive societies the world over, diminishes the richness and variety of human life, although it seems to be inexorable, and indeed wanted by many to whom it is happening.

* Initial research was sponsored by the Department of Northern Affairs and National Resources, Government of Canada, and 1966 field research was partially supported by Research Grant AINA M-46 of the Arctic Institute of North America. Printed here by permission of the author.

The Eskimos have welcomed some of the changes which have already taken place — those changes which have benefited their health and material well being. They have not welcomed many of the restrictions and controls which have been placed upon them by the Department of Indian Affairs and Northern Resources, however, or the consequent loss of human rights which has taken place in most Arctic communities. The evaluation of social and culture change described here is part of a larger systematic program of ethnological research initiated in 1956. The initial research was conducted along the Distant Early Warning radar line (DEW Line) between the Alaskan border and Boothia Peninsula — a distance of some 1200 miles, which contains relatively few settlements — for a period of about six months in 1956. It continued haphazardly during the winter of 1956-57 while I was an employee of the radar line construction company, and systematically for four months at Tuktoyaktuk, on the Mackenzie River delta, during the summer of 1957. The summer of 1958 was spent at Coppermine, on the western end of Coronation Gulf.

Following my first field trip to the Arctic I had vaguely conceptualized the research design which was to be followed. This came about through an awareness of the definite difference in Eskimo-European contact between the western area, where it had been intense, and the eastern area, where it was only becoming important at that time. Some of the older Tuktoyaktuk residents had first met white men in the 1890's, and there had been considerable numbers within the Mackenzie River delta area since that time. But Cambridge Bay, Coppermine, and the other more easterly communities had been in contact for not more than thirty years, and this contact had been much less intense. The study of Tuktoyaktuk in 1957 showed that, at least superficially, the traditional Eskimo way of life had been considerably altered. Most of the inhabitants had originally lived in other places, and the hunting and trapping economy was fast disappearing. Many of the other communities of the Western Arctic were located at or close to a DEW Line site and were being influenced by the same forces which had acted upon Tuktoyaktuk and its residents for a long period of time. Accordingly, the next community chosen for study was Coppermine, which was a distance from the DEW Line, was still relatively isolated and, presumably, had not undergone the same amount of social change. Coppermine was studied during the summer of 1958. While the earlier studies had been conducted by means of participant observation and the collection of existing documents and data, the Coppermine study proceeded by the use of a formal interview schedule and constant use of interpreters. Questions which had been asked informally by participant observation were now formalized into comparable interviews. I felt that my knowledge of Eskimo culture at this time was sufficient to eliminate participant observation as the only method of research and to concentrate upon particular subjects within the culture rather than continue broad-scale investigation. My wife and I returned to Coppermine and Tuktoyaktuk during the summer of 1966. As well as using different questionnaires for men and women — I interviewed the men, and my wife, who is also sociologist, the women — there were short questionnaires devised for male and female teenagers. The typical adult interview during the summer of 1966 took about an hour, and the teenager questionnaire about fifteen minutes. Approximately one hundred persons were interviewed.

Needless to say, the use of formal interviews does not preclude participant observation. On each field trip I have lived in a tent in the middle of the Eskimo community and have interacted with them to a high degree. This principle of field work has ensured that not only were Eskimo living conditions experienced, but that the Eskimos saw that all white men did not live in frame houses with oil stoves, and that white people could and would live in their style. This is particularly important at the present time when there is an overriding feeling among many Eskimos that the white man feels himself superior to the Eskimo way of life. During former stays I have gone fishing and whaling many times, and since this is known both at Coppermine and Tuktoyaktuk, it was not done during the 1966 field trip. We lived in a large umbrella tent at both locations and ate freeze-dried food that we had brought with us.

The locations of Tuktoyaktuk and Coppermine are very different, since Tuktoyaktuk is on a narrow sandspit projecting into the Beaufort Sea and Coppermine is located on a relatively sheltered bay at the mouth of the Coppermine River. Tuktoyaktuk is suffering from not only population crowding but from land crowding, while Coppermine has an almost unlimited amount of land for its town site. But both communities have the same problem of being located in a poor trapping area, and at a place where it is not easy to secure game animals for food. Neither location is particularly satisfactory for seal hunting and there are few resources except for fish. In both locations, this resource would appear to be sorely strained by the large population. The major difference is that Tuktoyaktuk, as a major port, has wage employment available, in a limited way, during the summer months, although the policy of not using Eskimo seamen, and the automation of cargo handling makes even this source of employment limited for the future.

CHANGE IN THE HISTORIC PERIOD

Changes in society are referred to by two different terms. Anthropologists tend to refer to culture change, and sociologists to social change. For the purposes of this paper, culture change means an enduring change in the basic values or goals of a society held by the majority of individuals.[1] Social change means a change in the relationships between individuals in society; a change in the methods of achieving the goals of the society, but does not necessarily imply a change in basic values. Presumably, one could occur without the other, but in reality social change usually precedes culture change. The occurrence of social change does not necessarily imply culture change, however, and many social changes have not changed the basic Eskimo culture, despite intensive contact with Europeans over long periods of time. For this reason the majority of changes which took place in Eskimo society up to the present would be referred to as social changes.

First contacts in this Western Arctic area were between the Eskimos and whalers at Herschel Island during the 1880's when the Eskimos were paid to hunt for food during the wintering over of those ships which did not return to their home port. Large numbers of Eskimos congregated there during the latter years of the nineteenth century. Considerable disease was introduced and the end of this period of whaling, about 1910, saw the depopulation of most of the Mackenzie River delta. This period of contact with Europeans did not greatly modify Eskimo society since the Eskimos were simply being paid to perform their normal activities. A majority did not yet have rifles and the caribou herds were still relatively intact. What had been started was more in the nature of a slow-burning fuse which would lead to explosive change in the present period when the original society has been in danger of being destroyed.

The period following initial contact — extending from about 1910 to 1950 — was one characterized by intensive application of the trapping technology. It had several consequences. First, it increased the need for store foods and other goods. The successful trapper had to spend relatively more of his time at trapping and less at hunting. This also changed the land use patterns and the areas of residence for most Eskimo bands, since the areas for successful white fox trapping were often different than those which were the best for caribou hunting, fishing, and sealing. As one result, the Eskimos tended to disperse from their traditional areas and occupy those that had been deserted for several hundred years. An example of this was the occupation in the 1920's of the coastline between Cape Parry and Clinton Point by several Eskimo and white trappers. But the Eskimos' integration into the larger economic system had disastrous consequences during the depression of the 1930's. The drop in fur prices suddenly caused great hardships among those who had become accustomed to a relatively high standard of living. Many Eskimos had constructed frame houses which required coal or fuel oil to heat; they owned large power boats or "schooners" of thirty to forty feet, and they had become accustomed to a large variety of store goods.

But the most important consequence was the effect upon Eskimo social organization. While the nuclear family was present in all of the

Eskimo communities of the Eastern, Central and Western Arctic, it was not the only, or even the most significant unit of social organization. Graburn[2] has correctly identified the importance of the Eskimo band as the major kinship form. This was normally composed of the original parents of two or more sons, their spouses and their children. It could range in size from five or six to as many as twenty or thirty persons. I had concluded that the typical Eskimo family form appeared to be of extended type but considering the analysis of Graburn, agree that it is necessary to consider a new type of kindred, as Graburn has done, when he describes the band as both a kinship and as a residential unit. Posposil has independently defined the Eskimo band as a political unit,[3] but did not place emphasis upon these kinship aspects. As described in the literature, the Eskimo band must have been necessarily exogamous, and that meant that marriage would always tend to create social ties between two bands which might otherwise be unrelated. In pre-contact times, those bands probably occupied traditional hunting areas and had relatively little contact with other bands except at specific times of the year, such as the spring sealing camps, and the gatherings for river fishing in the fall. Each band was not only a kinship group occupying a specified hunting area, but a cooperating economic unit, and a political group under the nominal direction of the head of the family — the oldest living man or woman whose sons were the active adults of the group. The fluidity of this group can be understood, since the death of the paterfamilias would tend to fragment the band. The active adults and their children would probably go to the wives' respective bands, i.e., the bands where the wives' parents were band leaders. Because of the amorphous nature of this kinship system, one could argue that the only stable form was the nuclear family. It might have been the most stable form, but it was not the most significant one. The introduction of trapping tended to break down the Eskimo band, since it placed a premium on the successful trapper, for the typical trapper did not share his furs with other members of the family as he would ordinarily share food. This tended to create nuclear family units, at least where trapping was a major part of the economy. The notion of "partnership" which was so common among Eskimos also tended to be eroded by the new trapping economy.

Trapping brought the intense individualism of the larger society to the Eskimo. He had been used to a certain individualism in his

[1] A. L. Kroeber and Talcott Parsons, "The Concept of Culture and of Social Systems". *American Sociological Review* (No. 23, 1958), pp. 582-583.

[2] Nelson H. Graburn, "Taqagmiut Eskimo Kinship Terminology". (Ottawa: Northern Coordination and Research Centre, 1964).

[3] Leonard Posposil, "Law and Social Structure among the Nunamuit Eskimo". *Explorations in Cultural Anthropology*, (New York: McGraw-Hill, 1964).

society but the introduction of a market economy intensified this. It tended to introduce new settlement patterns. Formerly, the Eskimo bands in the Copper Eskimo area had lived out on the ice in Coronation Gulf, during a greater part of the winter, hunting seals. Now the greater part of the winter was spent hunting white fox, which meant spending considerable amounts of time on the land, and travelling long distances. Brought into a trapping economy, they now found that their main source of income almost vanished. Accustomed to store goods and imported food, they discovered that they did not have the money to buy these commodities. In addition, although the price for fur continued low into the 1950's, largely because of the introduction of fur farming and synthetic substitutes, the price of all store goods continued to increase in the inflation that occurred after 1948. Most of the Eskimo population was afflicted with tuberculosis, and the average age at death was somewhere around thirty-five years of age, with an enormous infant mortality rate accompanying this. Christensen visited the Canadian Arctic in 1953 and made his assessment.[4] It was not a situation which would give anyone cause for great pride, and the Canadian government decided that something should be done. Nursing stations and schools were built and a concerted attack was made upon the major health problem — tuberculosis. Part of the reason for the great effort which was made in the early sixties was the growing interest in the north as a strategic area, and the model which was being provided by the U.S.S.R. in the development of large Siberian industrial cities. The comparison was not favorable there, nor was the comparison favorable even between the Alaskan and Canadian Arctic centers. Large amounts of money were spent during this period on the 10,000 or so Eskimo inhabitants of the Canadian Arctic.

Until the 1960's, the white inhabitants of the Arctic were either RCMP, missionaries, or Hudson Bay Company traders. The small amount of political power available for the inhabitants of this area was divided up among these groups, and most governmental decisions were based upon their viewpoints. Even now these groups hold a disproportionate influence in the administration of Eskimos. It was only in the 1950's that the Western Arctic — most of which lies in the District of Mackenzie of Canada's Northwest Territories — got any political representation through electing a Member of Parliament. His power was not a match, however, for that of the Department of Northern Affairs and National Resources, who expanded their Arctic administration enormously during the late 1950's and the early 1960's. Into most Arctic communities, or large areas with one settlement as the centre, they sent a Northern Service Officer, as he was first called. Previous to the late 1950's, most welfare was being administered by the Police, and effective government of each settlement was by the Police, the missionaries and the Hudson's Bay Company. Between about 1956 and 1966 the Northern Service Officers exerted influence in the community in several ways. All land use was controlled by the Department of Northern Affairs; all roads, and other utilities were built and controlled by them.

CHANGES IN BAND ORGANIZATION

While the family was broken apart, to a certain extent, by the introduction of trapping and the emphasis upon imported goods, what was disrupted more than anything was the system of band organization. Each band of Eskimos, which might number two or three to ten or twelve nuclear families, tended to hunt and trap in the same area, and for greater parts of the year lived in the same encampment. These bands would also meet in a larger grouping which one could call a tribe, although there certainly was no formal organization, at the spring sealing camps where trading and socializing would take place. Trapping tended to break up the band organization since it prevented the families in the band from remaining together for lengthy periods. Bands were usually formed about a dominant man or, occasionally, woman. They had as a core most often a man in his forties or fifties, two or three of his children, and their spouses and grandchildren. Because of the nature of Eskimo social organization, there was a fluidity to this band organization. Members might come or go at will and over the period of a year there might be several families that would leave or arrive, or both. The dominant bond was relationship to the band core members. Parent-child relationships were the strongest and in-law relationships probably the next strongest. These band leaders were frequently shamans and wielded more than a little of their power in this fashion. It would appear that there was also another type of shaman who wielded power through inspiring fear and through his ruthlessness. The power of band leaders was weakened by the hunting economy since they did not necessarily become good trappers, and younger men might outstrip them in wealth. So, during this period of intensive trapping their power waned, as did that of the other type of shaman because of the spreading influence of the missionaries.

In the traditional Eskimo community power had been in the hands of the band leaders who could sway public opinion through their role as paterfamilias and the respect that it engendered, and also in the hands of those men whose ability, daring, and ruthlessness were greater than average, men who were willing to take considerable chances with public opinion and were willing to risk public censure and possibly physical assault. There was not a situation of

[4] N. O. Christensen, "Some Information on Canadian Eskimos". (Ottawa: Department of Northern Affairs and National Resources, 1953).

anarchy, as van den Steenhoven suggests,[5] but simply a situation where order prevailed within bands except when someone was willing to step outside the accepted order and take the risks of individualistic action. Among the Copper Eskimos there were many instances of violence recorded since contact, and the Netsilingmiut and Mackenzie Eskimos also have records of violence. Jenness recorded Uloksak and Ilatsiak as two of the dominant shamans of the area.[6] They are still remembered with some fear by Copper Eskimos today. The situation with regard to Eskimo law was such that only the reckless would step outside it. When that happened, the man was literally *outside* the law, and could not be controlled by the normal sanctions. One method of legitimating such action was through sorcery and most of the "extra-legal" individuals were shamans.

Not only did the influence of the band leaders decline but that of the renegade, who set his own rules and practised witchcraft to legitimate it, also declined. Conformity became an increasingly powerful norm and there was almost no outlet for idiosyncratic behaviour. Almost but not total, for there was one new way in which a person might express individuality. This was through drinking alcohol. The whalers had taught the Eskimos in the West how to drink and how to make "homebrew". It became an accepted fact that a person who was drunk was really not responsible for his actions. This meant that belligerent behaviour was not the same drunk as sober. To this day, an Eskimo who wishes to injure another usually gets drunk first. Where shamanistic behaviour legitimated idiosyncratic behaviour in the traditional society, alcohol performs the same function today. It is not accidental that the best hunters are usually the biggest gamblers and the heaviest drinkers. They also tend to be the more individualistic Eskimos, and are relatively unconcerned about what public opinion decrees.

Most of the changes in Eskimo society which have taken place during the past decade could be described as social changes, not culture changes. In many respects Eskimo culture, its basic beliefs and values which are shared by most Eskimos, is relatively unchanged. Social changes which have taken place have resulted from two major factors, the continuing introduction of imported trade goods, the expansion of health and welfare institutions, and the great wave of modernization which occurred as a result of the Distant Early Warning (DEW) radar line being constructed through the territory of the Western Eskimos.

EFFECTS OF THE DEW LINE

The construction of the DEW Line had far-reaching consequences. It provided most Eskimos of the Western Arctic with their first experience at sustained wage employment. It drew large populations to the radar station sites located along the coast of the mainland, and when the construction was over, and there was no longer the employment for most adult males available, the experience of employment tended to prevent them from returning to their former hunting areas and pursuing their traditional occupations.

The majority of able-bodied Eskimo men between the ages of sixteen and sixty-five were employed at one time or another on the radar line in the Western Arctic. They saw and experienced employment for wages equal to those of white men for the first time. They ate and grew accustomed to the white men's food, and they grew to like the standard housing, and all of the other amenities of the typical radar station site. Many Eskimos had felt somewhat sorry for the fate of the white man in the Arctic up until this time since he seemed to eat poor quality tinned food all of the time. While most Eskimos did not grow to like the long hours of work or the sustained effort required as manual laborers at a heavy construction site, they all agreed that the monetary rewards were desirable, and the younger men frequently said that this was the life for them. The older men tended to look at DEW Line employment as a way to buy store goods at a time when trapping was relatively unprofitable. It was also a way to buy boats, outboard motors, and all other types of useful goods.

When construction ended and the labour force was reduced, everyone saw that Eskimos who got maintenance jobs were usually those who had gone to school, and could speak English well. Until this time there had been great resistance on the part of many Eskimo parents to send their children to school because they thought that it tended to spoil them for the life of hunting. This belief is still very strong, incidentally, at Coppermine. But now every parent in both communities wants his children to go to school because he says that they can then get good jobs, and the security of wage employment is seen as ultimately preferable to any other way of life. In order for children to go to school it was necessary for the parents to live in the large settlements during the entire winter. Until this time they had tended to live in the settlements only irregularly from spring to fall, and to move to a hunting and trapping area for a good part of the winter. If an Eskimo family lives in a settlement, it can neither hunt nor trap as effectively as when it does not live there. But the presence of day schools in such settlements as Tuktoyaktuk and Coppermine now became a very strong incentive for spending a good part of the winter there. A second very large attraction of the settlement was the nursing station, and these were established in all of the major settlements during the 1960's.

[5] Geert van den Steenhoven, "Legal Concepts among the Netsilik Eskimos of Pelly Bay" (Ottawa: Northern Coordination and Research Centre, 1959).

[6] Diamond Jenness, "The Life of the Copper Eskimo". *Report of the Canadian Arctic Expedition, 12.* (Ottawa: King's Printer, 1922).

At the beginning of the 1950's there were about fourteen settlements along the Arctic coast between Tuktoyaktuk and Cambridge Bay. In 1969 there were only six Eskimo settlements in that same area and of these three had ninety per cent of the population. Those who used to hunt over this vast area now live at either Tuktoyaktuk, Coppermine or Cambridge Bay, with a few going further north to Holman Island, and during the summer of 1966, a few returned to Paulatuk which had been deserted for eight or nine years. The process of urbanization which is so dominant in most countries of the world is going on apace in the Arctic. Even greater demands upon the resources of the area are being created by this concentration of population. When one considers that the three major communities have each between 300 and 500 permanent residents, one realizes that the traditional land use pattern of the Eskimo has been fundamentally altered. This may have been an inexorable process which was simply accelerated by the building of the DEW Line, but it has changed the settlement pattern and principal occupation of the majority of Eskimos within the Western Arctic.

At present the DEW Line is not a significant factor as an employer in any community, except that it tends to set the standards of employment. The wage rates are the highest and the rations and living accommodations perhaps the best. It remains as a model employer in many ways, and although it may have been built for defense, it served for the Eskimos as one of the first employers to give them more-or-less equal opportunities. It opened up a new way of life for them and at the same time it benefited the white residents. Up until this time there had been no landing strips at most Arctic locations and as a result only small planes could land there most of the year. Air freight rates were very high and they did not get fresh food. With the coming of the DEW Line there was air service almost every day at many locations, and it became possible to bring in fresh food regularly. There has been, then, a general upgrading of the standard of living as a result of the DEW Line. If it did nothing else, it set a standard of living that remains highly sought after.

THE CREATION OF A SATELLITE SOCIETY

The Canadian Arctic has appeared to be similar to colonial society in other parts of the world. Most Arctic settlements were made up of a large native population relatively indifferent to political participation, and a small European population made up of traders, missionaries, plus the RCMP as a symbol of government. This has been relaxed to a considerable extent by the extension of the franchise, at least in Territorial elections, to the majority of Eskimos, and the creation in some settlements of semblances of village councils. The white population has also increased dramatically, so that at both Tuktoyaktuk and Coppermine it is between one-fifth to one-sixth of the resident population. At the same time that the franchise is being extended the political power being made available is being concentrated into the hands of the new white residents of these communities. They are new not only because of their recent arrival, but because their type is something not seen before — the civil servant. There has always been a certain amount of discrimination between whites and Eskimos, but it has not been formalized until now with the actual physical segregation of housing that exists in both Tuktoyaktuk and Coppermine but which is most severe, perhaps, at Inuvik. As Inuvik serves as the "metropolis" for many young Eskimos, it also serves as the model for the new form of colonialism; the satellite society. What characterizes such a society is that the majority of crucial functions of local government are not performed by the indigenous population, that there is a large amount of material aid given in the form of welfare payments, that there is no economic basis for the support of the population in the region, and that there is a definite amount of physical segregation between the governing and the governed. It is colonialism infused with concepts of social welfare, and it depends upon large scale economic subvention from the parent society.

It should be added that the very large scale population increase at Coppermine and Tuktoyaktuk both by natural increase and by immigration have placed heavy loads upon the very limited resource base. Neither community has sufficient food resources, used in the traditional ways, to support the large populations. Tuktoyaktuk, located as it is on the edge of the Mackenzie River delta does not have an abundance of food about it. Seals cannot be hunted any closer than Warren Point; the whale population is definitely limited and would require a large increase in the amount of equipment available before any increase in harvesting could be done. Moreover, there has been a noticeable deterioration in numbers and condition of boats over the past ten years. Commercial fishing may be possible, but the only effort in that direction several years ago was badly conceived and organized by the Department of Northern Affairs and ended disastrously. Trapping areas are available to the East but the Eskimos say that the large number of oil explorers using tracked vehicles during the winter months have destroyed the muskrat "push-ups" and dimished the population. Marten may be trapped at Anderson River, but the distance is too great for most Eskimos to make the trip. The quality of dogteams has diminished greatly at Tuktoyaktuk, and there were few teams kept at all, while at Coppermine the typical Eskimo still kept three or four dogs, if not a large team.

Fur prices continue to fall while prices of store goods continue to rise. There has been almost no effort made to increase income from trapping, even though an increased rationalization of hunting and trapping techniques is possible. The greatest effort has gone into workshops for soapstone carving, or the making of fur garments. At Tuktoyaktuk the only industry consists of a fur garment project started as a government project, with a white furrier in charge. The white furrier had left the project during the winter of 1965-66, and at the time it was visited there were only five or six women working full-time. The quality of furs used was inferior, and the products which were currently being made did not show much originality of design. The women themselves complained that the parent organization in Inuvik was not supplying them with enough fur and that the quality was inferior. Most products were made of muskrat with a few novelty items made of white fox. The major question discussed among the women working in the project during the summer was whether it should remain as a government project, become a cooperative, or a partnership among the women. One of the main workers, Bessie A., had been sent away for a two week course in the principles of managing cooperatives, but the main problem seemed to be that no one in the organization had been sufficiently trained as a furrier.

The problem which was placed as uppermost in the minds of the women by the administration, however, was whether or not the project could be run as a cooperative. At its peak operation the fur shop employed twelve women full-time and each earned about $60.00 a week — a reasonable wage as far as they were concerned. During the summer of 1966, half of that number were working, and they were working around fifty hours a week to earn $30.00. The matter was not resolved during the winter of 1966-67 and in the summer of 1967 a government official told them that they could not turn it into a cooperative because it was not self-sufficient. Yet it was the government which initially encouraged the women to consider forming a cooperative and even sent one employee away on a course.[7]

At Coppermine, a large volume of soapstone carving is produced, but the actual amount produced by the average person is small, only one or two pieces a month. There are possibly three or four skilled carvers who might make $30.00 to $40.00 a week from carving, but it is not an industry which can easily be entered by the adults of a whole community. At most it could support three or four families. The systematic over-production of Eskimo carving and the steady debasement of the art is resulting in a market glut. Soapstone carvings were being sold in a clearance sale by the Hudson's Bay Company department store in Edmonton in the fall of 1966, and have made their appearance for sale in cigar stores in various parts of Canada. It does not seem likely, under the circumstances, that soapstone carving will ever be a source of continuous income for more than a few Eskimo families in any community.

There does not appear to be any stable economic activity at present which can give gainful employment to more than a handful in either community, and it seems unlikely that any industry can be created to employ this population. Tourism could not in the near future be anything but a minor business, something at the same level as handicrafts or the fur garment shop. Accordingly, it would appear that the majority of Eskimos will live from relief and other welfare payments, as they are doing now, and will not have any gainful activity other than casual hunting. One would expect that hunting and trapping will continue their decline since the density of human population is sure to cause reduction in many species.

Cut off from purposeful economic activities and living from various kinds of welfare activities, the typical Eskimo community will become more, and not less, part of a satellite society. For this is the last and certainly the most important factor in the maintenance of such a society — the lack of meaningful work for adults. Attendant with this will be many other social problems and one could expect that differing forms of deviance will develop. If one could develop a picture of what the society will be like, it would have to include a healthy, well-housed, population growing at a very high rate, fed only reasonably well on canned foods, having an enormous amount of leisure time, and little purposeful or gainful activity. To top off this picture, one would add that they would have almost all administration done for them, they would not get sufficient education to compete for the available civil service jobs, nor would they participate in politics. Accordingly, their resentment would increase proportionate to their status as second-rate citizens.

What would be desirable is a type of society which is the opposite of what has been described. It would be one where the natural and human resources are utilized satisfactorily, where there is opportunity to work meaningfully, where education is devoted to providing relevant knowledge and skills. There would be a minimum of administration imposed from the outside, and there would be an encouragement of political participation for the modernizing population. This type of society I have termed as developmental, meaning that it is the opposite of satellite. To some extent the situation at Tuktoyaktuk is approaching this, except where development is inhibited by present government policies.

There has been a constant devaluation of Eskimo culture by the Department of Indian Affairs and its predecessors. English is the sole language of the schools, and the white men's way of life is presented as the ideal. The values of Eskimo culture are being constantly undermined, and its content pauperized. This seems not only ethically wrong, but unrealistic in planning for the future. For there will always be a small population of Eskimo who will prefer to follow traditional life despite the hardships. The traditional values of their

⁷ *Coastline: Canada*, Vol. 2, No. 8 (1967), p. 3.

culture can only be preserved by placing positive worth on their language, mythology, socialization pattern, and other cultural features which define and give meaning to being an Eskimo. It is not satisfactory to turn the Canadian Eskimo into Arctic Hillbillies, but that is what is happening. Unless there is consistent planning for the future, and planning for change itself — a most difficult conception — the legacy of the present administration will be one of unhappiness, despair, and social disorganization.

BIBLIOGRAPHY

CHRISTENSEN, N. O. "Some information on Canadian Eskimos." Report to the Dept. of Northern Affairs and National Resources (trans. from Danish), mimeograph, 1953.

Coastline Canada 2:8, p. 3

FERGUSON, JACK. "A study of the effects of D.E.W. Line employment upon the Eskimos of the Canadian Western Arctic." Ottawa: Northern Coordination and Research Centre, Department of Northern Affairs and National Resources, 1958.

———. "The Human ecology and social and economic change in the community of Tuktoyaktuk, N.W.T." Ottawa: Northern Coordination and Research Centre, Department of Northern Affairs and National Resources (NCRC-61-2), 1961.

GRABURN, NELSON H. H. "Taqagmiut Eskimo Kinship Terminology." Ottawa: Northern Coordination and Research Centre, Department of Northern Affairs and National Resources (NCRC-64-1), 1964.

JENNESS, DIAMOND. "The Life of the Copper Eskimo." *Report of the Canadian Arctic Expedition, 12.* Ottawa: King's Printer, 1922.

———. "Eskimo Administration: Canada," *Technical Paper 14,* Montreal: Arctic Institute of North America, 1964.

KROEBER, A. L. & TALCOTT PARSONS. "The concept of culture and of social systems". *American Sociological Review 23:* 582-583, 1958.

POSPOSIL, LEOPOLD. "Law and societal structure among the Nunamiut Eskimo." *Explorations in Cultural Anthropology.* Ward H. Goodenough, ed. New York, McGraw-Hill, 1964.

VAN DEN STEENHOVEN, GEERT. "Legal concepts among the Netsilik Eskimos of Pelly Bay," Ottawa, Northern Coordination and Research Centre, Dept. of Northern Affairs and National Resources (NCRC-59-3), 1959.

3

The Eskimos
of Churchill, Manitoba*

George J. Vranas

Margaret Stephens

In Churchill, a deepwater port and terminus of the Canadian National Railway, one finds an Eskimo way of life which is rapidly beginning to characterize the Eskimo group as a whole. The Eskimo, however, is not the only group to settle recently in Churchill. This Manitoba port is the home of other native people — Cree, Chipewyan, and Metis.

Vranas and Stephens comment on the lack of organized leadership within the Eskimo settlement. The absence of a forceful community spokesman is understandable, however, given the fact that the aboriginal Eskimo unit was the family, not the community. As long as old patterns of social organization persist, the Eskimo may be at a disadvantage with respect to exercising effective control over his destiny.

INTRODUCTION

1. Spatial Layout and Physical Facilities

On a map large enough to depict northern Manitoba in detail a single dot at the mouth of the Churchill River on the edge of Hudson Bay is labelled Churchill. There are two main units to the place. The port town, Churchill, corresponds strictly to the map dot. Five miles to the southeast is a government establishment called Fort or Camp Churchill. The port town itself is fringed by satellite neighborhoods. The Tidal Flats are sandwiched between the railroad tracks west of the townsite and the river. Jocktown rambles over Cape Merry beyond the Harbour Board buildings to the north of town.

---

* Prepared especially for *Minority Canadians*.

Flanking the eastern boundary of the townsite a government settlement for Chipewyan Indians, Camp 10, balances on the rocks between the waters of the bay and the local cemetery. A few additional Chipewyan homes are located across the river.

Between Churchill townsite and Fort Churchill lie two additional government establishments. One, a Navy base, the "C.F.S. Churchill", is adjacent to the second, Akudlik, which serves the Department of Indian Affairs and Northern Development as administrative headquarters for the Keewatin District to the north. Twelve miles beyond Fort Churchill, Pan-American Airways maintains a missile base for the Canadian Research Council. Churchill Townsite and Fort Churchill are linked by five miles of paved road. The other roads in the region are surfaced only with gravel. Hourly buses shuttle between the two Churchills following the paved route and two local taxi services, as well as private vehicles, also make use of the road. During the summer boats are included in the local means of transportation while in winter, dogsleds, toboggans, motorized sleds, and other mechanized snow vehicles prove useful.

Akudlik's location bisects the pavement between the Churchills. Our research in this Eskimo community was conducted as part of a team project.[1] The team worked from June to September, 1966. A supplementary visit to Akudlik by Vranas was made for a period of six weeks during the following summer.

The world as seen from Churchill is divided into two basic categories, "north" and "out", which translates as southern Canada. Churchill is the point of transition between the two categories with connections linking the town to both designations. On three days a week train mail arrives from outside and on five days there is airmail delivery. One airline, Transair, operates flights to and from Winnipeg via Thompson and The Pas daily except Wednesday and Sunday while Lamb Airways arranges charter flights from Churchill to points north. Continental grain ships load at the town's five-million-bushel-capacity elevators from 28 July through the end of November and provide direct contact with Europe. The Canadian National Railroad sustains Churchill's most vital link with the rest of Canada. Trains bring wheat to fill the elevators, food and merchandise for stores, as well as mail, magazines, two-day-old Winnipeg newspapers, television tapes, and people.

Churchill townsite has a business district as does Fort Churchill. Food, clothing, hardware, lumber, real estate and insurance may all be purchased locally and the area boasts a beautician, barber, laundry, and a branch of the Royal Bank of Canada. The Townsite possesses a school with grades one through eight housed in a newly-constructed building and a collection of metal trailers. The Duke of Edinburgh School at Fort Churchill teaches grades one through twelve and serves the Fort Churchill and Akudlik children as well as the advanced students of the Townsite. The total urban complex shares three fire stations, two post offices, two Royal Canadian Mounted Police detachment stations and jails, and a small hospital.

The Townsite, Churchill proper, is the locus of a deep-water port and possesses docking facilities and a grain storage elevator. The chief commodity shipped from Churchill is wheat from the prairie provinces and bound for European ports. Smaller cargo ships from Churchill take supplies to coastal settlements in the District of Keewatin. The docking facilities, grain elevator, and oil storage tanks are actually about three-quarters of a mile from town but the looming hulk of the elevators dominates the surrounding landscape. The scatter of shacks in the vicinity of the port is known as Jocktown but does not qualify as a distinct residential zone of Churchill.

The center of the Townsite is a large, dusty, rectangle, called Hudson Square. Surrounding this gravel-strewn area are a number of retail establishments. The most imposing of these edifices is the modern Hudson's Bay store which includes a supermarket and various departments of dry goods. Next to this proud structure stands the "S and M" a rival supermarket and, unlike the "Bay" whose parent company operates branches throughout northern and western Canada, a local operation.

Metal trailer classrooms, the Royal Canadian Mounted Police Station, Churchill Federal Building which includes the post office, a movie theater, a bowling alley, a Canadian Legion Hall, and the railroad station roughly surround Hudson's Square. The square is also the Townsite terminus for a private busline which runs a maximum of two buses per hour between Churchill, Akudlik, and Fort Churchill. Off Hudson Square but in the business district are two hotels, The Churchill and The Hudson, and a small motel. The two hotels provide Churchill's nightlife. They have modern bars which offer live music as well as daytime eating places. A retail store selling televisions and other appliances, two gasoline stations, a beauty parlor and a barber shop all operate in the Townsite. An establishment supplying freighters is also in Churchill as well as a government liquor store selling wine and spirits.

Four religious denominations are represented in the Townsite. The Anglican and Roman Catholic missions are the two older, established denominations in Churchill. They have an extensive membership among aboriginal residents and claim, as well, most of the Eurocanadian community. The newer, fundamentalist denominations are the Pentecostals and the Christian Alliance. Their congregations are smaller and largely composed of Eurocanadians.

The Roman Catholic facilities are especially impressive, including a row of three modern structures near Hudson Bay, a rectory, the

[1] Funded by a training grant from the National Institute of Mental Health to the University of North Carolina (Grant # 5-TI-MH-8166-04), under the direction of Professor John J. Honigmann.

church, and an Eskimo museum. The Anglican mission, Saint Paul's, includes mission staff houses, a community center, and the mission church. The two evangelical churches have more modest structures.

The small often ramshackle wooden homes which comprise the bulk of Churchill residences are without plumbing since the Township has no waterborne sewage system. Central heating is also absent. Akudlik and Fort Churchill have all modern amenities, thus presenting a visible disparity to the residents of each area. The Townsite which is primarily Eurocanadian and its fringing aboriginal neighbourhoods have a fluctuating population roughly estimated as between 1500 and 2000, or about half of the total population of the area.

The Canadian National Railroad owns land along the Churchill River which is called "the Flats". Here reside about 300 people, mostly employees of the railroad and the majority of whom are Cree or Metis. A scattering of Chipewyan, Eurocanadians, and Eskimo inhabitants adds ethnic variety to this neighborhood, the houses of which differ little from those of the Townsite. Their arrangement, however, is more random and their appearance even less stable than those in town. Houses on the Flats rest on the ground and seldom sport even the slightest trace of paint; instead black tarpaper covers many.

A spur of the rail line slices into the Flats on its course to the whaling plant. This is the only industry in Churchill which derives its product wholly from the local environment. In summer, an American manager and part-owner comes to Churchill and runs the facility using local Cree-Metis and some Eskimo labor. Aboriginal fishermen catch white, or beluga, whale after the break-up of ice. The plant pays a set rate per foot and processes the whale into feed for mink ranches in the south. A tourist center has recently been established beside the whaling plant. It provides liaison between aboriginal guides and tourists who wish to hunt whale. The main unpaved road through the Flats has the same destination as the railroad spur. The smaller branch roads are also unnamed and unpaved.

Camp 10, inhabited until 1969 by a band of about 250 Chipewyan, was built by the Indian Affairs Branch. The small, wooden houses, built in rows, are set on the ground, most of them in a sad state of disrepair. In summer the area has two water outlets from the town pipe but in winter melted snow is the water source. Several sewage pits stand uncovered and are seldom pumped out, nor are garbage bins regularly serviced. Most of the poorly-insulated homes are heated by coal and wood-burning stoves.

Turning to Fort Churchill the visitor is confronted with as elaborate a bureaucratic system as might be found in any modern city. Chains of authority overlap and each structure is vigilant of its prerogatives. In this particular beaucratic matrix the various governmental agencies, as a result of decisions made in Ottawa, found their domains of authority reorganized during the interlude between our visits. A number of these administrative changes have particular bearing on our discussion of Akudlik. First the Department of Northern Affairs (D.N.A.), the Federal Governmental agency concerned with the welfare and development of the Canadian north and the country's Eskimo inhabitants, was reorganized into the Department of Indian Affairs and Northern Development (D.I.A.N.D.), thereby bringing all of Canada's recognized aboriginal population within its purview. Canadian treaty Indians were formerly under the jurisdiction of the Department of Citizenship and Immigration. Somewhat related to this change the Chipewyan residents of Camp 10 near the Townsite of Churchill were moved to improved housing less than one mile from Akudlik. The new site is called Dene Village.

Therefore our discussion of Eskimo and Eurocanadian attitudes toward the Chipewyan is not able to take into account the possibly significant changes in attitudes wrought by governmental policy.

Fort Churchill was built to serve the combined forces of the Canadian Army and United States Strategic Air Command. When the usefulness of a defense base in the area lessened military personnel abandoned the fort to the Canadian government and its buildings now serve to house a variety of Federal and related services. A rocket research range is maintained by Pan-American Airways. The Canadian National Research Council (C.N.R.C.) uses part of the base. The Department of Indian Affairs and Northern Development (D.I.A.N.D.) operates an Eskimo hostel for children in pre-vocational training programs. The Department of Transport (D.O.T.) occupies space in the fort, and the Canadian Broadcasting Company (C.B.C.) Northern Service broadcasts from there. The Department of Public Works (DPW) maintains the place. Residents of this encampment of official initials are usually on temporary duty in the area and hence turn over yearly or every two years.

2. The Unique Quality of Churchill

Churchill forms the meeting place of many very different natural and social elements. The tree line passes through the area, the resultant compromise between forest and tundra being symbolized by stunted conifers with branches on one side only. A riverine world joins a marine environment at the point of Cape Merry where the Churchill River pours into Hudson Bay. The whole coastal region constitutes a zone of transition from water to land accompanying the tidal changes. Even the atmosphere possesses a unique quality: Churchill is the point where the aurora borealis streams nearest to the surface of the earth. The variety of exploitable environments includes freshwater as well as marine fish and mammals, and a diversity of forest and tundra beasts. In summer Churchill provides a major nesting area for coastal, inland, and swamp birds.

The people are also varied, consisting of representatives of four major ethnic divisions: Eurocanadians, i.e., Canadians of European extraction; Chipewyan Indians; Cree and Cree-Metis; and Eskimo. Four major language stocks are brought together by these ethnic groups. Athapaskan, Algonkian, Eskimoan, and Indo-European. English serves as the usual language of intergroup communication. Class distinctions based on occupation cover a wide range. Dock hands and fur trappers have niches in the social environment as do nuclear physicists and aerospace engineers who work on the rocket range. Thus Churchill may be described as a collection of contrasts.

Churchill is a portal to Canada's central Arctic from southern Canada and a gateway to northern Europe, being the only deep-water port for Canada's prairie provinces. This rather strategic location gives it significance it would not otherwise have. Transportation and communication facilities are developed; governmental agencies operate from the site, and people are constantly coming or leaving, particularly in the summer.

The development of Churchill is unique when compared to other northern Canadian settlements. It is considerably larger and its economic base is more varied. It has a year-round surface transportation link to southern Canada, yet no road links it with points north or south. The nearest motorable road begins at Thompson, a new mining town in north-central Manitoba almost 300 miles away. The railroad connects Thompson and Churchill and, except for Gillam with 332 people, no other in-between settlement exists.

AKUDLIK AND ITS RESIDENTS

1. The Site

Akudlik in Eskimo means "the place in between", and was built, starting in 1954, as Federal regional administrative headquarters for Churchill and for the Keewatin District of the Northwest Territories. It used to be called "Camp 20"; and some people still refer to it by that name. The site of Akudlik includes a single story administrative building with a peaked roof. Another building is the modern looking arts and crafts center which displays and sells handicrafts, particularly soapstone carvings, by Eskimo from all over the eastern Arctic as well as from Akudlik. Through this facility handicrafts are shipped south to stores and for display and sold to tourists in Akudlik. The Department of Indian Affairs and Northern Development also maintains warehouses, a carpentry shop, and other such facilities at Akudlik, but not primarily for the maintenance of the D.I.A.N.D. local facility.

Akudlik also has a "transient centre", which provides a stop-over for Eskimo who are ill and being sent to the hospital in Fort Churchill or to larger medical facilities in southern Canada. Eskimo on their way back north also use the transient center as a stop-over, perhaps to recuperate, or merely to await transportation. Many hospital cases are maternity cases, the women usually arriving a week or so before the child is due, to be within reach of the Fort Churchill hospital.

Akudlik has a simple rectangular building that serves as a "community centre". Dances and other affairs have been held here and the Anglican mission at one time used the building for its Sunday Eskimo language services. But the building was not used during our field-stay, except one afternoon when a group of Boy Scouts from Minnesota, camping in Churchill, gave an amateur musical program for the local Eskimo population. Another D.I.A.N.D. building in Akudlik is the nursing station which administers injections and to which the Eskimos go for minor health services. The public-health nurse is in Akudlik two or three afternoons per week; and the nursing station is open at set times on those days. The nurse also looks in on patients at the transient center and the children's home. His office is at Fort Churchill Hospital and he must also serve settlements in the Keewatin.

The only building in Akudlik not owned and maintained by D.I.A.N.D. is the small Roman Catholic Chapel. Mass is said on Sunday afternoons in bilingual (Eskimo-English) services, in which English dominates through most of the first half (until after the Sacrament of the Eucharist is celebrated), after which Eurocanadians in attendance depart, and Eskimo prayers and chants begin, ending with a sermon in Eskimo by the priest. The priests are French-Canadian Oblates of Mary Immaculate. The priests reside at the mission rectory adjoining the church and Eskimo museum (which they maintain) at the Townsite and drive out to Akudlik on Sunday afternoons.

By far the largest part of Akudlik is taken up by one-family housing. The government designation for the housing style is "panabode," and the units are centrally-heated, single-story buildings with two or three bedrooms. There are four standard plans; and the regional administrator's home is simply a larger version of a panabode. These wooden buildings look like log bungalows from the outside, for long log-like beams interlock at the corners. The homes have hot and cold running water and plumbing lines are all subsurface, although the permafrost is only a few feet below the surface. The buildings themselves are raised about two feet above the ground, the exposed sides enclosed so that the illusion is of a wall even with the ground. Eurocanadian employees brought from southern Canada to any Arctic or sub-Arctic outpost have all their furniture supplied, since this has been found to be less expensive than shipping a family's belongings, at Government expense. Eskimo residents of Akudlik, although they usually live long distances from their places of origin, do not have furniture supplied.

There are forty panabode or modified panabode-type structures in Akudlik, thirty of which are one-family residences and eight of which were unoccupied in June, 1966. The nursing station is simply a two-bedroom panabode. It is really no more than an out-patient type of arrangement, since persons requiring bed-care are sent to the hospital or the transient center. The children's home is a larger version of a panabode. Should it ever be discontinued, the building could easily be used as a one-family residence. A number of years ago the health and welfare facilities operated at Akudlik were larger, the two panabodes next to the children's home also serving as health centers. At that time the three units were a prenatal care center for expectant mothers, an infant's home, and a children's home. The transient center served as a center for Eskimo adults who were ill. The children and infants' homes have been consolidated into the children's home, and maternity cases are handled at the transient center. A decline in cases of tuberculosis and other respiratory ailments may have led to a decrease in space needed. Also better transportation facilities may have eliminated the need for Akudlik as a stop-over place.

In addition to the panabode type of housing, D.I.A.N.D. has three single-room A-frame units, possessing electricity but no running water, which stand at the far end of the site. These are termed "welfare houses" by the Eurocanadian population, as Eskimo welfare recipients can be housed in them. Only one of the units is occupied: by an elderly Eskimo woman, and her fifteen-year old daughter, and a four-year old granddaughter. A second A-frame is used for storage, and the third provided temporary housing for a member of our research group.

2. The Eurocanadians

Only a small minority of the Eurocanadian population of the Churchill area lives in Akudlik. Only Eurocanadians who are employed by D.I.A.N.D., and their families, may reside in Akudlik. A short digression on the Eurocanadian population of the entire area might place the D.I.A.N.D. employees in better perspective.

The Eurocanadian population of Churchill consists of two main subgroups, the Townsite Eurocanadians, and the Ft. Churchill/Akudlik Eurocanadians. The latter group has the greater political influence as well as higher prestige, a higher standard of living, and more extensive educational background. It consists of people attached to the administrative, particularly federal, bureaucracy; the civil servants attached to D.I.A.N.D., D.P.W., D.O.T., etc.

The typical Townsite Eurocanadian came to Churchill from rural, southern Canada on his own initiative, with few skills, to work on the railroad or port to earn money, and then to return south.

Few were able to succeed in this dream, since Churchill seems, if anything, to have contracted during the 1950's and early 1960's. Although pay is higher than in the south, so are costs, and relief from boredom found in the form of alcohol and gambling is expensive. Few have been able to save. More recent migrants to Churchill still consider southern Canada as home, whereas old-timers often take pride in being "northerners," and "Churchillians".

The civil servant group has been sent to Churchill. Their stay is viewed as a tour of duty that can be terminated by a transfer without fear of financial loss, and without too much difficulty (particularly because large belongings, such as furniture and appliances, are provided). Whereas the Townsite includes many Eurocanadians who stay though they have not "made it" economically, civil service people tend to remain in Churchill over long periods of time only if they are economically satisfied, since the risks of moving are far less than for Townsite Eurocanadians. These Eurocanadians are sometimes characterized as seeing not Churchill but the Canadian North in general as home. Many young, unmarried individuals come north, often as teachers, lured by the notion of working in Canada's frontier. The notion of service beyond oneself and one's immediate family is a strong motivating theme among many civil servants, particularly in Akudlik. The Northern Allowance, of course, is also an attraction. Service may be directed to the Eskimo and other aboriginal inhabitants, or to Canadian wildlife and conservation.

The pattern of residence tended to change over the summer while we were in Akudlik, as new Eurocanadian families arrived to fill long-time vacancies, and as personnel were transferred to other settlements or to Ottawa. Movement is not uncommon for Eurocanadian personnel, and none regard Churchill or Akudlik as their "home". Quite a number identify with "the North", including Churchill, and with D.I.A.N.D. These people may spend many years in Arctic and sub-Arctic Canada, maintaining social ties with other D.I.A.N.D. personnel over a vast, sparsely populated region. All of the Eurocanadians are originally from southern Canada; family ties link them to the south and vacations are spent there. The adult Eurocanadian population of Akudlik is larger than the adult Eskimo population (about eighty-five people), although an exact census count of the former group has not been made. Out of thirty-one units in use (thirty panabodes and one A-frame), thirteen are the residences of Eskimo families, fifteen of Eurocanadian families, and 1 is the residence of a Eurocanadian head of household and his Eskimo wife and their children. Legally the Eskimo wife and their children have become Eurocanadian. Another panabode was, at the time of our study, the residence of a university student working for D.I.A.N.D. during the school holiday and yet another was occupied by four or five Eurocanadian electricians on call to Keewatin settlements and therefore quite often out of Akudlik.

TABLE 1

Resident Eskimo Population of Akudlik, June, 1966

Age	Males	Females	Total
60+	1	2	3
55-59	1	0	1
50-54	0	1	1
45-49	2	2	4
40-44	1	2	3
35-39	2	4	6
30-34	2	1	3
25-29	5	2	7
20-24	3	2	5
15-19	7	4	11
10-14	6	4	10
5- 9	10	8	18
0- 4	6	8	14
Totals	46	40	86

Since the Eurocanadian in Akudlik is only incidentally concerned with conditions in that settlement, focussing his interest and energy on the entire eastern Arctic, many of the more subtle emotional and psychological needs of the resident Eskimo population are not fully met. On this note we turn to considerations of the Eskimo population itself.

3. Eskimos of Akudlik

POPULATION

The Eskimo population of Akudlik, as of June 1966, numbered eighty-six individuals, ranging in age from eight months to sixty-seven years. Of this group forty-six are male and forty are female. The population is quite young, with not quite two out of every three individuals under age twenty (sixty-two per cent are less than twenty). Eighty-six per cent of the population is under forty. This figure includes the Eskimo wife and children of the Eurocanadian administrator. Including them again, the population is divided into fourteen households; two unattached, employed males are semi-officially resident in the transient center. No children from the children's home or transient adults at the center are included in these figures. Table 1 presents the age distribution of the Eskimo population.

This population is augmented by three households containing Eskimo that reside in the Townsite and on the Flats (Table 2). One household in the Townsite is headed by a Eurocanadian married to the eldest daughter of an Eskimo family in Akudlik. They have a

TABLE 2

Distribution of Eskimo in the Churchill Area

Neighborhood	Population
Akudlik	86
Townsite	8
The Flats	11
Fort Churchill*	300
Total permanent residents	105
Overall total	405

*The population refers to the approximate numbers of students in the vocational school hostel.

son, and the wife's grandmother resides with them. The second household also lives in the Townsite and consists of the male head, his wife, and their three children. This raises the Eskimo population by eight, to ninety-four counting the spouse and child of the Eurocanadian, who as a result of the marriage have no legal status as Eskimo. Both these households, however, are socially important to Akudlik. One family has close kinship ties there and the other at one time lived in Akudlik. The household on the Flats is a polyandrous unit headed by one Eskimo male, one Eurocanadian male, and one Eskimo female. Each male head lives in his own adjoining home, and the Eskimo female occupies both units, apparently equally. The family has eleven children, seven of whom live with their parents. Although each child receives the name of one of the adult males, based primarily on the appearance of the child and the judgement of the mother, all the children and the mother were unable to state which of the two buildings was their home. Sleeping arrangements vary, as does the storage of individual property (like clothing). Therefore, it seems useless to attempt to divide this polyandrous unit artificially into two households, despite the fact that each man maintains a separate, although adjoining home. This raises the Eskimo population by a maximum of eleven, including all children living in Churchill and vicinity, the Eskimo head of household, and his (shared) wife. Therefore the maximum population which is fully or partially Eskimo is 105. Extensive kinship ties exist between these individuals and households in Akudlik.

ARRIVAL IN CHURCHILL

Most of the Eskimo population in Churchill is of recent origin. Maps depict the southern limit of Eskimo habitation as roughly coinciding with the edge of the barren grounds (the treeline). This line runs through Churchill. Therefore Churchill is the point of furthest southerly advance of Eskimo aboriginally on the west coast of Hudson

TABLE 3

Year of Arrival in Churchill and Place of Origin of Eskimo Household Heads and Their Spouses

Year of Arrival	Identity	Place of Origin
1947	W.K.	Aivillik, Keewatin
1950	spouse	Eskimo Point, Keewatin
1950	P.T.	Tavani, Keewatin
1950	spouse	Tavani, Keewatin
1950	P.I.	Aivillik, Keewatin
1950	spouse	Chesterfield Inlet, Keewatin
1953	M.E.*	Chesterfield Inlet, Keewatin
1953	M.A.	Fort Chimo, Quebec
1954	spouse	Fort Chimo, Quebec
1953	S.G.	Fort Chimo, Quebec
1955	spouse	Fort Chimo, Quebec
1954	E.B.	Fort Chimo, Quebec
1955	spouse	Fort Chimo, Quebec
1954	L.A.*	Fort Chimo, Quebec
1958	A.T.	Great Whale River, Quebec
1958	spouse	Great Whale River, Quebec
1959	B.N.	Coral Harbour, Keewatin
1954	spouse	Fort Chimo, Quebec
1959	J.A.	Chesterfield Inlet, Keewatin
1950	spouse	Aivillik, Keewatin
1959	P.B.	Coral Harbour, Keewatin
1959	spouse	Coral Harbour, Keewatin
1959	N.K.	Keewatin (probably Coral Harbour)
1964	spouse	Eskimo Point, Keewatin
1961	L.P.	Coral Harbour, Keewatin
1961	spouse	Coral Harbour, Keewatin
1962	P.A.	Eskimo Point, Keewatin
1962	spouse	Eskimo Point, Keewatin

*Female head of household.

Bay. Present-day Eskimo residents of Churchill trace their origins to points further north. All heads of households were born further north as well as most children over ten. Table 3 shows the year of arrival in Churchill and place of origin of the present adult Eskimo population.

Only one Eskimo resident lived in Churchill prior to 1950 who is still resident today. Immigration has tended to come in waves, if such a term is permitted so small a population. In 1950 one couple arrived from the District of Keewatin at the instigation of a Eurocanadian who had known them there. The three settled on the Flats and are the polyandrous family unit discussed above. The other arrivals in 1950 are also from the Keewatin, and all are bound through kinship with the polyandrous family. Akudlik was planned and built between 1953 and 1955; because of too large a labor supply at Fort Chimo, in northern Quebec, a number of Eskimo men were persuaded by the Government to come to Churchill beginning in 1953. They brought their families in 1954 and 1955. Thus, of the two major bands of Eskimo at present in Akudlik, one came from the Keewatin around 1950, and the other from Fort Chimo in the period 1953-1955.

The Eskimo population, particularly of the Fort Chimo group, was once larger, but a number of families have moved back north. In 1958 a family came from Great Whale River, Quebec, apparently for health reasons, and 1959 witnessed the arrival of some more Keewatin Eskimos. The years 1961 and 1962 each saw the arrival of an Eskimo family, both from the Keewatin, and both apparently for health reasons. In 1964 a new wife arrived for a widower in Akudlik. Thereafter the population seems to have become fairly stable, with no immigration of families for the past four years, although an undetermined number of families are believed to have gone back to Fort Chimo, particularly since 1960. The important things to note are, first, that prior to 1955 the primary motivating factor in immigration was opportunity for employment; after that date health reasons brought people to Churchill. Second, it should be realized that movement from Churchill to coastal regions in the Keewatin, particularly from Chesterfield Inlet and south, is not an uncommon feature and occurred with relative frequency in the 1950's and 1960's. Fort Chimo is considerably more distant; and temporary visits there do not seem to have occurred as much, although ties are maintained through letters, and some travel has occurred. The wife in the family from Great Whale River has returned to that settlement once since the family's arrival in 1958. It must be emphasized that few Eskimo families today are confined to a single area. Government attempts to exploit natural resources at Rankin Inlet, have caused movement of Fort Chimo Eskimos to that Keewatin settlement in the 1950's. Today many Eskimo children who attend school receive secondary education at centralized boarding schools, such as the one at Fort Churchill. The Eskimo of Akudlik find that kinship ties can be maintained through school children who come from Fort Chimo and the Keewatin and the far northern islands of the eastern Arctic. Former Keewatin people also find that passage of relatives through the transient center gives them a means of renewing ties. Military needs since World War II have further disrupted Eskimo from their home settlements. Therefore, movement and contact between people over vast distances is not uncommon, and has become a fact of life for the Eskimo of Akudlik. The cause of this movement lies not so much with the Eskimo as with attempts by Government to develop the North, and to provide health, educational and other welfare benefits for the Eskimo population.

The entire Eskimo population is Christian: those from Fort Chimo and Great Whale River and one man from Coral Harbor are Anglican and Eskimo from the Keewatin coast are Roman Catholic. Relations between the two mission groups appear harmonious, and no attempts to proselytize by these denominations are visible. The Christian Alliance, situated at the Townsite would like to evangelize the Eskimo of Akudlik but has not been able to set up a mission for them.

KINSHIP STRUCTURE

An analysis of the kinship structure of Akudlik shows the dominance of a large kinship system centred around a family unit on the Flats. This system includes twenty-two of the eighty-six Eskimo in Akudlik, plus the nine Eskimo/Eurocanadian individuals on the Flats. The points of origin of this kinship system are Repulse Bay area (Aivilingmiut), Chesterfield Inlet, and Tavani (a settlement south of Rankin Inlet). Boas, in *The Central Eskimo*[2], describes the Aivilingmiut band as centred around Repulse Bay (Aivillik) and Committee Bay (on Melville Peninsula), and ranging as far south as Wager Bay, with hunting grounds extending to the northern shore of Chesterfield Inlet. Therefore it may be assumed that contact long existed between the Eskimo band north of Chesterfield Inlet and the band surrounding it. Furthermore, the writers believe that, although Tavani is claimed as the point of origin for some of the Eskimos under discussion, they are in fact Aivilingmiut as well.

Starting from the core residence area on the Flats, we have P.T., the Eskimo male of this polyandrous unit, and his wife, J.T.; each has siblings living in Akudlik. M.E. is P.T.'s adopted sister and W.K. is J.T.'s natural brother. J.T. also has M.A., a younger sister living in Akudlik, married to a son of M.E. (P.T.'s SiSo). M.E. is widowed and lives in Akudlik with L.E., her twenty-year-old unmarried son. M.E. also has a daughter, O.I., living in Akudlik, married to P.I., an Aivilingmiut who has no direct consanguine bonds to the rest. J.T. arranged this marriage between P.I. and O.I., her HuSiDa, and the couple lived for many years with J.T. and P.T. on the Flats, prior to moving to Akudlik. In summary, the Aivilingmiut Band in Churchill is situated in five residential units, four of which are in Akudlik. There is as well, a tendency toward group endogamy with only one conjugal unit including a spouse who is not Aivilingmiut .

The most affluent household among these Aivilingmiut is the group on the Flats, who have far more hunting and fishing equipment than any other Eskimos in Churchill.

When the known siblings of the T. family, M.E. and all of their children are included, a complicated picture results and the diversity of places in which these people are resident indicates the many movements of population which have occurred in this century. J.T. has two siblings at Eskimo Point, two at Akudlik, and one at Igloolik. P.T. has one sibling at Rankin Inlet and another, M.E., in Akudlik. Most of J.T. and P.T.'s children are in Churchill, although one son is working in Alberta. M.E. has three children in Akudlik, two at Whale Cove, one at Rankin Inlet, one at Eskimo Point, and one at Chesterfield Inlet. This group is too large and diverse to be termed more precisely than a kinship system. Realizing the bilateral nature of Eskimo kinship, let me call it the Aivilingmiut band in Churchill.

The second large bloc of individuals are Eskimo from Fort Chimo. Of eighty-six Eskimo in Akudlik, thirty-one are of the Fort Chimo group. An additional three are involved when an Eskimo-Eurocanadian household in the Townsite is included. These thirty-four individuals comprise two extended family systems and one nuclear family living in five households.

The Fort Chimo group also includes one household which is more affluent than the rest. This is the B. Family. Although the affluence includes such things as above average amounts of hunting and fishing equipment, the B. Family also finds it important to acquire material things, such as stereos, books, televisions, etc., which are not a part of traditional Eskimo interests. For example, while both affluent families have motor vehicles, the Fort Chimo family has an old station wagon, and the Aivilingmiut family has a pick-up truck, which is more suited to hunting. This distinction between Churchill's two most affluent Eskimo families, reflects, we believe two different adaptations to modernization which extend to all members of each group. The Aivilingmiut have not, it would appear, taken on as many aspects of the dominant Eurocanadian culture, with its values and goals, as have the Fort Chimo group.

The Aivilingmiut and Fort Chimo groups are the two oldest and largest blocs of population in Akudlik. The Fort Chimo bloc includes all of the Anglican Eskimo except the nuclear family from Great Whale River (husband, wife and adopted son), and one boy from Baker Lake who is the natural brother of a Baker Lake boy adopted by the B. family almost a decade ago. The Great Whale River family interacts far more closely with the Fort Chimo group than with the Catholic Aivilingmiut. This is particularly marked in the area of fishing. Yet another Anglican group is the legally white family of the Eurocanadian administrator about which I have little data.

The remaining individuals all arrived after 1959. All are Catholic and include two unrelated nuclear families from Coral Harbour. There are two other nuclear households from Eskimo Point, the K. and the A. families, linked by the fact that the wives are sisters.

---

[2] Franz Boas, *The Central Eskimo*. Lincoln: University of Nebraska Press, 1964), pp. 37-42 *passim*. (originally published in 1888).

The K. family head and his wife are old and only recently married, having no children from their union. Each has children from earlier marriages and Mr. K. apparently brought his present wife down from Eskimo Point to help manage the household.

EXTRA-MARITAL SEXUAL RELATIONS

The ethnographic and adventure-story accounts of Eskimo aboriginal culture often allude to a greater flexibility in sexual behaviour patterns than that alleged in Eurocanadian and Euroamerican culture. We do not have an aboriginal culture in Churchill but we have considerable data concerning extra-marital sexuality.

First we might briefly examine the genetic contribution of non-Eskimos to our legally Eskimo population in Akudlik. When first encountering the Eskimos of Akudlik, many people are struck by the obvious fact that a large number of them, although socially and culturally completely integrated into the Eskimo community, are not phenotypically completely Eskimo.

Eighty-one of Akudlik's eighty-six individuals having an Eskimo cultural and genetic heritage are legally defined as Eskimo. Of these eighty-one individuals, thirty-three have some known non-Eskimo genetic heritage. Fifteen of the thirty-three individuals have a non-Eskimo genetic contribution of fifty per cent or more. The most significant individuals for our purposes are those who are the direct result of biracial unions, i.e., those individuals who are at least fifty per cent non-Eskimo, the non-Eskimo contributing coming from one parent who is completely non-Eskimo and the other parent being at least partly Eskimo. Fifteen individuals out of eighty-one meet this requirement.

The legally Eskimo population of Akudlik are contained in thirteen households. The fifteen individuals who are fifty per cent or more non-Eskimo are distributed in nine of these households. There is no significant patterned difference in the geographical origin of these fifteen individuals. Eight are part of the Aivilingmiut group, and seven are part of the Fort Chimo group.

The non-Eskimo genetic contribution in the population is Caucasian and Negro. The entry of Negro genes into the community occurred in the first decade of this century. American whaling vessels sailed thoughout Hudson Bay prior to World War I. Negroes were included in the crews and had sexual relations with the aboriginal populations. At present, there are three generations of partially Negro Eskimos in Akudlik, all the descendents of a single individual. No cases of Indian-Eskimo crossings are known to have occurred.

With so small a population, it is impossible to determine any trends over time indicating increasing or decreasing rates of biracial unions from the first case in 1906 to the present. The fact that the cited figures include only children of unions which have been extra-marital indicates that a high frequency of casual sexual unions is common among Eskimos.

An examination of the genetic heritage of the population tells us little regarding rates of extra-marital sexual contact, which of course are far higher. No interest in birth control exists, either between spouses or in casual unions. Children are cherished; social paternity prevails over any biological considerations, and for the most part, although strains do exist at the husband-wife link, the Eskimo male who has an adulterous wife does not treat the children resulting from these casual liaisons any differently from his other children. Pre-marital sexual activity by adolescent females is also quite common. We have therefore, included it below in a general description of adolescent life.

Almost all extra-marital sexual activity crossing racial lines is between an Eskimo female and a Eurocanadian male, often only temporarily in Churchill. Extra-marital sex does not occur solely across racial lines but within the community as well. Contrary to the wife-lending arrangements institutionalized in traditional Eskimo culture, extra-marital sexual relations within and beyond the Eskimo community create problems for the husbands and wives concerned.[3] Husbands sometimes beat their wives; wives may use a liaison as a means of revenge. Such behaviour resembles the familiar Southern Canadian model.

One last point we might note is that, although Eskimos perceive the biological differences between Kabloona (Eurocanadian), Eskimo and Indian stocks, and can point out that an infant looks part Caucasian, there is no clear correlation of race and ethnicity, whereby a biracial individual might lose or dilute his Eskimo identity by the possession of non-Eskimo "blood". In Akudlik some of the children were genetically less than half Eskimo. Yet they were culturally fully integrated into the Eskimo community with no stigma attached to them because of differences in skin or eye color, or any other visible cues.

SOURCES OF INCOME

Having presented the major kinship structures existing among Eskimos in Akudlik, we can turn to a more general discussion of life in Akudlik, which attempts to bring to the fore the daily operations of the underlying kinship structure. Before this discussion is begun let us point out a fact of our fieldwork which must be borne in mind when considering life in Akudlik. We lived in Churchill three months, from June 1st to September 1st, which is from about three weeks prior to break-up until the weather begins to cool off again. This is the period of mildest weather and of longest daylight and is markedly different from the rest of the year. All the questions we could possibly ask could not make up for the fact that we were

[3] George Vranas, *An Ethnographic Account of an Urban Canadian Eskimo Community and the Problems of Extra-Marital Sexuality.* (M.A. Thesis, Chapel Hill, N.C.: University of North Carolina, 1968).

not present in the winter but lived there only during the warmest part of the year. We must, therefore, point out this imbalance in our presentation.

A total of twenty men from Akudlik, the Flats and Townsite are employed on a regular, full-time basis. This accounts for all married and single Eskimo men nineteen years of age and above, with one exception, who is seriously crippled. Therefore there is no male unemployment. Twelve of these men are employed by D.N.A., three by the Department of Public Works in Fort Churchill, two at the government-run laundry, two at *Steelgas*, a private concern selling liquid propane as heating fuel to residents of the townsite, and the last one is a barber who works in a government-supported shop in Fort Churchill. The older, married men employed by D.N.A. and D.P.W. are unskilled or semi-skilled laborers, truck drivers, one painter, and a plumbing apprentice. Laundry employees are also unskilled. Some of the younger, typically unmarried, men are hoping to be able to take a short vocational training course in a particular profession given by D.N.A. and Steelgas. The barber was trained in Winnipeg under the auspices of D.N.A. The important thing to note in these facts is that no one is on public welfare, although admittedly a D.N.A. type of featherbedding exists, with the strong possibility that efficiency would not suffer should some of the unskilled workers be laid off. Furthermore, these full-time, year-round jobs obviate going on the land and hunting for a livelihood. These jobs provide a steady income which allows plans to be made for the future. Therefore, these jobs are central to the lives of Akudlik's Eskimos. The younger men who are waiting to take, or have recently taken, vocational courses, probably will find employment in the north in the pay of the Government, as private concerns like Steelgas are rare. It appears that few are interested in living in the south; and the Government, in fact, would prefer that they remain north, because the Arctic must remain populated for a defensive and ecological reasons.

Another interesting pattern which emerges from the data is that the Aivilingmiut men, six in all, are noticeably absent from D.N.A., employment. Only one works for D.N.A., the other five hold all the positions in D.P.W. and Steelgas. This is no mystery, and the data should not suggest too much. The Aivilingmiut men arrived earlier than the others, before Akudlik was even built, and thus found employment with D.P.W. The two men at Steelgas are around twenty years of age, and close friends as well as kin. One tends to follow the lead of the other. All of the Chimo group works for D.N.A.

However, these jobs are not the only source of income for Eskimo men. A second source, in some cases financially quite significant, is soapstone carving. Quantities of soapstone are supplied free of charge to Eskimos who will carve it into art objects which are placed on sale in Akudlik. If the government supplies the materials, no Eskimo can sell his handicrafts privately, but must place them for sale at the Arts and Crafts Center run by D.N.A. Set prices govern the sculpture; and when a tourist or other party buys a piece of sculpture all of this money, minus a small percentage taken for the maintenance of the center, is given the Eskimo artist. This might run into sizeable sums of money for high quality work. Subjects range from traditional arctic motifs, such as seals, walruses, fish, "igloos", kayaks and Eskimos in traditional dress, to some more unusual subjects such as turtles and crustaceans, which are not indigenous to the north. Little time is given over to carving in the summer months, as most spare time is occupied in fishing or hunting marine life. But in the winter, when it is dark the greater part of the day and the weather is formidable, Eskimo men carve in soapstone. Accurate data are difficult to come by, since the Eskimos seem hesitant to talk about their finances, but a busy and reasonably good carver can make perhaps $100 for twenty hours' work. How often this is done is largely up to the individual Eskimo.

Fishing and hunting of sea mammals, done in the summer months, are not of primary economic importance to the Eskimos in the Churchill area. There is a whaling plant in Churchill that will pay for beluga whales that Eskimos sell to the whaling plant. However, this activity must take place after work or during the short vacation period. Whales are not easy to kill and retrieve; and many hours can go by without luck. As a result, only a small amount of money is gained through whaling. Seals and char, the other summertime targets of Eskimo hunting, bring no financial return.

In addition to this, one Eskimo has the distinctive job of being the Eskimo-language radio announcer on the local radio station, which broadcasts in Eskimo for an hour every night around six.

About half the adult women are housewives, dependent on their husbands. Some work part-time in the kitchens of the two hotels in Churchill, and two are employed as caretakers by D.N.A. at the children's home and transient center. Only one woman has anything near professional status. She is trained as an interpreter and nurse's assistant and works at the hospital in Fort Churchill. One girl, although actually an adolescent, is the Churchill representative of a cosmetic firm in southern Canada and sells cosmetics on a commission basis.

Women who do not have regular jobs usually have another source of income to augment family finances, the making of handicrafts. The women are supplied duffel, tanned caribou hide and other necessary items to make traditional articles of clothing as well as more innovative items. Boots (mukluks), parkas, gloves, hats, slippers and amautiks (used to carry Eskimo children) in all sizes are hand-sewn. In addition, items such as sealskin pocketbooks and grocery bags, seal-skin owls (ookpiks — a symbol of the north) and duffel wall decorations are made. All these items (unless kept for personal use) are placed on sale at the Arts and Crafts center, on the same basis as the men's soapstone carvings.

What should be noted from the above discussion is that most income is derived from full-time salaried positions. Carving and handicrafts merely augment this income, although in some cases considerably. Hunting and fishing are fairly unimportant economically, with income derived from sealskins being used for handicrafts and whale hunting. Furthermore, just about everyone in Akudlik is employed or at school. There are only two welfare cases, a severely crippled youth and an older woman. Although statistics are absent, Eskimo men do not appear from our observations to have particularly high rates of absenteeism, a problem among the Amerindian population of Churchill.

LEISURE ACTIVITIES

It is quite probable that carving and handicrafts-making are enjoyable pastimes for Eskimos, but we will not consider this to be "leisure" as the economic benefits are too important. Hunting and fishing, on the other hand, are almost completely in the area of leisure for the Eskimos of Churchill. In the fall, Canada geese are hunted; in the winter ptarmigan are a favorite, and Arctic fox and rabbit are available. Both sexes hunt the geese and ptarmigan. Caribou, although not far from Churchill, may not be hunted because of legal restrictions.

The greatest amount of hunting and fishing takes place in the summer months, when light is longer and the marine mammals and fish are close at hand. Seals, available much of the year, are particularly hunted from just before breakup until the next winter. The beluga whale is available from July until before freezeup; and char and other fish are caught after break-up.

For the men, hunting and fishing are limited to after working hours, weekends and vacation. At these times most men will have gone down to the beaches. Boats and equipment are usually stored on the beach, some men having small, locked shacks at the beach for their nets, harpoons, rifles, etc. The boats, which are sixteen to twenty foot wooden canoes powered by outboard motors, are kept on the beach for the entire season, Rifles, canoe, outboard motor and fuel and paddles aside, the special equipment needed is: for beluga, a harpoon and empty oil cans used as floats; for char and whitefish, four-inch gill nets with weights and floats; and for seals, nothing more than already mentioned. Equipment usually includes provisions for overnight stay, particularly bannock and tins of luncheon meats, tea, teapots, drinking mugs, knives, toilet paper, sometimes fresh water and often beer. Soft drinks are often taken for the children and adolescents. Life jackets are sometimes taken in the canoes. A tent is usually set up at the beginning of the season. Tents, bullets, rifles, canoes, outboard motors, and nets, are all store-bought, usually from the Hudson's Bay Company store in Churchill. Rubber boots and hipwaders are taken as well. Blankets serve for sleeping although some sleeping bags are used.

The Eskimos of Akudlik have two primary camping areas. One, which is frequented by women and children, is under one hour's walk from Akudlik, over the muskeg and rocks to a beach on Hudson Bay. The second area is across the river, at the point of land called Eskimo Point, just north of Fort Prince of Wales. Gill nets are placed on the far side of this little peninsula. A trip here is usually an overnight stay, and the place is frequented by the men, particularly on weekends. Younger men from the Keewatin who are not in the company of older adults prefer not to fish, but merely to seal and whale. These individuals do not own tents, and tend to lead a more spartan life when camping out. The Ft. Chimo group, dominated by three older men, is very much interested in char fishing, and this takes up the bulk of the three men's time on the land. In addition, the Fort Chimo women and the Great Whale River women all exhibit an interest in fishing not possessed by the Keewatin women who are employed part-time or are kept busy making handicrafts. The Fort Chimo women are sometimes absent from Akudlik three days or more, only to return briefly to make more bannock, get more supplies, wash and tidy the younger children, and then go back to the beach.

I have characterized hunting and fishing in Churchill as leisure because the Eskimo greatly enjoy the prospect of going out on the land, many supplies being prepared and taken, and often a case or two of beer added to make things particularly enjoyable. Although the fish usually are eaten, and the few whales are sold and seals provide food and their fur, the cost of hunting is far greater than the worth of the food supply caught. When large amounts of equipment or numerous children have to be transported, a taxi is called which costs $2.00, each way. Between tides the drinking of beer to excess is a common pattern, which tends to confine would-be hunters to their tents. All this makes hunting and fishing uneconomical but a great deal of fun.

Adult leisure time activities do not merely consist of hunting and fishing. Bingo games are in operation two or three nights a week at the townsite. A number of Eskimo adults are fairly regular bingo players, with the dominant position taken by the Fort Chimo group. A local television station has a "TV bingo" competition nightly; and many Eskimos, most of whom have television, play "TV bingo". Women seem particularly drawn to this, although the competition is broadcast in the early evening. Television itself provides limited leisure activity for adults, as facility in English, for most Eskimo adults, is limited, although numerals on the English system have long been adopted by Eskimo language speakers. Therefore, bingo does not offer the barrier posed by English dialogue. Some adults listen to the Eskimo-language broadcasts on radio.

Beer parties, leading to intoxication for the participants, might be considered as a leisure time activity in their own right, although they accompany other activities, such as hunting, and a visit to the bars in Churchill after bingo is not uncommon. The typical drinking pattern leads to drunkenness or extreme light-headedness. The Eskimos of Akudlik seem to be either heavy drinkers, who end up intoxicated after every drinking session and who typically consume all the beer at hand, or complete abstainers. The social drinker or moderate drinker, who might have a few cans of beer at one time, leaving some for another time, does not seem to exist. Twenty-two adults are moderately heavy to heavy drinkers, and seven are total abstainers by choice. One other abstains because of poor health. With one observed exception (a particularly heavy drinker), drinking tends to be a group activity, with anywhere from three to seven or eight adults drinking together at home, and smaller groups drinking while fishing or after bingo in the hotel bars. Eurocanadians sometimes drink with the Eskimos, particularly if the Eurocanadian hopes to make a sexual contact with an Eskimo woman.

Smoking is another activity which Eskimo adults enjoy. Just about every adult Eskimo smokes, and no negative sanction against smoking exists similar to the negative value felt by a minority toward drinking. In a number of cases children as young as thirteen smoke regularly, with their parents' knowledge. Usually the Eskimos roll their own cigarettes, since this is cheaper. Cigarettes by the pack are sixty cents in Churchill. Many, even those with long histories of respiratory problems and tuberculosis, are heavy smokers. Pipes and cigars are not noted. No other stimulants or drugs seem to be in use.

Contours of Eskimo Adolescent Life in Churchill

The greater part of the adolescent's day is taken up by school. Attendance is mandatory until age sixteen, and having to repeat a year is not uncommon. My data are not complete enough to assess the matter of education except at the most superficial level. I am believed by my Eskimo informants to have a high positive regard for education and staying in school, which I apparently project in my discussions with adolescents. Therefore, I tend to get expressions of positive valuations of school and occupational hopes which do not coincide with the student's standard of achievement in the classroom. For the adolescent group, the spoken language is no longer a problem in the classroom, since almost all have better facility in English than in Eskimo.

EDUCATION

Education of the Eurocanadian type is new to the Eskimos, and no strong motivation for classroom education exists in most Eskimo homes. It has developed in a few households, where it is viewed as a tool for success in a Eurocanadian-dominated world. But this presupposes a belief that a discontinuity exists between traditional Eskimo culture and the Eurocanadian world, and that somehow the latter will displace the former, so that most of adjustment will have to take place on the part of the Eskimos. In some homes, particularly those of families from Quebec, there are strong indications that such a complex of insights exists, but in most other homes this is not clearly indicated. In these other homes education is not stressed. These people appear to have few thoughts about the future. The assaults on traditional Eskimo culture by modern Canadian society and the readjustments and changes demanded of the Eskimos do not seem to be perceived by the Eskimos as posing problems in their lives. The more traditional Eskimos may note with some misgiving that their children are "less Eskimo" culturally than they are. But there seems to be little awareness of how or why this has happened. Some may be able to conceptualize "modern Canadian culture" as the cause of culture change; however, no one seems to feel that it lies at all within the power of the Eskimo to challenge modern Canadian culture.

No Akudlik Eskimos thus far have completed secondary school, although two will be entering the tenth grade in September 1966. Few children in earlier years were in the proper age category having started school later than Eurocanadian children. The fact that today more adolescents are going into the upper grades, and are completing more years of school in Churchill without being considerably older than their Eurocanadian classmates, suggests that in the next few years a number of students will complete secondary school. The school population of Akudlik, incidentally, attends a predominately Euro-canadian Manitoba school in Fort Churchill. The Eskimo hostel is a different institution, drawing upon pre-vocational students from all over the Eastern Arctic, but not from Churchill.

THE ESKIMO PRE-VOCATIONAL HOSTEL AT FORT CHURCHILL

In September each year, the Eskimo population of the Churchill area increases by approximately 220. These 220 individuals are Eskimo adolescents attending the Pre-Vocational School at Fort Churchill. The Franklin and Keewatin Districts of the Northwest Territory and Quebec supply these students.

Although the boarding school attempts to minimize the student's contacts with the community it is not possible to isolate them completely. Some of the Pre-Vocational students have relatives in Akudlik. Many others have family friends there. These students are permitted to visit Akudlik. The students at the boarding school attend church services in Eskimo with the Akudlik people and Akudlik teen-agers often attend the weekly hostel dances. Since seventy of the hostel students are in the regular academic program at the Fort Churchill school they have ample opportunity to associate with Akudlik Eskimo.

The policy of non-fraternization between the Pre-Vocational students and the Akudlik and other Churchill adolescents seems based on a theory that the hostel students would be corrupted by the local teens. The Pre-Vocational administrators take great pride in the very low pregnancy rate at their establishment. They express fear that the promiscuity of local adolescents could easily influence their Eskimo charges.

OCCUPATIONAL ASPIRATIONS

Occupational aspirations for adolescent boys tend to be generally manual and mechanical. Some want to take courses to learn how to operate large earth-moving vehicles, others want to drive trucks, or to learn a vocation such as carpentry, electrical work or plumbing by attending an intensive course in southern Canada. One boy wants to be a Royal Canadian Mounted Policeman. None of those questioned expressed any interest in any occupation requiring university training, and the suggestion of becoming a teacher is usually rejected outright. The adolescent girls, few in number, indicate some vague interest in nursing or an allied occupation; and one girl, already selling cosmetics on a commission basis, expresses some interest in becoming a beautician. The motivation for a job probably is not as strong in adolescent females as in males, as motherhood looms ahead. This is not necessarily considered an unhappy end.

LEISURE ACTIVITIES

Leisure-time activities for adolescents in Akudlik must be considered rather separately for each sex. Social maturation seems to occur at particularly distinct rates as to sex among the Eskimo of Akudlik. Boys tend to lag quite far behind girls in their social development. Here, I am particularly concerned with sex and dating habits, but there are indications that juvenile attitudes to other matters persist longer in boys. Four of the five unmarried Eskimo girls in Akudlik have had sexual intercourse. Of these four, two are pregnant; and the other two have been treated for venereal disease. The fifth girl is believed to be a virgin; her father attempts to be very strict with her, although this procedure leads the girl to date under various pretexts. Furthermore, her older sister, now married, had conceived her child before marriage. Sexual experience of this magnitude simply does not exist for the Eskimo boy of the same age. Sexual needs just do not effectively express themselves in the boy between 15 and 19. By 19 and into young adulthood, boys may have girlfriends in the hostel or at school. But these girls are fairly closely watched so that sexual activity is probably not common. The physically attractive Eskimo boys between twenty and twenty-five seem to have no trouble finding sexual outlets within the resident community, sometimes with a rather disruptive result.

For the Eskimo girl in Akudlik the situation is different. Dating and sexual contacts tend to be with Eurocanadian young men in their twenties. These young men often have cars and drive them slowly through Akudlik, planning to attract the attention of the Eskimo girls. The girls seem to expect them, and are prepared for their arrival. When a parent is away, perhaps down at the beach for the night, a few of the girls will have a house party with some young men usually resulting in sexual intercourse. Contacts are made in other ways as well. Community dances, which are held in early summer, are an important source of dates. Girls go in groups but tend to meet Eurocanadian boyfriends, by a prearranged plan, at these dances. Along with this behavior, girls usually drink although they are below the legal drinking age and are, therefore, barred from taverns.

The boys from fourteen to nineteen years of age seem far more interested in hunting and fishing, in athletics and obtaining a Honda motorbike. These are very popular, and boys take girls for fast and daring rides over the back roads of the Churchill area. Many Eurocanadian boys have Hondas as well, and the Eskimo boys tend to become friendly with these white boys. In Akudlik, friendship patterns across racial lines seem much more marked among adolescent boys than among girls.

COMMUNITY LEADERSHIP

The literature of Eskimo ethnography makes much of the apparent absence of political organization above the kinship-centered band level. The only references beyond kinship refer to the existence of camp headmen, or *ihumatar* (lit.: "he who thinks"), as described by van den Steenhoven.[4] Briefly, the camp headman assumes the role of leader on the basis of experience and respect. Since he has no formal political authority, others are free to follow or not. His leadership usually is concerned with movements of the band, or with hunting. Looking at the Eskimos of Akudlik for individuals in any way structurally definable as leaders yields only scant results. One man might be characterized as a good hunter and provider for his family. He is generally spoken well of by both Fort Chimo and Aivilingmiut Eskimos. However, except for the fact that adolescent youths want to go hunting with this man and use him as an example of a good hunter, decision making for a group larger than his family is not needed in the town of Akudlik.

Instead of trying to find community "leaders" in Akudlik it is more productive to conceptualize human links between the Eskimo community and the Eurocanadians, particularly the D.N.A. administrators. Akudlik has such a "human link". He is the most acculturated and consequently the most prosperous Eskimo in Akudlik. He speaks English with considerable fluency and is the Eskimo-language radio announcer. He emerges as an Eskimo leader in the area of "white ways". He has many acquaintances in the Eurocanadian community, and seems to invite these contacts. His eldest daughter is married to a Eurocanadian and lives in the Townsite.

The Eskimo groups see in this person a man who knows how to get along in the Eurocanadian world; and he is, therefore, useful as a

---

[4] Geert Van den Steenhoven, *Leadership and Law Among the Eskimos of the Keewatin District, Northwest Territories.* (Rijswijk, The Netherlands: Uitgeverij Excelsior, 1962), p. 54.

link between Eskimo and Eurocanadian. He may also be asked for money on loan; and his extensive hunting and fishing equipment may be used, at least by other Fort Chimo Eskimos.

Although he has this linking quality, it should not be assumed that he is an individual to be imitated. Most Eskimos see this man as important in a practical sense, not necessarily in a charismatic sense. Furthermore, he emerges as a leader because the Eurocanadian community sees him as a leader and finds this human link convenient in dealing with or organizing support among the other Eskimos. It is important to note that a "link" can carry with it few notions of actual power or authority, and this is the case here. Eurocanadians disregard or are not aware of this man's lack of actual authority in the Eskimo community, possibly because Eurocanadians have difficulty accepting the notion of acephalous social systems, and confuse Eskimo social organization with tribal or patriarchal peasant societies elsewhere in the world.

CONCLUSION

Links to the larger community are an important structural feature of the Eskimo community. The Eurocanadians, controlling the power and very much present, must be adjusted to via human links so that a resolution of Eurocanadian cultural demands and traditional Eskimo behavior can be achieved. The result is that, although links exist, it cannot really be stated that Akudlik has any Eskimo leaders, in a political sense. Certain individuals, because of special abilities, may emerge as somewhat more important than others; but any "leadership" which may derive from these abilities is of the most ephemeral variety. Ultimately, the power rests with D.N.A.; and, although the administration is benevolent toward the Eskimos, no encouragement is given the Eskimos to govern their own local affairs. The present situation may persist for some time.

4

The Eskimo
of Frobisher Bay*

John Honigmann
Irma Honigmann

The Eskimo townsmen in this southern Baffin Island community are "people under tutelage". According to the Honigmanns, cultural change has been accomplished with considerable success. On the one hand, change may be attributed to such alleged Eskimo character traits as "resourcefulness... [and] confidence to experiment," and on the other hand, to "an active and interested [Euro-Canadian] administration."

Since most of the adult Eskimo population was not born in Frobisher Bay, learning in the new environment has involved every aspect of living. For example, the scope of Eskimo learning has ranged from the consequences of an unpaid telephone bill to the penalties — formal and informal — surrounding the immoderate consumption of alcoholic beverages. Much of this new learning creates stress, to which a characteristic Eskimo response is withdrawal. Such behaviour is often typical of minority members who cannot or choose not to conform to the demands and expectations of the dominant group.

Although much learning is taking place in Frobisher Bay, it tends to be one-sided; the Eskimo receives instruction from and mimics the Euro-Canadian. What might this trend portend for the future of the Eskimo as a culturally distinctive and viable ethnic group?

*An abstract of the book, *Eskimo Townsmen*, prepared by the authors for *Minority Canadians*. *Eskimo Townsmen* was published by The Canadian Research Centre for Anthropology, Ottawa, Ontario, 1965.

In January, 1963, when the RCMP completed their latest count, 906 Eskimos made Frobisher Bay in southern Baffin Island their home. There, among other goals, they pursue what they themselves identify as a goal of happiness. In order to achieve things that bring happiness in the modern world, many families send somebody out to a job; or somebody produces something at home that will earn income. For those who cannot find remunerative work, a satisfying life in town depends on social assistance, and for those physically unable to hold jobs, the environs of the Rehabilitation Centre provides a sheltered environment.

There are 261 men between fifteen and sixty-nine in Frobisher Bay, and about one-third of them are steadily employed. Eskimos who are full-time employees work in a variety of occupations. One man assists a chef; a woman bakes bread, cake, and pastry in the bakery; several men drive trucks, tractors, and power graders; some help the electrician and plumber; many more work in the carpenter shop; garages are staffed by motor and heavy equipment mechanics; a number of men collect garbage and sewage from houses; several are painters; four young men sit behind desks in offices much of the day; in the laundry men and women fill a variety of tasks, including that of licensed stationary engineer. The Northern Canada Power Commission has Eskimo trainees in its generator plant. By the time we left Frobisher Bay the RCMP had imported a special constable from farther North, and an airline serving the town uses two trainees to load and unload aircraft and to work around the airdrome.

Jobs set goals for the Eskimo that contrast, sometimes sharply, with the demands exercised by such traditional roles as hunter and housewife. Weather no longer controls his activities as it does on the land. He must show up for work even if it is blowing a blizzard (provided work hasn't been called off). His basic workweek demands that he be on the job forty-four hours to forty-eight hours. His job starts at a given time and be there he must, even if he stayed up late the previous night. Being mostly repetitive, jobs also require a certain tolerance for monotony.

We calculated the net or take-home pay (what remains after deducting taxes, rent, and in some cases groceries) of fifteen Eskimo employed by the Federal Government, the town's largest and best paying employer. Their earnings, which include overtime pay, range from about $2,705, earned by a widower with grown children who lives in a married daughter's house to $5,644, earned by a road grader-operator.

Thanks mainly to Government-operated facilities, even the socially and physically handicapped manage to be incorporated in useful and, at least sometimes, congenial roles. The Federal Governments Rehabilitation Centre provides artists of both sexes, especially carvers, with remunerative opportunities to pursue their bent. The Centre not only advances capital, in the form of material that individuals could only with difficulty secure for themselves, but in the winter of 1963 guaranteed a cash market to practically every craftsman. If the artist is also a rehabilitant, the Centre subsidizes him to the extent of providing housing, clothing, food, and meals.

Both wage earners' and hunters' families in their homes also turn out duffel-lined parkas, stuffed dolls, embroidered duffel socks, slippers, and an unending stream of soapstone carvings. Home industries earn extra cash for families receiving social assistance and for retired men who live with married children. Some products are purely utilitarian, like sealskin boots sewn with watertight seams, but many women and the carvers, who are mostly men, execute work that clearly betrays their own aesthetic sensibilities.

The extent to which home industries augmented family income can be gauged from the fact that the Centre, from April, 1962 through March, 1963 paid 288 craftsmen a total of $40,686 for their crafts. Most producers earned less than $100 throughout the year, but a handful received $1,000 or more. Two local shops retail handicrafts (the U.S. airbase supplying many customers while it was in Frobisher Bay).

I. COMMUNITY ORGANIZATION

One of the fundamental characteristics of Frobisher Bay community life is the living together in town of two ethnic groups, Eskimos and Eurocanadians. Mostly the two segments work together harmoniously. Occasionally they run into conflict of a nonviolent kind that rarely gets a thorough airing. Such conflict occurs over discordant values concerning school or the sale of alcoholic beverages, over competition for the same goals, and over power.

Bases for class distinction are present among Eskimos to a degree never before true in the Eastern Arctic and they are increasing. For example, some Eskimos live in one-room prefabs or huts without electricity while others occupy multiroom co-op houses with brand new amenities. Although evidence of poverty can not be discerned, hunters with low cash incomes head some families and men steadily employed with earnings of $3,000 or more annually head others. Yet up to now inequalities in income, jobs, and housing have failed to promote social classes, partly due to the possibilities for mobility available in the town to which came people of relatively equal backgrounds. Practically everybody could get a job or gain a livelihood through a combination of home industries, welfare, and family allowances.

Power, however, is unequally distributed, both within the community as a whole and among the Eskimos as a group. Officials of the Department of Indian Affairs and Northern Development, of course, possess the lion's share of power in community affairs, but they use it judiciously and circumspectly, keeping a firm hand covered by a velvet glove. Often administration does not use its overwhelming power to do things *for* the Eskimos but employs its talents and other resources to help the people accomplish aims that both parties see as worthwhile. The housing co-op, Community Council, and Community Association constitute large-scale, successful examples of this type.

Eskimos share in community decision making mainly through participating in the Community Council and the much livelier Apex Hill Community Association. That those organizations have been initiated and are guided by Eurocanadians should not deter us from considering them as part of modern Eskimo life. By participating in those organizations, Eskimos in fact maintain them.

So far there have been thirteen Council sessions. These have discussed the following major issues: paychecks; payment of hospital bills; plans for a consumer co-op; use of hereditary family names for Eskimos; new elections to the Council; improvements for Ikhaluit, a neighborhood of the town; control of alcohol; keeping dogs tied; role of the police; hunting regulations, and promiscuity. A number of these matters originated with Government, though in the minutes they may be reported as being presented by the chairman. Until now the Council has largely been reactive, and usually has assented to suggestions put before it by officials. Significantly, however, it has also at times assumed a more positive role, criticizing the Government and requesting certain administrative actions, such as a curfew on young people and better housing facilities and amenities in Ikhaluit.

Providing movies, dances, and other recreation keeps the Community Association's board of directors one of the liveliest Eskimo-manned bodies in Frobisher Bay. The group operates through a board of directors which appoints committees to run social affairs. Services go unpaid and the Association has shown an annual profit of close to $2,000. In 1963 it planned to operate a public bus line between the scattered neighborhoods of the town, a venture that threatened competition for the white-operated taxi company.

The Community Council, the Community Association's board of directors, as well as the Anglican Church Council are channels that facilitate the emergence of a local elite. To highly motivated individuals, offices in these bodies provide opportunities to exercise and develop leadership.

II. SOCIALIZATION: PEOPLE UNDER TUTELAGE

At almost every turn, the town exacts learning by Eskimos as the price of surviving in their town roles. Eurocanadian-set laws and administrative policies are among the foremost conditions that call forth learning. For example, a series of legal and administrative acts brought alcohol within Eskimo's easy reach, thereby initiating a vast educational situation. A Government-sponsored housing co-op led more than a dozen families to change their style of life, and official sponsorship of a proposed consumer co-op would similarly alter buying habits. Since Eurocanadians apportion many desirable rewards of town life, they also possess powerful means of sanctioning learning. An Eskimo who will not acquire correct work habits loses his job; if he doesn't pay his bill, the company disconnects his phone, and so on.

Change in the Eskimos has proceeded with considerable success. Why? The Eskimos' successful adjustment to a new culture depends on many mutually reinforcing elements in their current situation, including their curiosity, resourcefulness, a readiness to "try it", confidence to experiment, intelligence to benefit from experience, and on other character traits acquired in early life. Eskimos are given to testing their ability to master some new experiences and in doing so even venture beyond the bounds envisaged by Eurocanadian tutors. Change is aided by the fact that Eskimos participate in many areas of town life as if they were fully entitled to those resources of the town. The previous culture's stripped-down nature itself promotes change. With less to unlearn, no vested interests to be placed in jeopardy by new learning, and little of a hallowed tradition to conflict with new behavior, change can go fast. Then, too, the very fact that change proceeds on a broad front, simultaneously affecting many areas of life, probably facilitates cultural transformation. One new element (for example, wage labor) is quite compatible with several others (schooling for children, commercial recreation, house ownership, and furnishing the house). Joining the Sisi Housing Co-op and building their own houses gave several families a heightened incentive to modernize, but it is very significant that all married men in the co-op are steadily employed and have chosen the town to be their home. The home owners' good income permits them to gratify their wishes for a new style of life and gives point to their wives voluntarily attending sewing and cooking classes. That many Eskimos voluntarily came to, or remain in, Frobisher Bay suggests a largely self-selected population, and one highly motivated to experiment with new lifeways. Finally, instead of being left alone, the Eskimos are helped, encouraged, guided, goaded to change by an active and interested administration, many of whose employees genuinely support the transition for which they consciously feel responsible.

For all its broad front, tutelage goes on unevenly, some areas of life being relatively neglected. Experience teaches the Eskimo how to act in court, but nobody instructs him on his legal rights. No sanctions are put on the putative fathers of babies born out of wedlock to make them assume financial responsibility. Individuals, too, learn at different rates and then go in different directions. Few, if any, women know how to drive. Young women between sixteen and twenty-five, compared to their male peers, speak English better and more readily, are far more sophisticated in dancing and habits of dress, and show greater ease in meeting whites. When girls of this age group have also had opportunity to live in southern Canada, they emulate flawlessly many tastes of Eurocanadian girls of the same age .

A. The Rehabilitation Centre

Two major local institutions are deliberately designed for socialization: The Rehabilitation Centre serving primarily teenagers and adults, and the school. These two groups build in tutelage as their official mission.

We watched the Rehabilitation Centre closely, for its ambitious aim of guiding Eskimos' resocialization (rather than, as the name might suggest, providing physical rehabilitation), intrigued us from the beginning of our stay. Organized around a core of income-producing projects, including a coffee shop, bakery, carving room, sewing centre, and kitchen, "Rehab" gives its clients useful things to do as they develop their potentialities under the superintendent's close, personal direction. Residents who can benefit attend classes in English, arithmetic, and other subjects taught by a special teacher as well as learning such income-producing skills as sewing, carving, gem grinding, and print making. Eurocanadian technical experts, notably a carpenter, crafts instructor, and cook, assist the pivotal superintendent. The superintendent is an exceptional man, fluent in Eskimo, with a long northern experience first as a Hudson's Bay Company employee and later as a D.I.A.N.D. officer.

People enter Rehab because "something is wrong with them" for which they can compensate or that can be corrected. Rehabilitants fall into two classes: those whom illness or surgery have rendered incapable of any longer living on the land as hunters and trappers, and others diagnosed as suffering from psychosocial problems whose conduct alarms the community; for example, promiscuous girls. Residents in the first class are assisted to become self-sufficient through mastering congenial new skills and work habits. Those in the second class, while able to benefit from enhanced self-sufficiency, need encouragement to develop moral obligations and acceptable social roles — a much harder task for the Centre's staff. In both cases a rehabilitant's family may have only recently come off the land, so that they have room to learn new habits appropriate to town life, like housekeeping routines, preparation of new dishes, English, and elementary hygiene.

In an informal way, everyone joining the Centre undergoes evaluation for three or four months, during which the superintendent closely scrutinizes his conduct. The period is long enough to disclose a case of a person whose profound indifference can't be budged, whose impulsiveness won't be controlled, or who avoids even the simplest rules. As a result, he is quickly dropped. That happened to Simigak,[1] a twenty-one-year-old, illegitimate child of a transient white man, and adopted daughter of an Ikhaluit family. In 1961 she had been convicted of theft and sentenced to serve a short term in a southern reformatory. Rehab admitted her briefly as a social problem, promiscuity being included in her troublesome behavior. A friendless girl, she speaks good English and dresses neatly, two skills that may have helped her find part-time housework at the Airbase. We have heard her referred to as peculiar subnormal, a compulsive thief, and as bidding to be arrested again so that she could return to the reformatory. Such characterizations signify little more than a difficult person, someone whom no one has succeeded in understanding, and whom the Centre could not "work with".

Diagnosis of a newly-admitted client allows the superintendent to plan a program compatible with the client's formal education, skills, and physical condition, but one inevitably limited by the Centre's physical resources and social skills. Pudloo, a man nearly forty years old, returned North after 9 years in a sanitorium, minus one lung. Although he once ran a vessel between Frobisher Bay and Lake Harbour, he can now do only light work and has been assigned to the carpenter shop. The men here, at least when they have a specific job to do, work well, responding dutifully to their Eurocanadian supervisor's orders, given in English. Learning in the shop depends on practice and example, rather than on formal instruction.

Women attend sewing classes three mornings weekly, as well as cooking and baking classes, which co-opt the professional cook as teacher, on two mornings. In the sewing room they are put through a regular sequence of instruction, including pattern making, cutting, sewing, and embroidery. Two afternoons each week, women meet in the art shop to learn silkscreen printing. Each pupil is supposed to draw her own design. Frequently she makes scenes of traditional Eskimo life, featuring snowhouses, dogs, and people clothed in traditional garb. The attractive cards that the women then print find a lively local market. On two other afternoons, women work in the gem room, located behind the men's carving shop, learning to design and fashion pins. They also grind Baffin Island gems and gingerly operate other machinery. Friday after lunch is unassigned, women being free then to use any facilities they choose. Also that day is reserved for group meetings, when the goals of Rehab are re-explained, the necessity for discipline emphasized, and rehabilitants' attention focussed on their goals.

With respect to the more personal aspects of re-socialization, particularly for clients admitted to the Centre primarily as social problems, Rehab efforts remain much less focussed, and nobody talks too happily about achievements. Hopefully, such residents absorb habits of responsibility, learn something of demands to be faced in the job world, and become accustomed to the regime and dependability on which white employers insist. Young men, at least, will have to make

[1] All names and other identifying characteristics in this section have been altered.

such standards their own before they can become reasonably well-adjusted townsmen. Some do adjust, though as the following case of Poulat illustrates, the role of Rehab may be hard to fathom. This young man was born twenty-three years ago in southern Baffin Island. Following a technical course in Manitoba, completed in 1957, he came to Frobisher Bay where he worked until 1960. Although judged capable, his work habits proved so unreliable that once he received a month's suspension as punishment for absenteeism. At this time he also married, but drinking and infidelity are credited with quickly spoiling his relationship with his wife. She tried vainly to persuade him to leave Frobisher Bay, threatening that otherwise she would leave him. In October, 1960, moderately advanced pulmonary tuberculosis sent him South. In the sanitorium where he recovered, he practiced good carving, dropped a typing course despite having made fair progress, and refused to master English. Word received from Ottawa in the spring of 1961, reporting that his wife had quit Frobisher Bay, apparently deeply depressed him. On his return to Frobisher Bay in October, 1961, he sought "work" in the Rehabilitation Centre. Three months later the court punished him for wilful damage. He proved so uncooperative and unreliable in the Centre that the superintendent, who also suspected he had pilfered a cash box, soon released him as unrehabilitated. Dismissal left him bitterly resenting the Centre and its staff. For seven months he drifted, in the spring of 1962 being arrested for public intoxication. Then in September, 1962 he seized a chance to apply for on-the-job vocational training. Since then, as everyone admits, he has attended to his responsibilities faithfully, in addition to restoring good relations with the Rehab staff.

No staff member employed in the Centre conceives of his role over-optimistically. In fact, staff members carry a persistent image of difficulties they encounter. Employees emphasize the dearth of economic opportunities in Frobisher Bay to which rehabilitants can be successfully graduated. They regard the town as an unfavorable environment in which to accomplish rehabilitation, one especially unsuitable for young people who have been admitted to the Centre as social problems. Disorganized, the town tempts young people to drink excessively and encourages crime and illicit sex. They maintain that the Centre's limited effectiveness is due to the fact that rehabilitation alone cannot fit Eskimos who have come off the land for a place in Frobisher Bay society. The society, too, must change if Eskimos are to enjoy greater economic mobility. Other difficulties that complicate their attempts at re-socialization they acknowledge less readily, or not at all, like being forced to work without aid of a professionally trained therapist or full-time social worker; having to work cross-culturally with divergent values and expectations, and being confronted by the Eskimos' tendency to withdraw under relatively intense social pressure such as the rehabilitation process, for all its permissiveness, necessarily entails.

B. Childrearing and School

The school aims to transmit to Eskimos a substantial portion of the heritage of western civilization, the portion deemed appropriate for mastery by children. By its very nature, the official aim allows very little if any scope for suiting the school's curriculum to local conditions and problems, neither to the Eskimo's traditional role on the land nor his newly-found career in town. The official goal also prevents school from utilizing the Eskimo child's own language during the first few years of schooling. While individual teachers vary in their educational philosophies, some firmly agree that their duty requires preparing the Eskimo child to become aware of the world beyond his local environment, a world he can only encounter directly by going south.

An Eskimo youngster who starts school at five does so at a time when his previous extreme dependence on his parents, particularly on his mother, has ended. In that sense he is ready for school. Since he was three, an older sibling or some other older child living in the household, has not only cared for him by carrying him in an *amawt,* but has taken him within the borders of the active children's world to which the caretaker belonged. In infancy and during years immediately following, at least until a sibling came into the world, the youngster could hardly escape playful adult attention. Adults made him a cynosure and bent their efforts to stimulate him, to make him notice them, to evoke in him a happy, emotional response. Eskimos, who believe that small children urgently need secure affection, cherish a baby carefully. Although extremely tolerant of adoption, they deplore emergencies that require a child to be passed rootlessly from hand to hand. Yet, as devoted as a mother is, she is never so wholly engrossed in her baby that she lacks time for the town's manifold interest. Occasionally her attention becomes so intensely concentrated — say on her print making in the Rehabilitation Centre, on a movie, or on a bingo game — that the toddler is left unattended and unheeded to cry alone, so that she can go on with whatever she is doing as long as possible. Her behaviour foretells the relatively high degree of independence that the youngster will enjoy in a very few years.

By age five, the child's independence is real. Though he already visits other homes, it is perhaps a little too soon for him to be roaming around his neighborhood in a peer group; but the age when he will be incorporated in a children's world, the axis of his waking hours, is not far off. The five-year-old is ready for school in the sense that he has been weaned emotionally from his parents, though they are still important figures in his life. He was weaned easily, largely at his own speed, spurred much by his own impetus to growth, aided by his basic security, and drawn by the attractive activities of other youngsters in camp and town. In other words, he broke his dependence in quite an independent fashion; a fashion consistent with the dominant emphasis on independence which colours almost every element in Eskimo childhood.

One thing the school-age child is unprepared for: the discipline enforced in the classroom. The children have grown up with minimal rules and flexible routines, privileged to enjoy considerable emotional spontaneity. We never observed children being trained to inhibit emotion; only in church did we ever see one being restrained if he became over-excited. Parents are easily persuaded to give in to a child's wishes, for instance, generously buying him candy and soft drinks at a movie even if they believe that "too much" candy is bad for the teeth. Physical punishment occurs rarely, though on occasion it does happen that children are spanked. Parents scold much more frequently, but it too takes on the distinctive colour of the culture, so that it supports rather than interferes with the youngster's increasing independence and resourcefulness. For a child never needs to become penitent or submissive before his parents, nor is punishment unrelentingly dragged out to humiliate him. Parents may even follow scolding by offering candy to a small child. Only if a youngster moves too near danger does discipline grow sharp and utterly imperative.

Eskimo children beyond six or seven have relatively little to do with adults, even in their own family. They contrive to be away from home much of the day, especially in summer. Eskimo child culture is a peer-group culture, and the growing individual continues to be bound closely to his peers throughout adolescence, until his late marriage. The peer group provides a rich source of socialization, one that may easily compete with school and even oppose Eurocanadian authorities in town. But it is too strongly locked away from adult outsiders for us ever to have succeeded in penetrating it. From what we could observe and what we heard, there can be no doubt that in the peer group children and teen-agers carry on far more animated and emotionally uninhibited lives than they reveal in school.

In teen-age years make-believe play more or less ceases. Boys begin to turn their enthusiasm to the real thing, hunting. They also talk darkly about the Sevens and Thirteens, rival gangs with duly appointed leaders and hand-printed membership cards inspired by that desirable franchise, the driver's license. Not that children at this age don't have some responsibilities at home; they do, though work is not consciously assigned to provide deliberate training for later-life industriousness. We have spoken of caretakers of small babies; such employment starts when a girl is seven and lasts through her early teen-age years. Both boys and girls are recruited to serve as baby-sitters. Even if a household contains a girl old enough to help with housework, a boy of twelve may be asked to wash dishes and to sweep. Such services aren't very burdensome, especially not for boys; they don't long keep him away from his peer-group.

Eskimo parents instruct their children with a minimum of accompanying explanation; they seldom try to explain why some task should be done or a skill mastered. An explanation, presumably, will be found in the situation by the child itself as he learns to understand it through becoming practically, rather than theoretically, involved in it. Of necessity, the school's curriculum forces teachers to ignore this educational technique — learning by doing — which many American-Indian people follow. Instruction in school is highly rationalized, with children constantly being given reasons for certain rules and expectations.

The school's greatest flexibility and boldest attempt at cultural integration occurs with respect to absenteeism for hunting and fishing. In spring the principal permits children, whose families are going to coastal camps, to leave school before the end of the academic term in order to accompany their parents. At other times, too, she allows boys to enjoy the educational experience of accompanying a father or other relative on a hunting trip. The play of small children, even in town, reflects boys' early orientation to food gathering, just as girls' play revolves around housekeeping routines that are often carried out in small tents rather than in replicas of wooden, town dwellings. Since he was ten a boy has very likely owned his own gun, has accompanied men on sealing and other trips, and has been allowed to shoot at game. On these trips he left his sister and mother behind, thereby quite firmly establishing in his own personality his like-sex identification.

Adolescence brings with it several difficult years, especially for town boys who, having already identified with jobholding men and with the hunter's role, mostly find themselves without any useful career or meaningful identifying role. Adolescent boys' personalities struck us as complex, even conflicted. In one or two growing youngsters we could watch the tension and conflict accumulate, even in the six months we were there. Girls impressed us as being more comfortable in their adolescent years than boys. They seem to accept puberty more easily than boys do, although that generalization hides the several morose girls we knew and also the problems of the promiscuous ones, and those who have been in trouble with the police about drinking. Between twenty and twenty-four, young Eskimos run the greatest risk of breaking the law. In the eight months from January to August 24, 1963, a total of sixteen young adults of both sexes were in trouble with police. Almost one-third of the thirty-seven boys in the twenty to twenty-four age bracket and fourteen per cent of the thirty-seven girls were arrested. Four of the sixteen made their first appearance in court during this period but twelve had previous records of arrest going back to at least December, 1961, which is when our records cease.

Compared to white children, Eskimo in several respects participate in school to only a relatively limited extent. No Eskimo has yet registered for the one-room high school, whose student body, therefore, is entirely Eurocanadian. None has yet begun eighth-grade work.

Despite compulsory education, a number of Eskimo children start school at only a relatively advanced age. Not until age ten do all eligible boys and girls in the population go to school. As a result, classes contain a great age-spread for Eskimo pupils. Dropping out begins after age eleven. At age sixteen, only sixty per cent of boys of that age and twenty-nine per cent of girls go to school. No girl of seventeen attends and two boys still registered constitute only a quarter of the town's seventeen-year-old male population. Even during the years when children come, absenteeism constitutes a chronic problem against which principals and their staffs have long tried a variety of remedies. Teachers are equally troubled when children physically present in class hold back from full-fledged participation. Shyness constrains Eskimo children, teachers say, though the phenomenon may also be withdrawal.

C. Learning to Drink

So far we have spoken about tutelage as it occurs in organized groups, guided by teachers of one kind or another. We now propose to analyze other, conspicuous topics and contexts that have called forth learning, starting with alcohol.

Prior to January 19, 1960, Frobisher Bay Eskimos saw or heard of their Eurocanadian military and civilian neighbors using alcohol, but only illegally could they themselves possess or consume it. Then practically overnight, in consequence of a far-reaching court decision that freed all Canadian Eskimos from discriminatory injunctions concerning drinking, they acquired precisely the same privileges as the white man. They can go to the counter of the Territorial Liquor Store on any of several afternoons and evenings weekly, show their permit, and order wine, rum, whiskey, gin or beer (including ale) for delivery three weeks later, paying with their order. Almost any evening they can sit down in the tavern in the hotel, and drink beer or hard liquor, hoping that the waiter won't take it into his head to detect drunkenness and refuse to serve them before they are ready to leave.

We must rely mostly on hearsay and police records for what happened when alcohol at not too steep prices[2] became legally available to Eskimos. Eskimos and Eurocanadian spokesmen both agree that a number of Eskimos, both men and women, embraced the new opportunity with the same alacrity and enthusiasm they have shown for other promising new experiences. They purchased mostly beer and apparently drank it without full awareness of its consequences, lacking a tested pattern of drinking that would have regulated the speed and amount consumed at any one time. In 1962, drinkers in a population of approximately 380 adults consumed 6,588, 5,520, 3,516, and 4,200 cans of beer from the liquor store alone, in May, June, July, and August respectively, plus sixty-five ounces of spirits in May and twenty-five ounces each in July and August. Then, in September, 1962, a three-week period between the time liquor was ordered and when it could be picked up (already in force for spirits) came into effect for beer as well. In that month beer taken from the store fell to 540 cans but liquor remained the same. In the following three months Eskimos consumed only 864, 1,188, and 1,140 cans bought at the store; spirits rose to 245, 750, and 565 ounces. As might be expected, heavy drinking between January, 1960 and September, 1962 fostered much public drunkenness and allegedly contributed to considerable fighting and many other offenses. Police estimated that ninety per cent of all offenses heard in court in some way involved the excessive use of alcohol, mostly by Eskimos. Most arrests, in fact, represent offenses against the Liquor Ordinance. Between 1959 and 1960, total convictions (Eskimo and non-Eskimo) jumped from fifty-three to 155, and in 1961 reached 190; a very large proportions of persons arrested must have been Eskimos.

The town took various measures to curb excessive drinking. Police vigilance, fines, and jail sentences constituted pressure to control alcoholic indulgence. Townspeople also received literature written in Eskimo describing difficulties that could arise from excessive use of alcohol and explaining the relationship between drinking and offenses committed against the law. Sometime before March, 1962, the superintendent of the Rehabilitation Centre helped produce six radio plays in Eskimo, many of which dealt with drinking and its connection with violence and other social problems. Radio station CFFB aired the tape-recorded plays. The plays presented drinking with an unequivocally moral tone, giving drinkers and the tavern a disreputable air. Efforts like these to combat the Eskimos' enthusiastic response to alcohol proved discouraging, but two measures administratively introduced in September, 1962 proved more effective. The tavern could no longer sell beer to be taken off the premises, and at the liquor store customers had to wait three weeks before they could pick up their paid-for beer or any other alcoholic commodity. These measures have greatly pleased officials and police with the way they slowed down Eskimo drinking. Reportedly public drunkenness declined. Offenses against the Liquor Ordinance, which totalled ninety-six from December, 1961 to August, 1962 dropped to forty-two between December 1962 and August, 1963. Criminal offenses also fell, from twenty-six in the first period to eleven in the second period. Police and others connect these drops to the decline in excessive drinking.

D. Recreation

Eskimos have taken some of their greatest strides in assimilating new behavior in recreation: in dancing, card playing, gambling, bingo, hopscotch, pool, boxing (dropped from Community Association activities after a serious knockout), guitar playing, motorcycle and motorbike riding, "reading" comics (young adults as well as children enjoy

[2] In 1963 a bottle of good Scotch whiskey cost $6.75; a bottle of sherry, $1.85; a dozen cans of beer $3.25.

them), and ice-skating (largely by children). In addition many people snap pictures (including with Polaroid Land cameras).

During our stay we saw young men respond to an opportunity to play a relatively new sport when the Naval commanding officer volunteered to help coach a softball team. Like us, this man had seen boys and men play a game closely resembling baseball. Two sides play that game. As many men and boys play on each side as want to. Even boys seven or eight can claim the bat and men in their forties joined in on Sunday afternoons. In its spread of ages, the game resembles keep-away and one night even women tried to play. Each player gets his turn to bat and he may take as many swings at any available ball as he needs in order to get a hit. Nobody strikes out. In fact, there is no umpire. After hitting the ball, unless it is caught before it bounces, the batter runs in a clockwise direction around the field from first, to second, to third base, and then home. The diamond resembles the standard baseball diamond, as does the equipment of bat and gloves. A batter runs, regardless of where the ball flies; there are no fouls. In order to be put out of the game, he must be tagged by the ball while he is off base, either when it is held in an opponent's hands or when it is thrown and strikes him as he runs between bases. He may dash from one spot to another trying to escape being tagged, while all the other players watch, enjoying the two-man contest. Each side plays until all its players have been eliminated, after which the other side gets its turn at bat. Players keep no score, indicating that the sides are not thought of as corporate groups that win or lose. Nor are there fixed innings. The game continues until the evening light fails or too many players have been called away on other matters. Contrary to the opinion of Eurocanadians who watched this game of "Eskimo baseball", rules certainly exist, but compared to official baseball they are few, broadly defined, and not strenuously insisted upon. In those respects as well as in the game's tolerance of players of all ages, it seems to be closely integrated with the informality and other qualities of traditional Eskimo culture.

Once teen-age boys and young adult men began to play regulation softball, rules became paramount. Whenever they showed up for practice, two coaches, one the Navy officer and the other a young RCMP constable, carried the official rulebook. They insisted that the rules be followed. The players learned to respect the rules and tried to apply them faithfully, even when the coaches did not show up. Now they needed an umpire when they played, and usually sought one, including the male anthropologist. The coaches explained the importance of skill and swiftness and the boys practiced long, frequently, and with concentration to become increasingly skillful and to play a faster game. Playing for the sake of playing and for individual success ceased, and they began to play for their team to win. One of the best players was a youth who had learned to play ball while in a southern jail. Other youths with baseball experience in the South also shone compared to others. None of these boys, however, became captain.

The formal rules and the premium placed on skill converted ball playing into a relatively closed game. Whereas formerly anybody who came along could join the side that was up or in the field, now no more than nine men could play on a team. Formerly nobody evaluated a player's skill, certainly no side considered skill or experience before admitting a player to the game. Now teams sought men with ability. Youngsters could hardly play regulation softball competitively, so they, like older men, found no welcome. When we saw Eurocanadians begin their sharp, concise, and sometimes mildly harsh coaching in June, we predicted that the game would not last. But the boys took criticism in good grace and steadily improved their performance. They wanted to learn to play by the official rules and sought to measure up to the standards that the coaches demanded.

III. PERSONALITY: BEING AN ESKIMO

Eskimos are people who have been able to learn from the intensive situation of tutelage created by Frobisher Bay town and able to adopt the substantial changes that have revolutionarily transformed their former culture. Optimistic and venturesome, their personality is both compatible with, and supportive of, the town's incessant built-in change. It is not a personality reared for routine and repetition; therefore, local work habits and other customs reflect Eskimo flexibility with respect to time, routine, planning, and assertive leadership. But Eskimos in town have learned to be dutiful about social obligations. They are also learning to surrender a measure of their impulsiveness and insistent independence and to accept subordination to job supervisors, police, and even to the formal principals of social groups which they form. However far these growing tendencies have gone, the dominant pattern consists of a considerable measure of traditional atomism, weak and informal leadership, patience of people with one another, and a reluctance to press too closely on one another in expecting conformity. Behind their disinclination to press one another is a reluctance to idealize the world, to see it as the blueprint says it should be, and to measure people and situations by whether or not they come up to standards.

A. Atomism

Despite the multiplication of organizations, people's social relations retain an atomistic quality (though perhaps not as extreme as in some northern Indian cultures), particularly if for the moment we overlook Eurocanadians' impinging roles. Eskimos, of course, depend on each other; for example, husband and wife, parent and child. But each individual tries to retain a large element of independence. In childhood, independence increases rapidly as a child becomes increasingly closely affiliated with his peers in groups where no member formally owes any obligation to the others. A person conceives his primary responsibility to be to himself and his immediate kin group. If he spreads his services beyond this narrow circle, it is usually entirely at his own volition, and not because of any compelling values that make him recognize responsibility to a larger, more impersonal circle. Individualism also manifests itself in how leadership is exercised. People neither claim nor notably exercise sustained power over others.

Inroads on atomism are being made. Eskimos have begun to learn that individual interests can run counter to formally specified group interests and that the group — even an all-Eskimo group — can acquire power over individual members, forcefully coercing them. For example, Eskimos in the Sisi Housing Cooperative use fines to compel cooperative effort and the group, ignoring latent kinship sentiments, once even expelled a recalcitrant member, two of whose brothers also belonged to the organization.

B. Ego and Ego Ideal

Overtly the Eskimo evidences a degree of security in the world which is buttressed by the confidence he has in the resources of his ego. He is characteristically optimistic rather than inclined to worry or expect trouble. He is even over-confident and, therefore, likely to take risks that sometimes turn out fatal. The earliest source of security in the setting of a relatively strong ego consists of abundant nurturance in childhood together with other aspects of good parental care. Whatever the rigors of his physical world, the Eskimo child starts life in a richly gratifying and protective social environment in which no abrupt break terminates dependence on his true or adoptive parents, especially his mother. Mothers do not attempt to wean children emotionally. Yet the character of childhood is such that it allows a youngster many opportunities to test his growing independence. These help him prove his gradually maturing resources. As he proves them, he widens the orbit of his activities, simultaneously reducing his emotional dependence on parents. Independence comes at the will of the child, not through the forceful push of his mother, a push whose implications the child might misunderstand and perceive with anxiety. Until the youngster has been firmly integrated in his peer group he frequently returns to his mother to receive affection — characteristically in the form of food but also in caresses — that reintegrate his security.

The Eskimo's pronounced readiness to imitate and emulate follow from his security and ego strength and forms one basis of the Eskimos' rapidly changing way of life. They readily adopt the clothing, hair styles, make-up, automobiles, cameras, radios, hi-fi sets, and other appurtenances of Eurocanadians, as well as fads that start up locally. We doubt very much that Eskimos emulate whites out of insecurity. In our judgement, positive rather than deficiency motives instigate the Eskimo's imitative tendency and draw him into groups and fads. Emulation also springs from an avaricious desire to experience striking and otherwise gratifying new experience; from impulsiveness. A willingness to try, also founded on ego strength, likewise motivates change. Eskimo adults deliberately encourage children to try new things. Eskimo conversation is studded with frequent references to trying. To put forth effort courageously in an effort to succeed constitutes an approved value in Eskimo life.

If anything, Eskimo childhood is too kind. The first five years only poorly prepare the person to deal with some of the threats, setbacks, and challenges he encounters in life. People *are* venturesome, but if they venture into an unfamiliar situation for which they feel unready, they may shirk the effort to cope. They resist trying some things whose parameters they don't fully know, in part because they are not sure that they can manage. If a situation involves more direction than is compatible with a person's insistence on remaining individually responsible for his own actions, he holds back or gets out. People fear appearing ridiculous, or being made ridiculous by a companion's antics or social clumsiness; for example, a drunken dancing partner. Women especially reveal such fear. Withdrawal and suicide also indicate that the Eskimo is readily overcome by psychological threat and hurt by social rejection. Against his easy vulnerability, he possesses few and paltry defenses, other than fight or withdrawal. Withdrawal, however, is not a defense calculated to bolster a person's ego and enable him to deal with threat. Bluffing, denying that a threat exists, and other of the well-known defense mechanisms prove difficult to adopt because, the Eskimo is also unprepared to reinforce his inner convictions through rationalization or by magnifying himself. He can't lie or brag. The Eskimo's ego ideal is an elemental thing. Early childhood led him to depend upon and expect the ready acceptance of others, with the result that when occasional rejection inevitably occurs later in life he is unprepared for it, bewildered, and unable to cope. Seeking the approval he expects sensitizes him to shame and public approval.

C. Patience with One Another

Eskimos are patient with one another, beginning with the relationship of parents and children. Because they are non-interfering, they don't try to tell others what to do or how to do it, unless help is requested. In Eurocanadian society, people's dependence on each other (employer and employee and co-workers for example) accompanies intense demandingness in interpersonal relations that often leads to resentment and open friction. Eskimos live together far more equitably, partly because they demand little of one another. We do not deny that personal and destructive violence occurs (especially when people are drunk) and that some men try to gratify sexual impulses by forcing themselves on women. Such deviant acts occur, but they don't represent the dominant pattern of either Eskimo personality or culture. To stress them would be to stress the untoward side of life with which every social group has to deal, the libidinal impulses which no society is consistently able to manage but which some cultures, by extolling the strong, violent person, indulge more than others.

Since Eskimos give small thought to the ideals to which behaviour should conform, they give little thought to reforming social relations. Logically, then, they must find puzzling and irritating Eurocanadians who seek to compel them to behave in certain ways and who authoritatively impose their own values. They themselves withdraw from difficult social relationships that prove unpleasant, thereby giving an impression of fatalism. But here, too, changes are taking place. Fixed property like private homes purchased through co-ops, and steady jobs, plus other satisfactions inherent in town living combine to restrict people's mobility. They induce the Eskimos to stay in Frobisher Bay. Conditions in the past allowed flight from an uncongenial situation or person. Now they must live with him, and it might pay them if they could reliably alter his behavior or improve conditions.

Society, of course, cannot exist unless people maintain some boundaries beyond which their actions must not venture. By themselves, Eskimos leave it largely to individuals to recognize when they have exceeded limits of permissible behaviour. Eskimos rely heavily on shame and on guilt to signal that they have done wrong or merited disapproval. By definition, shame occurs with reference to others. That is, we are ashamed because something we did arouses unpleasant attention from others. Guilt, on the other hand, operates more autonomously; it registers disapproval through the voice of conscience and does so regardless of whether anybody witnessed our trespass or its consequences. A comparatively high development of the sense of shame, compared to guilt, coincides with several conditions of Eskimo life, especially with the earliest circumstances in which children form superegos. The early independence that children easily attain, the relatively light discipline exerted by Eskimo parents, and the highly complimentary quality that distinguishes the relationship of Eskimo parents and children all favor a comparatively stronger sense of shame than guilt.

D. Withdrawal

Withdrawal means shutting down responsiveness to social stimuli; in that sense it is like an Eskimo's capacity for extreme concentration. Withdrawal behaviour varies; an individual may simply respond in monosyllables or he may physically quit the scene, so that nothing can be forced upon his reluctant ego. For a person who did not in the first place find a certain role meaningful, and whose ego therefore didn't respond pridefully to the skill with which he or she played his role, such withdrawal after seeming commitment is evidently an easy thing to do. Exaggerating the Eskimo's degree of commitment, Eurocanadians fail to see disenchantment and resistance build up. As a result, an employer does not know how deeply an Eskimo is offended, or how far he has transgressed on the Eskimo's feelings, until suddenly the Eskimo's attention can not be riveted to the task, or he does not return.

Withdrawal occurs not only in response to external, social situations in which the individual feels himself pressed, constrained, or threatened. A depressed mood sometimes envelops a person without apparent environmental threat, suggesting that internal conflicts, intense shame, guilt, or depression are motivating the ego's withdrawal. In extreme degree, such overwhelming emotions drive an individual to attempt to take his own life, an attempt wherein he may succeed. Suicide, like other symptoms of ego withdrawal, integrates closely with a personality that lacks skills for creative lying, pretense, and substantial rationalization. Such an ego is poorly endowed with defensive resources for erecting complex devices through which to defend itself against external stress or which would help it to cope more resourcefully with stressful moods and impulses arising with the organism.

E. Thinking Concretely

Compared to middle-class Eurocanadians, these Eskimos do not tend to idealize behaviour or cultural situations. In fact, most seem unaccustomed to appraising situations and people qualitatively, though each individual attempts to govern his own public behaviour. Eskimos evaluate concrete events and things, condemn specific wrongs, and praise individual, meritorious accomplishments. They appreciate moral goodness and physical comfort and dislike physical inconveniences and know that things do not have to stay as they are, even though they lack a blueprint which specifically defines what life should approximate. Unlike Eurocanadians, Eskimos do not constantly appraise performance, ready to see it deviate from norms. They do not deliberately test artifacts to see wherein these objects fall short of some ideal blueprint sharply defined in their consciousness.

Eskimos think concretely in another sense. They concern themselves more with doing, with action, rather than with reasons why people act as they do. From our somewhat limited perspective it would seem that they take slight interest in the psychological aspects of behaviour. Answers to questions concerning motivation tend to be answered superficially by our standards, somewhat like saying, "He eats because he wants to eat." People find it difficult to detach themselves from action situations. Answers to hypothetical questions or conditional questions like, "What if you were . . ." are not readily forthcoming. We asked a woman who spoke English, "Where would you rather live, in Frobisher Bay or Pangnirtung?" (She had come from Pangnirtung.) The question confused her although she responded lucidly to others. We interpreted her action as not being able to detach herself from the present situation to place herself in another.

His anchorage in concrete and immediate experience (plus certain ego characteristics already described) makes creative lying nearly impossible for an Eskimo. He may deliberately withhold facts or allow someone to draw a conclusion about his behaviour that he finds convenient yet knows to be untrue, but he finds it difficult to build fictional edifices.

CONCLUSION

People who do not objectify their culture and who concern themselves little with abstract thought will have small interest in history. Eskimos are not timebound nor are they generally moved to conserve tradition for the affection they bear it. Eskimos are present oriented, with a strong interest in becoming. Their involvement with the past (together with the traditional culture's slight inventory, which left little room for vested interests to promote its perpetuation) facilitates change. If Eskimos still have babies at home rather than in the hospital, it is through no emotional attachment to the old ways. If they maintain that children should learn skills of camp life, they offer a concrete, practical reason: Eskimos must be able to survive on the land doing what they like, hunting. They enjoy hunting as a present satisfier, not for its symbolic associations with the past.

Growing, nativistic sentiments in favor of perpetuating hunting and other land-based skills by teaching them to children, sentiments which several men communicated to us, represent a conspicuous exception to our generalization that Eskimos don't idealize. As a consequence of having broken contact with their former existence and come into the town, Eskimos are beginning self-consciously to romanticize certain, selected aspects of their former culture.

5

Eskimos of Canada as a Minority Group*

Frank G. Vallee

The Eskimo is among our most disadvantaged minority groups. Vallee describes factors historically related to the present low status of the Eskimo relative to other ethnic groups. The imbalance between the Eskimo and Kabloona ("white") with respect to power, prestige, and general well-being is of such magnitude that the Eskimo culture is in danger of extinction.

Minorities tend over time to assimilate to the majority culture. Minorities in Canada other than the Eskimo and Indian may also have their ranks replenished by additional immigration from the "old country." The Eskimo group, small in numbers to begin with, cannot tolerate as high an assimilation rate as groups still receiving immigrants. Thus, the total Eskimo group is currently "under fire." Continuance of a depressed minority status for the Eskimo will assure the demise of the traditional culture pattern of a genetically unique people.

An ethnically plural society is one in which ethnic origin is used as an important component of identification and where the ethnic groups have some distinctive social and cultural characteristics. Of course, most modern states are ethnically plural in this sense. In Canada, regional and ethnic diversity co-exist with an overall French-English linguistic dualism. The prevalent sentiment expressed publicly by most national leaders in Canada is in favour of this pluralism, often called the *Canadian Mosaic,* an important component in the Canadian ideology.

A number of students of Canadian society have concluded that the mosaic is not arranged horizontally as a combination of equal and

*A longer version of this paper was presented at the Conference on Cross-Cultural Education in the North, Montreal, August 1969. Revised for *Minority Canadians.*

distinct parts, but is to a large extent hierarchical. John Porter, who invented the term *Vertical Mosaic,* and others have shown that there is inequality in the distribution of prestige, power, resources and facilities among Canada's ethnic groups.[1] Most pertinent to this paper, on every index of prestige, power and command over valued resources, the native peoples of Canada are the least advantaged of our ethnic groups. The position of Indians and Eskimos at the bottom of the hierarchy insofar as education, income, health and power are concerned is well-known.

Even where they form a numerical majority, the native people occupy a minority status, and are a rural, non-agricultural *proletariat.* To amplify this point, I cite a formulation of Bierstedt's

> *As Bierstedt points out, there are three sources of social power for groups: numbers, organization, and access to valued resources* [and facilities]. *All other things equal, the numerical majority is more powerful than the minority. Where two or more groups are equal in number, the one with the most control over crucial resources is more powerful than the other ... In the context of Canada as a whole the* [native people] *are a small* [feebly organized] *minority with very limited access to significant resources. In the context of the local region and community in the Arctic, the* [native people] *outnumber the non-native, but they are comparatively unorganized and, by and large, have access to little more than subsistence resources. There is little which they can withhold which would cause the non-native people much discomfort, except their services and their co-operation in helping the non-natives achieve their goals.*[2]

One consequence of the imbalance between natives and non-natives in access to facilities and resources is the emergence of a kind of Disestablishment. In this respect the situation in Canada's north is a special case of a more general, if not universal, feature of modern society. With rapid advances in technology, thousands become unemployable because the skills they have are obsolete. Should they live in economic backwaters, they become alienated from the mainstream of social and economic life. Those who guide the system attempt in different ways to prevent the disestablished from remaining outside, by giving them a "stake" inside. These ways vary from grassroots community development to large scale retraining programs. The native population of Canada's north is not unique in being served with such programs, but a special feature of that population is that it is differentiated *racially* from the non-Eskimo minority in its midst. This physical factor accentuates the cultural, economic, and social distinctions between groups enjoying different levels of prestige, power and well-being in the society.

One further distinction between Eskimos and those who are not a "native people" is the special legal status of the former in federal statutes. With the exception of Eskimos in Labrador, who come under the jurisdiction of the Province of Newfoundland and who do not have any special politico-legal status, the other Eskimos in Canada are defined for some purposes as a tribe of Indians and for these purposes come under the Indian Act. The point is mentioned to underline the distinctiveness of the Eskimo element within the Canadian polity and society.

THE ANCIEN REGIME IN THE ARCTIC

During the first quarter of the twentieth century there emerged patterns of residence in the Canadian Arctic which would become stabilized and would characterize the human scene in the Arctic for up to fifty years. In other words, during that period there developed what in the 1960's is regarded as the *ancien regime*. Dotting the coastal areas and barren lands were scores of tiny settlements, most of them dominated by the trading post. In some of these tiny posts, the trader would be joined in permanent residence by the missionary and policeman.

Before the fur trade period, the location of Eskimo living sites was determined by whatever animals they were exploiting at a given time. The most important factor in the placing of the trading posts was access to the outside world, places which ships could visit to deliver their goods and to pick up furs.

Actually, the only native people encouraged to settle in these places were those who served the outside agencies: the trader's post servant, the policeman's assistant or special constable, the missionary's catechist. The remainder of the population continued a nomadic life in scattered camps, from which regular, but widely-spaced visits would be made to the posts. Some of these land camps would be visited by traders, missionaries and policemen on their occasional tours between posts.

The trading system introduced an element of structuring into Eskimo groupings, such as extended families and camp groups, because the traders preferred to deal with one or a few Eskimos whom they regarded as representatives or leaders of the nomadic people who lived on the land. Some missionaries, policemen and, later government administrators, reinforced this tendency.

[1] John Porter, *The Vertical Mosaic*, (Toronto: University of Toronto Press, 1965).

[2] Frank G. Vallee, *Kabloona and Eskimo in the Central Keewatin*, (Ottawa: Canadian Research Centre for Anthropology, 1967), p. 196.

Because the Canadian government had scant interest in the Arctic regions until after the Second World War, native affairs were left to the agencies with personnel resident in the Arctic; namely the churches, the Hudson's Bay Company and the Royal Canadian Mounted Police. Except for the latter, who represented the federal government, and many of whose policemen were Canadian citizens, the outsiders among the Eskimos were mostly from Britain, Newfoundland, and French-speaking parts of Western Europe, with a handful from Scandinavia. They can hardly be said to have been strongly oriented to the Canadian polity. Indeed, the bulk of the Arctic population, Eskimos and outsiders, were Canadian in only the technical sense of inhabiting geographical space to which Canada laid claim. Each of the communities and sub-regions of the Arctic was a self-contained little world whose frail and tenuous connections with the centres of the Canadian polity only highlighted its isolation and autonomy.

In this situation the outsiders interacted directly and personally with the Eskimos around them. From this interaction developed relationships between the settlers from outside and selected Eskimos and their families. The latter became intermediaries, the forerunners of a kind of elite of native settlement dwellers about whom more will be said later. During the *ancien regime* these intermediaries broke from their camp and band networks to move from post to post, in some cases ending up in regions far distant from their original homelands. This mobility was in a sense sponsored by the agencies with which the intermediaries were affiliated, thus enhancing the dependence of the intermediaries on their agencies or, more specifically, on the local representatives of the agencies. They were more oriented to the agencies they served than to the communities in which they happened to reside at a given time. They were the first Eskimo cosmopolitans in the Canadian Arctic.

To summarize, the typical communities into which outsiders moved were isolated, tiny, with only a few Eskimo people sharing living space with the outsiders over most of the year. Each place was dominated by one or two men representing outside agencies. Settlement organization was simple. The small population and lack of a complex division of labour required little coordination and structure.

THE CONTEMPORARY ARCTIC

Surveying the scene in the late 1960's we find that many of these small posts have been abandoned; a handful of others survive with minor adaptations to the new world, such as the addition of a new school and nursing station; a few have been modified and expanded beyond recognition; besides, many new settlements have been established, some of them planned by experts. Although there are no large towns by outside standards above the Tree Line, even places with from 300 to 500 people are 'urban' areas by the traditional standards. Most Eskimo people live in settlements of this magnitude. There are four communities with between 500 and 1000 and two, Inuvik in the West and Frobisher in the East, with more than 1500 each. By any standards these are small urban centres. This urbanization which channels Eskimos into larger aggregates and sees them become sedentary village dwellers is only one, albeit an important one, of the changes which occurred in response to the suddenly heightened significance of the Arctic for Canada.

After the Second World War, the Canadian Arctic, which had been a twilight zone hardly within the span of Canadian consciousness, rather suddenly became the centre of much attention. The military significance of the Arctic was demonstrated during the War when airfields were set up as part of a staging route for planes and material between North America and Europe. With the postwar development of tensions between the Soviet Bloc and the West, the Canadian Arctic assumed further military significance as a kind of no-man's-land between the potential belligerents. Defence installations and warning systems were spotted across the Arctic. Military units conducted exercises in the Barren Lands. The most advanced technology suddenly appeared in more than a dozen places, vastly improving the systems of transportation and communication.

The military intrusion itself, although important, was not as crucial in propelling the process of change as was the advent of government. The government followed the military and took over direct responsibility for Eskimo affairs, providing facilities and services that touched on every aspect of native life.

The Eskimo's material standard of living has been greatly improved since government intervention. Housing standards are far below those typical of the country as a whole, but are vastly superior to what they were. Famine is a thing of the past, what one hopes to have been the last one occurring in 1959 in an area far removed from a settlement. A sweeping health program cut deeply into the very high death rate, although this is still much higher than for the Canadian population as a whole. The continuing high birth rate and the small amount of out-migration brought the population from about 8000 Canadian Eskimos in 1948 to about 12,000 in 1968, so that in terms of its traditional wildlife resources, this vast desert region is already overpopulated and will continue to be so until large scale economic development materializes.

Within a generation the whole economic base has shifted. A minority still make a living from the more or less exclusive combination of hunting and trapping. The majority earn a little from these pursuits and this is supplemented by income from sources which did not exist a generation ago: wages, sales of handicrafts, family allowances and various pensions, and relief. For most Eskimos the economic sphere is unstable, unpredictable. Less than twenty-five per cent can be regarded as fully employed in some occupation. The single largest employer of full-time and casual labour is the federal government. Like the Indians of the Northwest Territories, the Eskimos have been able to take only minimal advantage of mining and other developments taking place on their own doorstep. There are several reasons for this, the chief one being lack of training and experience in industrial occupations.

While there has been a rise in the standard of living, it has been accompanied by a rise in the level and number of wants and the gap between income and wants has been widening. In the settlements where a substantial number of outsiders now live, the Eskimos see what the outsiders regard as a normal 'standard package' of possessions for a family. Furthermore, in the settlements the more acculturated Eskimos, many of them descendants of the intermediaries referred to earlier, enjoy a standard of living which, while inferior to that of the Kabloona[3] in their midst, is far superior to that of the average Eskimo. The latter, and the younger among them in particular, come to compare their lot with the Kabloona and the better-off Eskimo, and while their standard of living is higher than it was a decade ago, they tend to feel deprived.

This is not to say that the contemporary Eskimo is highly acquisitive and materialistic. I suggest that the gap between the average Eskimo and Kabloona families is of most significance symbolically, in that it serves to mark off groups from one another. To use the terms of an earlier section, the imbalance in access to resources marks off the established from the disestablished.

As long as Eskimos lived in isolation and in contact with only a few outsiders, their distinctiveness from the outside world was of little or no significance to them. But that distinctiveness becomes salient and is thrust into one's awareness in the settlements where Eskimos are exposed to a wide range of outsiders, such as nurses, teachers, administrators, mechanics, anthropologists, engineers, and their families. To these government sponsored outsiders are being added private entrepreneurs, small businessmen, insurance agents, merchants, and so on. The latter are not so numerous in Eastern Arctic communities but are coming to form a sizeable segment of a few Western Arctic settlements. We know that the outsiders are differentiated among themselves in terms of occupation, class, commitment to the North, government department, and so on; we also know that Eskimos in these settlements are differentiated among themselves in terms of region of origin, closeness to the outsiders, religious denomination, and so on. However, more impressive than these internal divisions is the overall division noted by so many writers: to oversimplify, there exist two sub-communities, one Eskimo and the other Kabloona, in the new-style settlements, with the Eskimo one definitely subordinate to the other.

In the process of differentiation between groups certain qualities which are used initially to identify one or the other, such as style of life or standard of living, can become relatively *fixed* attributes, regarded as inherent and inevitable. This is most likely to occur where segregation between the groups prevails. The many studies of Arctic settlements describe the marked tendency to segregate unofficially along lines of native and non-native.[4]

Now this would not be so serious if it were not for the fact that individuals and groups have histories. That is, once a pattern is begun — for example a pattern of segregation between two groups, one of which looks down on the other — the pattern does not disappear in one generation but survives and even is nourished in a kind of vicious spiral. Subordinate groups have a way of adjusting to their condition, to their lack of power, through hostile withdrawal, passivity, submission, fantasy, displaced aggression, and other means. Superordinate groups have a way of accepting the rightness of their advantaged position and of accounting for the imbalance between themselves and the disestablished, sometimes in terms of heredity. The latter, like the established, have families and transmitted to younger generations in the families of both groups are the subtle ways of assessing and evaluating their social worlds. The vicious spiral, once begun, is very difficult to halt.

To some extent this vicious spiral has already been set in motion in the Northwest Territories and Arctic Quebec. I have referred chiefly so far to the economic sphere, perhaps putting too much emphasis on it; but the same point could be made with reference to organization and to participating in decisions that affect one's family and friends.

Here again there has been a one-sidedness, with the Eskimos usually in a dependent position — almost always the client or go-between, almost never the patron. Deliberate attempts have been made at several levels to involve Eskimo people through including on such bodies as the Northwest Territories Legislative Councils, Community Advisory Councils, and the like, to some extent changing the traditional passive role of the native people vis-a-vis the outsiders. However, representation is one thing, meaningful participation another. I refer here to participation in decisions in many spheres of group life and not only the official ones. In most of the community studies with which I am familiar, it is the outsiders who are presented as the key decision-makers in a wide range of matters.[5]

---

[3] Kabloona is the term used by the Eskimos to denote white man.

[4] See, for example, A.M. Ervin, *New Northern Townsmen in Inuvik*, (Ottawa: Department of Indian Affairs and Northern Development, 1968), Esp. pp. 11 ff.; and John and Irma Honigmann, *Eskimo Townsmen*, (Ottawa: Canadian Research Centre for Anthropology, 1965).

[5] See, for example, J. Mailhot, *Inuvik Community Structure*, (Ottawa: Department of Indian Affairs and Northern Development, 1968).

This is partly due to the persistence of traditional social patterns. Living in small, egalitarian, nomadic groups the Eskimos had no need for formal organization. The process of formal debate, of voting, of majority rule, which many outsiders take for granted, was unknown and was imposed from outside. The Eskimo style was that of *consensus* in decision-making. It might take a long time to achieve that consensus on particular issues, but that time would be so invested and what we would regard as highly developed human relations skills brought into play to achieve consensus. In the modern settlements, the imported practice of formal debate and resolution by voting leaves many Eskimos unenthusiastic. Their silence is sometimes mistaken for assent by the outsiders.

Besides the lack of precedent in Eskimo culture and the traditional asymmetrical relations between Eskimos and outsiders, another reason for the relative passivity of the Eskimo people has been that the very local affairs about which they could have been deciding were the responsibility of a remote government administration, even for day-to-day matters, such as the allocation of relief, repairs to small sewers and roads, new windows for the school and so on. While these functions were, and in many places still are, carried out in local settings by government administrators, until recently the ultimate responsibility and decision-making was located in Ottawa. Implied in this one-sided allocation of local government functions is that the Eskimos are incapable even of deciding about trivia.

The federal government has recently taken a step to remedy this situation by investing local authorities with more powers and by shifting much of the administrative machinery into the Northwest Territories. The involvement of the Eskimo people is now very much a matter of how the Territorial Government (and in its region the Quebec Provincial Government) and residents in communities respond to this shift in powers. A key element in this situation is the resident non-Eskimo.

As I have already indicated, one reason for the minor role of Eskimos in community affairs was the availability of non-Eskimos who were only too eager to bear the burden of decision-making. In an earlier period these were the traders, missionaries, policemen. In more recent times, in addition to these, there are the government administrators, teachers, nurses, businessmen, and so on, as well as the spouses of some of those. The very presence of people eager to play a role in community affairs militates against Eskimo participation, *unless* a special bid is made for that participation.

I suggest that crucial to the issue of integration of ethnic groups is the way in which people who are from the outside, but who settle permanently or on a long term basis, exert their power and influence. I refer here to the growing significance of those who, unlike most people connected with government and big industry, make such a commitment and regard themselves as Northerners through and through.

Many traders, trappers, and missionaries made this commitment in the past, some marrying Eskimo women and raising families. But as I noted earlier, there is an increasing number of 'new' people who have put down roots in Arctic communities as businessmen, contractors, publishers, and so on. The most common stance of this element is anti-federal government. Within the Territories, many of them are milder equivalents of passionate French-Canadian nationalists in Quebec.

The passion of the New Northerner is correlated with the presence in some communities of people who work for the government and who receive what the non-government people regard as very special treatment: fine housing at low rents, various allowances, linkages to such services as sewers and power. On this particular issue, the New Northerners at times ally with the Eskimos or at least try to see things through the eyes of the latter. On the other hand, there is the possibility that many among the New Northerners, because of their initial head start as controllers of local economics and government, will discourage real Eskimo participation and themselves fill the power vacuums left by the federal government, creating a kind of settler-native imbalance familiar to many parts of the world. We can only speculate on this possibility. I mention it only to drive home the point that issues in the Arctic will be resolved not only in terms of what the Eskimos do with Eskimos, but *what they do in interaction with other elements in the population,* in particular with those who settle there permanently.

So far I have dwelt on the historical origins of, and the social structural reasons for, the segregation between Eskimo and non-Eskimo people in Canadian Arctic communities. Another dimension which has been only touched upon needs to be added, the dimension of culture. The creation of a true pluralist society, along the lines laid down in Canadian myths and beliefs, requires the bridging of cultural gaps. This in turn presupposes that the people in whose hands lies the power give some attention, credence, and credit to the culture of the Eskimos, the topic of the next part.

ASPECTS OF ESKIMO CHARACTER AND CULTURE

There is no doubt that the material culture of the Eskimos in Canada is doomed to the museum, with a few elements surviving in isolated areas. Even in these areas, items which were widespread in the early 1960's, such as dog teams, are being replaced by imported vehicles. To the extent that a people's identity is tied to their distinctive material culture, Eskimo identity is rapidly losing that reference and criterion.

Some material objects with a primarily symbolic or expressive function continue to serve as definers of Eskimoness. Carvings and prints deserve special mention, because they are not only objects of economic value, but also symbols of Eskimoness. Purists may decry the departures from tradition and the outside influence on styles, claiming that the majority of these objects are not 'really Eskimo', but if the people themselves perceive them as Eskimo and if the outsiders define these objects as Eskimo, then they are indeed Eskimo in terms of their significance for Eskimo identity. In one community in Arctic Quebec where carving is an economic mainstay, carving as an activity is used to sort out those of Eskimo descent who have abandoned their Eskimo identity from those who, no matter what their style of life, still regard themselves as primarily Eskimo. A man who carves even infrequently is an Eskimo in this place. This kind of symbolic significance of activities and objects usually escapes the outsiders who deal directly with the Eskimos in Canada. I have known teachers to discourage youngsters from carving on the grounds that the carvings are imitative of outside influence or that it interfered with their school work. These outsiders tend to view carving and print-making either from a purely aesthetic or a purely instrumental point of view.

The same point should be made, even more forcibly, with regard to the most important expressive aspect of culture — language. On the basis of my experience, I must say that a majority of educators in the Canadian Arctic regard the question of language primarily from an instrumental point of view, illustrated in the question, "how is this language going to help the person making a living? How is it going to help him fit into the larger society?" These are, of course, valid and important questions. But language is a fundamental structure and process. Upon it is built much of the way of experiencing and thinking about reality. It is also a symbol of group identification and solidarity. Rules that forbid speaking Eskimo in the classroom or schoolyard get across to the Eskimo child that the language of his home is something to be ashamed of, something bizarre which, like the spears and kayaks, will survive only in museums.

Other expressive features of Eskimo culture have been discouraged, especially by missionaries, who equated them with the manifestations of the devil's control in pre-Christian times and with what they regarded as an undue preoccupation with 'sex'.

Because so much of the oral literature, song, and dance had to do with the supernatural, as defined by the Eskimos, its open expression is now taboo; again, because so much of this tradition is now defined as 'obscene' by the new moral guardians, those Eskimos who cherish certain vestiges of the tradition are reluctant to pass it on to their children and reluctant to express it publicly, i.e., in the presence of Kabloona. In short, many Eskimos have become ashamed of a large part of their own oral and musical tradition.[6]

Very recently there has been a revival of drum dances and other traditional performances in public, but I have the impression that these have been drained of their original symbolic meaning and are presented as cultural specimens for the gratification of outsiders, especially tourists.

So far I have talked about fairly explicit manifestations of what used to constitute Eskimo culture. Except for the viable language, these are definitely on the wane. But what of the massive part of the iceberg of culture, the part that is submerged and about which few people are conscious? I refer here to the ways in which people unselfconsciously know and evaluate the world around them. Authorities on the subject agree that these aspects of culture and personality are the most resistant to change. They also agree that where these basic conceptions differ among people who are forced to interact with one another, the resulting faults in communication have serious consequences. Let us look briefly at some Eskimo ways of knowing and evaluating the world.

Many writers have provided examples of Eskimo ways of thinking about the world, ways of explaining happenings which are different from the explanations of the outsiders. These ways of explaining things make up what are called *cultural thought models*. A favourite example from my own experience will be cited here, paraphrased from another publication. The example pertains to a certain theory of disease held by some Eskimos. If the outsiders in the community concerned had known beforehand about this particular theory, much misunderstanding and tension could have been avoided.

During the late winter of 1962, there was a serious epidemic of rabies among the dogs of an eastern Arctic settlement with a population of about 500 Eskimos and thirty whites. The settlement was only about six years old and, like so many other settlements, was inhabited by people who had formerly lived in small land camps. There was no clear policy about chaining dogs, and some Eskimos new to settlement living refused to chain their dogs, or refused to take precipitate action when a dog broke loose; they had not chained them in the small camps in which they formerly lived. No less than 600 dogs were distributed over an area of just more than a square mile. The spread of the rabid virus among the dogs was speeded by the many loose dogs, and within three weeks of the outbreak, more than 100 had to be destroyed because they were rabid.

The white element in the community and some of the more acculturated Eskimos made passionate appeals to the people to keep their dogs tied. Most responded by making special efforts to do so, but several were indifferent to the pleas and threats. The whites accounted for this indifference in terms of stupidity, hostility, or their own

⁶ Vallee, *op. cit.*, 1967, p. 29.

failure to communicate their passion on the issue. Much tension was generated in the community.

Six weeks after the outbreak the epidemic was over, with a high casualty rate among the dogs; but no people had died. As soon as the rabies epidemic subsided, an influenza epidemic broke out; ten people died and scores were violently ill.

It was during the influenza epidemic that I learned about the Eskimo theory of disease.

Some Eskimos in the community, but not all, believe that there is always a constant amount of disease in the world. This amount of disease is channeled onto certain species at a given time for a given period. For example, if there is an inordinate amount of sickness and death among seals for a period, other species will be relatively free of disease for that period. The reasoning seems to be that if one species is under the disease gun, other species should consider themselves fortunate in being outside the range of that gun.[7]

Applied to the situation I described, this meant that while the dogs were overwhelmed by disease, the people were comparatively well-off. The dogs were consuming much of the constant amount of disease in the world. As soon as the rabies epidemic ended, the human species became the biggest consumer of disease — witness the influenza epidemic — and the 'fold theory' was thus confirmed for those Eskimos who believed it.

The attitudes and behavior of some of the Eskimos during the rabies epidemic would have been comprehensible in terms of the logic of their way of thinking if the non-Eskimos had understood that way and had taken it into account in their efforts to combat the epidemic of rabies. We conclude then, that systematic investigation of the thought models of the Eskimos is not just an academic exercise, but has practical value as well.

Certain Eskimo values and character traits can be inferred from behaviour. For instance, many have remarked on the value which Eskimos put on independence and autonomy, as evidenced by their reluctance to coerce or speak for others. Their techniques, which they employ unself-consciously, for inducing conformity made little use of overt punishment and much use of nurturance as a 'reward'. Educators brought up in a society where adults make it obvious who is in control, where classroom regimentation is viewed as essential, where parents and teachers speak for 'their' children, are often disturbed at what they interpret to be the Eskimo parent's lack of concern for his children.[8] In their opinion the children should not be allowed to stay out so late at night, to accompany parents on just about every kind of event, to stay away from school without a reason acceptable to the teacher, and so on.

In the eyes of the tradition-oriented Eskimo, the Kabloona world is excessively rigid and concerned with discipline, too ready to invade an individual's zone of privacy. They view the Kabloona as relatively insensitive in the sphere of what we call 'human relations'. For instance much resentment is felt over the policy of taking children away from their families and removing them to a distant hostel-school. Should the children be removed and placed with another family, there is little, if any, resentment as long as it is understood that the youngsters will return.

The question has been asked on many occasions: Why is it that the Eskimos show so little hostility and resentment openly? As I mentioned earlier, Eskimo silence and show of indifference are often interpreted as positive assent. However, in terms of traditional values it was considered improper to display strong feelings unless one were extremely frustrated or extremely moved. Eskimos have ways of 'reading' one another's behaviour and feelings, of course, and the cues used to display feelings are usually unobserved or misinterpreted by the Kabloona. Related to this traditional trait is the oft-noted smiling and happy front which Eskimos display for the Kabloona. It has been suggested that this front is an exaggeration of the traditional one, and is used consciously by some and unconsciously by others to conceal strong feelings, both negative and positive, which if expressed might disturb the kind of accommodation which has been developed between Eskimos and Kabloona.

What is perhaps best regarded as another aspect of the trait of repressing displays of strong feeling, is the stoicism which has frequently been described as an outstanding Eskimo characteristic. This stoicism is inferred from the apparently resigned way with which the Eskimos have accepted terrific hardships and crises. The tendency is to accept things as they are or, to be more precise, to give the impression that one accepts things as they are.

Accommodation and compliance with Kabloona rules of the game are widespread, but this does not imply that there has been a wholesale identification with the values which underlie these rules. In fact, Eskimos who comply with the Kabloona rules at work, in meetings, in school, or in the administrator's office are given to acting out, in the privacy of their homes with their friends, hilarious imitations of what the Kabloona regard as normal behaviour.[9]

This brings up the question, which we cannot answer conclusively, of the extent to which Eskimos do indeed nourish the values

---

[7] Frank G. Vallee, "Stresses of Change and Mental Health Among the Canadian Eskimos," *Archives of Environmental Health*, 17, 4, (October 1968). p. 568 ff.

[8] Honigmann & Honigmann, *Op. Cit.*, esp. p. 174 ff.

[9] Norman Chance, *The Eskimo of North Alaska*, (Toronto: Holt, Rinehart and Winston, 1966), p. 92.

attributed to them. If we based our conclusions on actual behaviour, then we would have to say that because so many Eskimos in the larger settlements behave in most ways like the Kabloona, they have abandoned their cultural values. Many observers have expressed the opinion that those Eskimos who have had the most contact with the outsiders identify with the Eskimo social groupings but not with the Eskimo culture in the sense used here. They argue that it is only among those families which have only recently moved into settlements and among those who live mostly in isolated camps and small settlements that anything like the traditional cultural values survive. In the absence of systematically gathered data on the subject of values in the Canadian Arctic, one can only guess as to their distribution and viability.

Many more examples could be given of the hardly visible, intangible, subjective values which we infer from behaviour. However, I think that enough has been presented to conclude that in Arctic communities account must be taken of more than meets the eye if productive relationships among the different sub-cultures are to be developed. Individuals have expressed admiration for traditional Eskimo values and have observed that non-Eskimos would be wise to adopt them in their own lives. However, many of the currents running through the mass society in which the Eskimos are moving go in the opposite direction and favour centralization, impersonality, and regimentation. The pressure is on the Eskimos to abandon their customary ways of viewing the world. This pressure is deliberately applied in the schools and work places. It is unwittingly or unintentionally applied in most spheres of life and disseminated through the mass media.

6
Indian Island:
A Micmac Reserve*

Fred Gross

Before culture-contact with the Euro-Canadian, Canada's Indians for the most part did not share the same language, mythology, artifacts, or social organization. The erosion of the indigenous Indian cultures, however, has resulted in their coming to share to a greater or lesser extent the "culture of poverty", characterized by dependency and despair.

Fred Gross examines the impoverished state of the Micmacs, a former hunter-gatherer tribe, inhabiting the woodlands of Atlantic Canada. The Micmac dilemma is viewed within the framework of Maritime poverty; that is, as part of the larger problem of "regional disparity".

Indian Island is the home of about two hundred Micmacs in one of the Maritime provinces. These Indians, together with an equal number of their relatives who live away from the Reserve, constitute a Band under the provisions of the Indian Act of Canada. Those who live at the Reserve, when contrasted with those who have left, tend to be either more traditional in their behaviour, or incapable — for reasons of health, personality, or lack of developed skills — of supporting themselves in accordance with the expectations of non-Indian Canadian society.

A. THE ABORIGINAL MICMAC

Aboriginally, the Micmacs were subsistence hunters and gatherers. Their techniques for environmental exploitation rarely produced an abundance of food and they had limited means for food storage. The traditional band included between two and six nuclear families; i.e., a total population varying between approximate limits of ten

* Written expressly for *Minority Canadians*. "Indian Island" is a pseudonym.

and forty. Each band was, for most of the year, geographically and socially independent from any other band.

Formal political institutions showed no more than rudimentary development. As a rule, leadership was exercised by individuals whose opinions were valued, whose recommendations had usually worked out well. This leadership, however, was subject to a consensus among all of the adult members of the band. Since the techniques by which the band coped with its environment required cooperation from all participants, the absence of a consensus would threaten the survival of the band.

During the past two hundred years, hereditary chieftanships were established under the sponsorship of the government, but the powers of these chiefs were severely limited. In large measure their responsibilities were to represent the band in its dealings with governmental authorities. However, since they lacked any capability for sanctioning actions which the Canadian or provincial governments might take, these chiefs can best be understood as figureheads who satisfied the expectation of the non-Indian that every group had a leader who could legitimately represent the group.

B. THE CONTEMPORARY MICMAC

At the present time there are no traditional Micmac communities; none could exist in the late twentieth century. So many changes have occurred in the environment which the earlier Micmacs exploited that there is no possibility of re-establishing an ecosystem which would support a hunting-gathering population. Furthermore, so many of the traditional practices have been forgotten that the present-day Micmacs would probably view the old way of life as alien and uncongenial, just as their non-Indian neighbors would.

Thus, in characterizing the Reserve residents as relatively traditional, reference is being made to a group of traits and patterns which in many instances have been manifested only during the past half century. When contrasted with ethnographic accounts of the Micmacs up to the beginning of the twentieth century (e.g., Wallis and Wallis), the present residents of Indian Island appear to be almost fully acculturated to Eurocanadian patterns. For example, their clothing and diet is not easily distinguished from that of the rural population throughout the Maritimes. Their religious affiliation, as with virtually all Micmacs, is with the Roman Catholic church. Although most are familiar with Glooskap, the central figure in Micmac oral tradition, few can retell any of the numerous legends that have been recorded. Although most of the adults are in varying degrees bilingual (Micmac and English); most of the children can only speak English. While members of the older generations make baskets, most of the residents show no knowledge of traditional handicrafts. Houses are of frame construction and contemporary Canadian design. A chief and band council are elected in much the same fashion as, for example, a college student president and student council.

Thus there are few clues by which a casual observer might identify these people as being culturally distinctive. A more thorough examination, however, yields a number of behavioral patterns which are distinctive of this and other Reserve Micmac populations. In part, these are modifications of earlier Micmac traditions; in part, they are responses to the special legal status of Indians, as determined by the Act and its implementation.

C. THE INDIAN ISLAND BAND

Today the Indian Island Band (in the legal sense) consists of more than 400 members, approximately fifty per cent of whom live at the Indian Island Reserve. The Reserve population is divided into about forty nuclear families, each in its own home. Virtually all of the residents derive their principal support from government-sponsored social assistance programs. These include the Indian Affairs Branch's Welfare Program, old age, veteran's and other pensions, and salaried occupational training and educational upgrading programs. Those few living on the Reserve who are regularly employed hold positions which relate directly to the maintenance and servicing of the Reserve, for example, the operation of the boat to the mainland.

During August and September many Indian Islanders follow the now-traditional Micmac pattern of migrating to Maine for work on the blueberry and potato fields. As Bock has noted in his discussion of the Micmacs at Restigouche Reserve, the Indians consider this to be more than a job; it is an entertainment and diversion from the ten months during which they are isolated on the Reserve, with few opportunities to make new acquaintances and engage in activities which they consider exciting.

On the Reserve there are few opportunities for employment or amusement. The natural resources are limited and the means for exploiting them on a profitable basis are not presently available to the Indians. Of the Reserve's 1500 acres, only two or three hundred acres are presently in use. These contain the house plots, the school, church and recreation hall, the garden plots, and a ball field and outdoor hockey rink. The rest of the Reserve is part salt marsh, part bog, and part thickly-overgrown secondary forest.

Some fruits grow semi-wild on the Island, many of which are gathered and provide seasonal variety in the residents' diet. Included are wild strawberries, blueberries, apples, and cranberries. Small garden plots are maintained by a number of the people, the produce — various vegetables — usually being consumed at home. A few of the Indians cultivate potatoes as a cash crop, but all farm less than five acres. A small number of domesticated fowl are also kept, principally for domestic consumption.

In the waters surrounding the Indian Island reserve oysters, clams, quahogs, lobsters, eels, mackerel, and smelt can be found, although no resident of the Reserve now has the equipment which would be needed for commercial exploitation of these resources.

While the Reserve residents make some use of the local fruit and fish, in no sense can the Band or its members be viewed as *subsistence* hunters and gatherers. Cooperation and consensus are no longer requirements for group or individual survival, on or off the Reserve. Even an individual who is socially alienated from other members of the Reserve community will receive his welfare cheque if he is entitled to one.

A principal factor in understanding the dynamics of this community is the very fact that the Reserve is an island, separated from the mainland by a channel which, at the usual point of crossing, is almost a mile wide. The only ways to reach the mainland are the government-maintained diesel-powered boat and, during the three or four months when the channel is frozen, a snowmobile or a good pair of legs. In consequence, communication between the Reserve and the mainland is severely restricted. Access to medical services, employment centers, and commercial establishments is difficult. Integration of the children into provincial schools would require their boarding away from the Reserve for about half of every school year.

Thus their isolation has ramifications throughout the economic, educational, occupational, social and legal-administrative spheres of activity.

D. THE RESERVE'S LEGAL STATUS

Indian Island, as with the Reserve land of every registered Indian Band in Canada, is superintended under the Indian Act by Indian Affairs Branch personnel. While the degree to which superintending represents controlling may vary, in general the Branch serves to mediate relations between a Band and all other governmental agencies, both federal and provincial. In addition, the Branch assumes some responsibility for the well-being of individual registered Indians. In many areas these responsibilities are legally the exclusive province of the Branch; in some, the Branch has a shared responsibility with other agencies of the federal government.

In contrast to the long-held attitude that Indians were wards of the Government, Ottawa's policies in 1970 acknowledge and encourage the possibility of the Indians becoming full participants in the larger Canadian society. Many of the Branch programs are directed toward the total assimilation of the Indians, generally through the realization of economic development to a level and in a mode equivalent to that found in neighboring non-Indian communities. The expectation is held that such development would culminate in the elimination of the Reserves and of the special status of the registered Indian.

Regardless of governmental policies in these respects, it is apparent in the case of Indian Island that the rate at which persons leave the Reserve — note that every ethnically distinctive group in North America has seen some of its members leave the home community, minimizing or losing their ethnic identity — is unlikely to exceed the rate at which the Reserve population naturally increases. There exists, and will continue to exist for many years, a large population of individuals who have little desire to leave the Reserve. For these the Reserve serves as more than a home; it serves as a refuge within which they are protected by the various welfare and other services which the Branch — they believe — is committed to provide indefinitely.

These people, constituting a large majority at Indian Island, can be characterized as participating in a poverty-welfare cycle, i.e., it can be predicted that the adults will continue as welfare recipients, and many of their children will join the welfare rolls upon attaining adulthood.

E. THE POVERTY-WELFARE CYCLE

There are a number of factors which have influenced the establishment and maintenance of this cycle at Indian Island. Some can be understood in terms of traditional culture of the Micmacs; some in terms of Branch policy; some through examination of similar phenomena in other communities.

A number of Micmac actions and attitudes can be observed which would at one time have been highly functional for the Indian, but which have become, in the context of the reserve, highly dysfunctional to the general goals of the Branch. For example, it was noted that the traditional way of life required a high level of consensus and cooperation among the band members. This degree of cooperation is unnecessary on the reserve. Yet a superficial pattern of consensus is expected, and typically achieved, in dealing with matters presented for consideration at Band meetings. While almost every vote taken will be unanimous, private conversations with the Band members reveal the existence of a diversity in opinions, values and aspirations, among the reserve residents.

That the apparent consensus is often mythical, and diversity of opinion is present, is evidenced by private expressions of dissent and by the frequency with which, under the influence of alcohol, fighting occurs. Alcohol does not cause fights but permits latent hostility to come to the fore. Many people — and this includes Indians at the Reserve — drink, even to excess, without engaging in fisticuffs. Fighting at the Reserve can be viewed as an acceptable (within the community) means of expressing dissent, justified by the values associated with drinking. Such dissent if expressed verbally and while sober would constitute unusual public behavior at Indian Island.

The mythical consensus has some unfortunate consequences. Many of the Band members, once having expressed their assent at a formal vote, subsequently behave as though the expression of approval constituted the totality of support they were obligated to provide. For example, forty-odd Band members might agree to hold a series of meetings to discuss various aspects of Band affairs. But at the next meetings, where the agreed agenda is to be considered, very few of the forty are present.

As a repeated pattern, this has left many of the Indians with the sense that "nothing ever gets done", that concerted and continuing action is an impossibility. The parallels with the situation which Bock describes for the Micmacs at Restigouche are striking:

> I don't understand the people at Restigouche. They can't get together to do anything. And if they do start anything, they get tired of it in a few days and say, "forget it . . . it's too much trouble". [p. 65, an informant speaking].

Branch policy, even when considering its more enlightened aspects, has served to perpetuate these traditional, but in the context of Branch goals, dysfunctional attitudes. For example, new or changed benefits under the various Branch programs are likely to be granted only if the Band presents a unanimously-supported petition. Professional community-development workers display an expectation that all members of the community should participate in the planning and implementation of any programs for change.

The Branch and its agents support sentiments to which the Micmac has traditionally subscribed. However, given the Branch's principal goals, these policies are self-defeating. If the Indian is to leave the protection afforded by the Reserve system, he will be entering a society in which individual initiative is highly valued, and large-scale consensus is rarely encountered. If the Reserve is to be transformed into a politically and economically independent community, its residents must receive some encouragement for political and economic independence of action. The case of the general store at Indian Island will illustrate this point.

A few years ago the Branch established a general store at the Reserve. This store was managed by a local non-Indian merchant, and when it lost money, the Branch officials felt compelled to terminate the enterprise.

Today there is strong sentiment at the Reserve for the re-establishment of the store, but under Indian management. Two alternative means for accomplishing this are through collective action or through individual initiative. If the former approach is adopted, all matters of organizational and operating policy would necessitate establishment of a "consensus" in the community. The cost of such consensus would likely be an attitude of non-responsibility on the part of the Reserve residents. Having voted for a particular procedure, the individual will feel his responsibilities have ceased. Likewise, those charged with the daily operation of the store would tend to lack a personal sense of commitment toward the successful operation of the enterprise. If going to work were an inconvenience, the store would probably remain closed for the day. The Branch-approved procedure yields no psychological investment from those who should be most concerned. Alternatively, if an individual were to receive the encouragement and assistance necessary for establishing a general store at the Reserve, both his training and his sense of commitment would tend to result in those entrepreneurial attitudes and practices which a profitable operation usually requires.

The combination of traditional Micmac values and governmental paternalism, as exemplified in the operation of the Reserve system, has resulted — at least in the case of Indian Island — in a population which manifests virtually all of those patterns which Oscar Lewis (1968) has associated with the "culture[1] of poverty". Lewis has noted a cluster of diagnostic characteristics for this phenomenon, none of which is absent from the Maritime provinces. These are:

1. A cash economy, wage labor and production for a profit;
2. A persistently high rate of unemployment and underemployment for unskilled labor;
3. Low wages;
4. The failure to provide social, political and economic organization, either on a voluntary basis or by government imposition, for the low-income population;
5. The existence of a bilateral kinship system rather than a unilateral one.
6. The existence of a set of values in the dominant class which stresses the accumulation of wealth and property, the possibility of upward social mobility and thrift, and explains low economic status as the result of personal inadequacy or inferiority.[2]

While Lewis has perceived these characteristics principally in urban contexts, he argues that they can also appear in the rural setting. He suggests that where this cluster of characteristics is present, it is likely that a low-income group will respond to their situation through the development of attitudes akin to those which have been manifested at Indian Island. Ultimately, he maintains that the possession of these attitudes will result in the perpetuation of the group's condition of poverty.

[1] or more properly, "subculture."

[2] Oscar Lewis, pp. XLIII-XLIV.

The distinction between the culture of poverty and the state of being poor, or poverty-stricken, is crucial to an understanding of the Indian Island situation. Simple lack of affluence does not require the adoption of a set of values which will tend to perpetuate the condition of poverty, denying the individual any sense of personal dignity and worth.

Termination of a culture of poverty culture situation of necessity involves more than simple economic inputs. It involves the education of the members of the community: supplying them with formal education and generating in them those values which would enable them, when economic inputs are available, to use these inputs for their long-term benefit.

F. THE RESERVE AND THE MARITIMES COMPARED

Breaking the poverty-welfare cycle at Indian Island in many respects is parallel to eliminating the "regional disparity" between Upper Canada and the Atlantic provinces. Many of the impediments to development which afflict the Reserve are also present — sometimes in milder form — throughout the Atlantic Region.

As certainly as physical isolation and poor transportation facilities have been obstacles to individual initiative at Indian Island, they have also impeded the commercial development of such provinces as Newfoundland and Prince Edward Island.

Low educational levels, lack of job opportunities for the skilled, low wages for the unskilled, limited natural resources, and the exportation of the most capable citizens to Upper Canada and the States are all characteristics of the Reserve and the region. Also, both the Maritimes and the Reserve have high incidences of welfare payments to persons unable or unwilling to provide for themselves.

At this point the parallels begin to break down, and points of divergence come to the fore. In most respects, Indian Island is non-self governing; each of the provinces has an elaborate government. But the outside agency which effectively governs the Reserve has been much more generous to its clientele than any provincial government can afford to be.

Thus the Indian can receive free education through college and graduate school. He receives free medical care (when medical attention can be had; some practitioners avoid treating Indians, claiming that the government's payments are generally inadequate and tardy). He receives free on-reserve housing if unable to supply his own. He also receives welfare payments if they are needed to cover the costs of food and clothing.

In a very real sense, the registered Indian lives in a welfare state — albeit a very imperfect one. It should be noted that his non-Indian neighbor frequently expresses envy and resentment of this situation.

Unfortunately, this welfare state has developed at the cost of individual initiative and effective group cooperation: the conditions under which it operates tend to encourage the Indian's dependency upon the government.

There are other respects in which the Reserve population differs from the rest of the Region. There is only a rudimentary development of the neighborhood political system, through which a community is able to communicate its desires and fears to the government. When the government is not responsive, the Indian cannot go out and join the other party.

Patterns of cooperation within the Reserve community vary from those of nearby non-Indians. In particular, cooperative activities are generally organized on very short notice, with goals involving immediate rewards for all through their own efforts. In contrast, the rural non-Indian Maritimer engages in cooperative activities quite regularly, with exchange of labor on a continuing basis providing assistance alternatively to one and another of the cooperating group. In such circumstances there is a felt obligation to participate; at the Reserve there tends to be a spur of the moment decision.

For the rural Maritimer there is usually a leader who will set the time for doing the project and assign duties while the project is in process. For the Indian, leadership tends to yield to individualism. While one person will indicate that he hopes to undertake some project at a certain time, he can rarely know before that time who will show up, or what constraints on duties each participant may establish for himself.

In understanding these distinctions it should be recognized that the Micmac Indian rarely operates in a competitive situation; the rural non-Indian typically runs a farm or boat as a competitive economic enterprise.

Thus the conditions under which the Indian is likely to be engaged in cooperative activities are of a sort that do not demand a sense of responsibility to the group; the welfare of the group or its members is not dependent on each individual. Failure to manifest a sense of responsibility is unlikely to result in the group's disapproval.

Related to this lack of group responsibility is the Indian's conception of time. For the non-Indian time must be carefully allocated to meet occupational commitments. The Indian typically has time on his hands. The non-Indian must often plan ahead; he must operate within a system of delayed gratification. The Indian seems to expect immediate gratification. Planning, for the Micmac Indian, often appears to be principally a verbal activity which is enjoyed in itself: there is a low expectation of any plan coming to fruition. And whether or not this is an instance of the self-fulfilling prophecy, his low expectation is demonstrably realistic.

CONCLUSION

The Indian Island Micmacs have developed a relatively success-ful set of behaviours and attitudes for accommodating themselves to their Reserve situation. This situation is such that virtually all of their physical needs are met through the direct operation of the various Branch programs. But the operation of these programs has allowed these people to escape any responsibilities relating to their personal well-being.

In large measure they have behaved quite rationally within a social, economic and legal context which has been imposed upon them. That which the Branch is prepared to give, they are prepared to take. But give and take are understood primarily in terms of im-mediate personal gain.

In some respects, this had yielded them material benefits which exceed those enjoyed by many of their non-Indian neighbors. But though many of their neighbors are poverty-stricken, it is the Reserve community which most closely confirms to the *culture of poverty* pattern.

The pattern is discernable not only in the measurement of socio-economic variables; it is manifested in repeated expressions of the sentiment that life at the Reserve is neither productive nor satisfying. In effect the Micmac Indian finds himself discontented with his life style, but is incapable of conveniently and comfortably changing his world and his ways.

BIBLIOGRAPHY

BOCK, PHILIP K. "The Micmac Indians of Restigouche: History and Contem-porary description," Ottawa: National Museum of Canada, *Bulletin 213,* 1966.

HAWTHORNE, H. B., ED. *A Survey of the Contemporary Indians of Canada,* *Vol. 1.* Ottawa: Indian Affairs Branch, 1966.

———. *A Survey of the Contemporary Indians of Canada, Vol. 2.* Ottawa: Indian Affairs Branch, 1967.

LEWIS, OSCAR. *La vida: a Puerto Rican family in the culture of poverty, San Juan and New York.* New York: Vintage, 1968.

WALLIS, WILSON D. AND RUTH S. WALLIS *The Micmac Indians of Eastern Canada.* Minneapolis: University of Minnesota Press, 1955.

7

A Cree Indian Reserve*

John W. Bennett

The Cree became Plains Indians in the mid-19th century by moving from the forests to the prairie. The need to adapt to a new environment was necessitated at this time by white encroachment in their native land. Bennett considers the adaptive strategies the Cree use when faced with contemporary white power.

The status quo on a regional level is maintained by minority-majority interaction in which Cree and white play stereotyped roles. The identities of both sets of actors — minority and majority — are formed in large measure as a result of a mutually-exploitative interaction pattern.

The Cree's self-esteem is especially dependent upon adroit one-upmanship with the larger community, a skill which is also rewarded within the Indian Reserve. In fact, the social organization of the Cree community is held together by "personal networks of influence and manipulation."

I. HISTORY AND CULTURE

The northern Great Plains portion of Canada was a transition zone for Indian tribes inhabiting the northern forest and the Plains proper. By the middle of the eighteenth century, the Gros Ventre and Assiniboine lived in the eastern portion and the Blackfoot and affiliated tribes in the west. To the north were bands of people speaking an Algonquian language, collectively called *Cree*. The former tribes

*Written in collaboration with Niels W. Braroe, who did the basic fieldwork on the Indian group. The chapter is excerpted from John W. Bennett, *Northern Plainsmen: Adaptive Strategy and Agrarian Life*, Chicago: Aldine Publishing Co., 1969. © 1969 by John W. Bennett. The book is a general treatment of the results of Bennett's Saskatchewan Cultural Ecology Research Program, a study of a 5,000-sq. mile region in western Saskatchewan, made in 1962-65. The chapter is reprinted here by permission of the author and publishers, with some minor changes and omissions. "Jasper" is a pseudonym.

were, by the seventeenth century, bison-hunting, horse-riding Plains nomads, while the Cree were still forest hunters, only occasionally moving out onto the Plains. The first written accounts of the Cree in the seventeenth century, by Jesuit missionaries, describe them as hunting and gathering peoples centered mainly on the west coast of Hudson Bay, where the modern Woodland Cree Indians still live. During the early nineteenth century, portions of the Cree people moved south, into the lake country and out on the Plains. By the end of the first quarter of this century, the Cree were a true Plains people.

This movement was caused mainly by the fur trade. As the Hudson Bay Company expanded its activities, all of the tribes were affected, since most of the furs were obtained through them. The vigorous Plains tribes were less influenced by this business, since they could always retreat into their organized bison-hunting life. The Cree, however, with ties to the forests where the fur-bearing animals were found, were drawn into the traders' orbit, and by the end of the eighteenth century had become greatly dependent upon European tools, weapons, and consumption items of all kinds, including food. As the eastern forests and streams were denuded of beaver, the Cree moved west in search of furs, and some of the bands became horse-bison Plains Indians in the process, largely severing their contacts with their forest-hunting relatives, though a few continued to move back and forth. For a time, the Cree were middlemen in the trade between whites and tribes further west. As this happened, a kind of no-man's land developed between the Plains Cree and the other tribes to the east and south: the Cypress Hills and the Jasper region were in the heart of this zone. The Blackfoot eventually dominated the area, maintaining garrisons in or near the Hills in order to keep other Indians from permanent habitation. The presence of numerous grizzly bears in the Hills also discouraged Indian occupancy. The Hudson Bay Company more or less collaborated in this policy, since they were anxious to maintain the bison herds, to ensure the supply of bison meat (in the form of pemmican) for the posts and make profitable sales of guns and other articles to the Indians who did the hunting and trading.

By the early part of the nineteenth century, the situation had developed into a stable military frontier, with the Cree and their occasional allies, the Assiniboine, raiding the Blackfoot, but generally fleeing before the implacable Blackfoot could retaliate in force. But the no-man's land policy held, and the long delay of white settlement of the region was due to Blackfoot hostility and collaborative desire of the Company to keep whites out.

The culture of the Plains Cree Indians by the mid-19th century was thus already a product of a century and more of culture change: the ecological move from forest to Plains; and the involvement with the fur trade and the Hudson Bay Company. This was not an "aboriginal culture, but one already adapted to a Euroamerican frontier society. Moreover, the population of the "Cree" bands was actually quite diverse: individual Indians and whole families could move freely between bands; members and families of other tribes might find a home in a Cree band, and people with French or English names — Metis (half-breeds) — could live in the bands as Indians. hunt bison for cash payments, or join white society as employees of the Company; or, after about 1880, serve as scouts for the North West Mounted Police.

1. Social Organization

The bands were loosely organized aggregates, varying in size and geographical range over short periods of time. Each band claimed an imprecisely defined territory, usually along a river valley. All of the bands in the vicinity of Jasper were more or less adapted to bison-hunting, but occasional hunting and gathering forays into the Cypress Hills, and dealings with the fur traders to the east, preserved the flexible, relatively unspecialized nature of their adaptation. Life was migratory, with the bands moving on the Plains in search of bison, deer, or in and out of the forested islands and brushy coulees and river bottoms, as the food quest, fur trapping, or fear of the Blackfoot dictated. There were, however, certain rhythms: about late June one or several bands would come together to hold the annual Sun Dance — one of the great Plains ceremonials the Cree adopted along with the other features of the culture. Bison drives were usually associated with the Sun Dance. Late in the summer, the coulees and Hills were searched for edible vegetable foods, and in Fall, deer and elk were hunted in the valleys and the Hills. If fur trapping was contemplated, bands would head for the northern forests at the onset of winter, and would camp near the Company posts and bring the pelts to the factor, receiving European articles and food in return.

The Plains Cree had been forest hunters with an exceedingly simple social system based on kinship and loose bands, with informal chieftanship — features which persisted after the adoption of Plains culture. There were no formally recognized procedures for selecting chiefs, no fixed membership number per band, no formally organized constituency. A man was recognized as a leader if he had demonstrated ability in hunting and war. He was expected to be generous, providing for relatives and financing ceremonials like the Sun Dance for the whole group. Decision-making among the Cree was implemented by holding gatherings of the responsible men of the band whenever the occasion arose — legal processes and formal authority were flexible and informal.

A feature of the Cree social organization derived from Plains culture was the Warrior Society — one for each band. Those ambitious young men who showed promise were given recognition of special status and eventually were invited by the older men to sit in the Warrior Lodge — a kind of men's club, police force, and planning council for hunts and raids. The Warrior Lodge was headed by the War Chief, who exercised authority during the spring and summer when large encampments were built, and during the hunts and bison drives: that is, only in connection with Warrior Society activities.

The big hunts or drives were always collective operations, and individuals were not permitted to hunt alone while the official hunting camp was in existence. This rule applied to the hunting of bison and deer primarily, but was not observed when the Cree hunted smaller and more isolated game in the forests or elsewhere. An effort was made to equalize the hunting operation so that the men with the fastest horses would not have the advantage. Animals hunted collectively were divided evenly between all participants in the hunt, to ensure a food supply for all family units. Formal punishment was meted out by the Warrior Society to anyone who violated these rules. Punishment usually took the form of destruction of the culprit's property, but if he mended his ways, restitution was made after a few days. The purpose of the sanction was to restore an individual as a functioning member of the group, and was not vindictive.

This sketch of the Plains Cree social organization focuses on those features which were critical in forging attitudes toward the individual and the group, since these are key factors in understanding the socio-economic adaptation of the reserve Indians to modern Jasper environment and culture. As a way of life, the bison-driving and slaughtering episode lasted only about two human generations after the Cree had emerged on the Plains.

2. Breakdown of the Plains Culture

In addition to the gradual disappearance of the bison, another factor which hastened the breakdown of the Plains culture and the integrity of the tribal groups were the great smallpox epidemics of the late eighteenth, and nineteenth centuries — caused by the increased contacts of whites with the tribes, and by the large concentrations of Indians brought together by the stepped-up bison hunting operations. Historians of the epidemic have pointed out that the debilitating effects had by 1873 virtually eliminated warfare among the old contenders in the northern Plains, the year of the last battle between Blackfoot and Cree. The Cree were never again able to muster a coherent front for tribal warfare. These epidemics depleted the ranks of the tribes, reduced their vitality and determination to control their involvements with whites, and discouraged their resistance to contact and settlement. It was not until after the 1869-1870 epidemic that American whiskey and fur-traders were able to open a post in Blackfoot country in southern Alberta, not far from Jasper, and to use the area as a channel for hide shipments south into the United States.

Thus as the bison vanished and smallpox sapped the vitality of the tribes, the whites moved in, and by the mid-1870's, the whiskey trade became a major factor in the northern Plains. The Cree and

Assiniboine became dependent on the Indian officials of the Canadian Northwest Territories, after 1871 the successor of the Hudson's Bay Company in the area, and a few bands began to move north into the reserves allotted to them. The whiskey traders, moving into the vacuum created by the withdrawal of the Company from the whiskey trading, instigated a series of disorderly episodes, one of the most famous of which was the Cypress Hills Massacre; a slaughter of thirty-odd Assiniboine by a dozen wolf-hunters from Montana, in a coulee in the Hills in the heart of the Jasper region. In 1873, the Canadian government decided to organize a frontier constabulary, and in 1874, Colonel Macleod's 300 pioneer North West Mounted Police rode west to establish a fort in the Cypress Hills and one in southern Alberta. This stopped the whiskey trade.

But it did not solve the Indian problem. The tribes, now augmented by refugees from the Indian wars in the United States, congregated around the forts by the thousands, rioting drinking, begging, demanding support, and refusing to head north to the new reserves. White settlers — mainly the pioneer ranchers, began filtering into the area, and the Mounted Police succeeded in preventing Indian attacks on these people. Thus the Canadian Plains did not become the setting for major and destructive Indian wars for a combination of reasons: the smallpox, the destruction of the bison herds, and the law-enforcement of the Mounties.

In 1885 occurred the Riel Rebellion. Louis Riel was a sometime schoolteacher, reformer, politician, and agitator who had aroused the Metis in 1869, was defeated and exiled, and then returned in the 1880's to rally the Metis and their Indian allies against the land survey and settlement policies of the new Dominion. These policies, developed by Eastern politicians out of touch with the history of the old West, were working out so as to deprive the Metis of their control over lands along the Saskatchewan River system. The Metis were a "non-people:" they had signed no treaties with the government and had no access to food or free distribution of agricultural equipment. Riel invited the Indians to participate in the Rebellion in the hope of securing better terms with the government, and Poundmaker, a Cree leader, accepted. After a series of small battles, which generally ended in favor of the Cree or Metis, the latter were defeated decisively in a major engagement by General Middleton, and a mixed force of militia and Mounties, and the Rebellion was over. Louis Riel, an eccentric with genuine heroic qualities, was hanged — an act many Canadians continue to regret.

The end of the Rebellion marked the end of the relatively free Indian occupancy of the Plains. The policy of forcible removal, delayed for want of adequate preparation in the northern reserves, now had to be carried out to clear the way for settlement. For a few years after 1879, there had been an Indian agricultural graining farm near Jasper, on the north slope of the Hills, but this was abandoned in order to remove all Indians comfortably north of the Canadian Pacific

Railroad. However, small groups of Indians returned to the Hills, saying that they had been promised a reserve there. A small reserve was eventually established for them about 1915 — although to this day the Jasper Band is listed as "non-treaty." The population was, and remains, a microcosm of the ethnic composition of the Plains Cree in the last days of the 1870's and '80's: many French family names; mostly Cree-speaking; with at least one Assiniboine family.

II. JASPER INDIANS TODAY

The 1960's population of the Jasper reserve had few connections with the original group that remained in the Hills after the removal. Only two families could be considered to be descendants of the original band; the remainder were Indians or transitional Indian-Metis who had joined the Jasper group in the subsequent decades. In fact, during the period of the research, at least three Jasper Indians departed and as many joined or "drifted in", as the whites have it, from northern reserves or Montana. (There is a comparable reservation of half-Cree, half-Cherokee people south of the Jasper region, across the line in the United States.) All of these people migrate relatively freely, when the spirit moves them or when the promise of a job invites, from enclave to enclave in the northern Plains. Without a permanent footing in the economy — no cash surplus to permit roots — there is nothing to stop them from doing so.

The Jasper reserve was considered by the Indian Affairs Branch as a marginal and very difficult case. Too small to attract massive support, and its society too disorganized to absorb the limited help that slender budgets could give it, the bureau felt that the reserve would be better disbanded and its members distributed to the northern Cree reserves. This plan was offered the Jasper Indians in the early 1950's, but they rejected it on the basis of the poverty and immorality of the northern reserves, and probably out of general mistrust of white authority. By the 1960's, the condition of the Jasper Indians, and their role in the regional society, had deteriorated considerably.

The official residence of the Jasper Indians was their reserve in the Cypress Hills, about twenty miles southeast of Jasper town. The altitude is 3,700 feet; much of the land is covered with a dense aspen forest consisting mainly of very old and very young trees: the middle-size specimens had nearly all been cut by the Indians to sell as fence-posts. The area has a number of springs and running brooks, and does not want for water, although some of these sources have become polluted. The forest is alive with colorful wildflowers from June through October, and a variety of edible berries abound, some of which are picked and eaten by the Indians, or sold to the ranchers nearby. (However, wild foods do not form a significant part of Indian diet or income.) At the edge of the forest, great vistas of the Plains can be seen, and to the north, the town of Jasper can be picked out far below by the flashes of light reflected from its aluminum-painted grain elevator along the CPR tracks.

The few neighbors of the Indians consisted of the ranchers with pasture land on the "Bench": a local name used for this part of the Hills. These people were considered to be the "rougher type of rancher" by other Jasper residents: their "spreads" had small pasture areas, they used casual methods of management, and had a reputation for cheerful violence and horseplay, much of it carried out with the Indians. To the southeast of the reserve was a Hutterian colony, but at the time of the research, the Indians and Hutterites had no dealings with each other: Hutterites regarded Indians as pagan savages, beyond the pale, though they also pitied them.

At the time of the study, there were about 100 Indians on the reserve, but most previous census reports indicated that this was a low point: the average population appears to have been relatively stable since 1885, with the number about 125. In 1963 there were twenty-five Indian children under five years of age; forty-six from six to twenty-five years; twenty-four persons from twenty-six to fifty-five; and four who were fifty-six or older. The somewhat disproportionately large number of children reflects an increased birth rate and, since Indian women now have their children in the Jasper town hospital, decreasing infant mortality. The sex ratio favored men over women: about seven more males. The population was divided into twelve fluid household units of which about six were parent-child groups, the remainder mixtures of different relatives: mothers alone with children and an older person; grandmothers and grandfathers with or without assorted grandchildren from broken marriages. Residence had a marked ambulatory pattern: individuals and groups would move from household to household after quarrels or after protracted drunken sprees in town. Or, relatives from other reserves might "visit" for periods lasting up to five years. Children ate or slept in whichever house they happened to be visiting or playing in at the time. Many people lived in tents during the summer, others would remain for days at a time in a tent/jalopy camp on the town dump, or in one or two shacks at the edge of town owned by Metis families or those few whites who associated with Indians. The population was divided into six surname groups, most related to one another by marriage. While the entire group had an official existence as a Band, with each person's name entered on an official document, there was at the time of study no band chief, and no implementation of the corporate existence of the group (indeed, the "Band Fund" administered by the Indian Affairs Branch contained less than ten dollars). There was an amorphous sense of group identity defined largely in terms of the discrimination and segregation patterns practiced by whites against the Indians, and implemented by common language and culture and such mechanisms of free sharing and transfer of possessions.

The looseness of the social structure was reflected in the constant going and coming of Indians. The whole population was rarely on the reserve at any one time: individuals and families would be travelling in their old cars, to pow-wows, Sun Dances or festivities at other reserves; to temporary laboring jobs; cutting trees in the woods on or off the reserve ("off" was illegal, but constantly done); or simply cruising around. Their mobility was historically a part of the old Cree migratory culture, but functionally a response to the lack of roots and a sustaining economy of the contemporary reserve culture. It was, in another sense, a part of the "jalopy culture" of contemporary Indian reservation life everywhere in North America: the automobile confers mobility on people without definite ties to the larger community. The car is not only a means of transportation, but a means for amusement, a way to kill time, and on occasion, a place to live and sleep. Indians could be seen living in these old cars on the town dump, on the reserve, or occasionally in the yard of a Bench ranch, while the Indian was working for the rancher. Jalopies could be seen on every day coming down off the reserve for the spree in town, and returning the next day or so, full of sleeping, laughing, quarreling Indians. "Beer bottle Indians" was a local term applied by some whites to the practice of Indians throwing the empties out of the car windows at night, and then returning the next day to pick them up to sell them to beer parlors.

None of the Indians were Christianized, although one or two had been married in a town church, not out of religious attachment, but to legalize the union for financial gain (to obtain the government family allowance). The majority believed in fragments of Cree and Assiniboine folklore, magic, spells, and various conceptions of spiritual beings. Little rituals accompanied many daily events: often before drinking a bottle of beer, Indians would pour a little on the ground as an offering to the generations of dead Cree. Songs and chants were sung in both Cree and Assiniboine; drum beating and singing was a regular part of the "pow-wow" demonstrations the Indians invariably put on (for a fee) for Jasper town festivals. Rain Dances were held nearly every year on the reserve; the tattered old lodges were one of the interesting sights of the district. The words and music for the Rain or Sun Dance ceremonials were known by all of the older men and one or two of the younger.

The educational situation on the reserve had been a source of anxiety for the Indian agents and white friends of the Indians for years. There had been really no education at all until the Indian Affairs Branch built a school on the reserve in 1958. Attendance by children at the school was intermittent and casual, and very little had ever been learned, according to the white teacher in 1963. In 1965, the school was finally closed in an admission of defeat, and the children were bussed into the consolidated schools in Jasper town. By 1966 it was evident that the practice was having its effect: one or two

Indian children took part in school functions and scholarly competitions, and the dress and behavior of most of the children had begun to change toward the white model. There were, however, no children of high school age in school. It was believed and hoped by some Jasperites that the change in educational procedure was devised in part as a means of gradually liquidating the reserve.

The following excerpts from a brief oral autobiography of a forty-four-year-old Indian man provide a typical life trajectory:

I can't remember much before I was seven years old. Things have changed a lot in the last twenty years — the Indian's life, I mean.

We used to haul wood into town . . . . I was about ten years old, I guess about '28 or '29. We used to use horses; it would take six hours to take a team to town; we used to camp for the night, then in the morning we'd cut up the wood for burning. We did this year 'round; we used to charge one dollar a wagon box load. We went sometime with my Dad, sometime with my Mother's Dad, sometime my Mother, or Charlie or Joe [brothers]. We buy some stuff in the store — everything, sugar, butter, flour. Everything was cheap that time. That time Father was live this place. Lived in a tent. We had log house that time like this too, but we used tent when we went to town. Stay sometimes two nights when we finish selling wood.

My father he was cuttin' posts, tryin' livin' that time. That time there was no help at all [government relief]. I think my old grandfather was workin' over here — we call 'im that Gus Andert, but he died. He worked for 'im twenty years, eighteen anyway. Haul hay, help plowing', everything; feed cattle Winter and Summer. He [Andert] live there eighteen years, had three [Indian] girls live with him, and some boys. My Dad was one of 'em.

There was no school then. Old Indian fellas didn't want us to go school in town. Old folks was afraid we would go to war then. That time was war — 1919. I guess lotta Indians went that war — lotta Indians kill 'em up East. Young fellas they learn to read they go into Army, that's what the old fellas afraid.

There was lotsa Indians that time, more than now. All pull out around '29 or '29, '30 I think. They can't live very much — this place no good, no work, long ways to town, that'sa reason. Round 1919 there was a big Flu here, too, and in town. Lotsa Indians, they die then. Lotsa white mans die too.

We was pull out from here. Left 1936 with my old Dad and Mother. We went Moose Mountain. At that time die my old Grandmother. My Mother's Mother died in the States when we were at Rain Dance, same Spring died that old fella. Lived there about two years. After that two years we come back from Moose Mountain. That time was 1940. We don't like that place, water no good, lotsa sickness. No good place.

In '42 died my old Mother. So we scattered all over. We tried workin' here, workin' all over the place. My father got married again in '41. That's his own sister-in-law. No more kids with that lady. He met her Moose Mountain, she Jimmy's wife. He went back there again that year and married her. I went then too.

About '39 I start ride horses in stampede. I rode all over. Last time was '57 up here in Greenfields [a famous Jasper amateur rodeo in the Hills]. Then I quit. I made maybe $140 the whole time. I rode bareback and saddle bronc, and wild horse race. That's all I ride.

I was start bronc riding that time — '39 — when I met wife that time over Moose Mountain. Live with that girl there. I was stay with that father-in-law. Had a kid about one year later. Wife catch cold and die pneumonia in that winter — that was about 1940. Then I come back here. The baby stayed with that grandfather. Indian Agent ask me sign paper so that baby stay with old folks. He was supposed to stay there and come here when he twenty-one, but he didn't do it. I think he married now, but I don't know when. See him five years ago, we went down Moose Mountain for Sun Dance, in 1958.

So I come back here by myself. I stay with Dave [friend] and we cut posts, we live that way. Was huntin' a little bit — deers and coyotes. I live with that Dave until 1942. He die 1953. For while I work for old George Carson, nice guy, he treat us pretty good. His wife nice woman too. We start at seven o'clock and quit about five o'clock evening — right time to work and right time to quit. They didn't work us too hard.

But then I was bronc ridin', so I went East maybe two-three weeks. We work out winters, maybe sometime Spring, Summer. Then we go ridin'. Lotsa work then, but not no more. I guess the ranchers got lotsa machinery now, they don't need no man now . . .

Several patterns are typical and important: the ambiguousness over dates and the imprecision of relating movements and experiences; the lack of roots in any one place and willingness to roam, making a living where one can; the casual ties between relatives; the sense of a deteriorating role for the Indian in Jasper.

III. ECONOMIC ADAPTATIONS

Jasper Indians seem to have made a low but steady income down to about World War II. While their economic behavior was casual and intermittent, there were a number of income-producing activities which were always available. At different times, they concentrated on farm and ranch labor, manual labor in town, cutters and salesmen of firewood and fenceposts, trappers, hide-tanners, and craftsmen who made beadwork moccasins, and polished bison horns for local sale and for travellers on the CPR trains stopping at Jasper, or for tourists at the Park in the Hills. With a more assured income, and with memories of the old frontier still fresh, they also appear to have been treated by whites with greater respect. Many of the old pioneer ranchers and farmers had firm friends among the Indians; more than one claimed to have been in the habit of inviting Indians to dinner, and of providing gifts at Christmas or at the birth of a new baby — customs almost unbelievable in the deteriorated situation in the 1960's. Indians were always invited into town to appear at festivals (they still were, but it was now a matter of a perfunctory performance for a fee), and receive honors along with whites. The Indians were an important symbol of the old frontier and the pride the pioneers took in its development: the Jasper Indians were "our Indians" as more than one old timer put it, invariably concluding their stories by deploring the contemporary sad state of affairs.

For the Indian by the 1950's and '60's had lost whatever meager socio-economic status he might have had in Jasper society, although he retained a little of his symbolic or ceremonial significance as "our Indians". But many merchants in town discouraged Indians from coming in their stores; restaurant proprietors, by tacit agreement, confined the Indians to one café, and of the two hotel beer parlors, only one received Indians regularly. Their low incomes forced the Indians to be very selective in their business dealings: only one garageman in town would repair their cars, usually knowing he would rarely receive full payment; only one grocery store manager would give them money on credit, letting them use relief chits as collateral (an illegal practice) — and so on. Indians "hung out" in vacant lots, in the laundromat, behind the beer halls or garages, in one old empty building, or in a shack or two on the outskirts of town.

In the period of the study, the Jasper Indians received a small cash income from the following sources:

a) A monthly relief allowance from the government. For a household of two adults and four children this would provide about $85 per month. In the case of families with husbands and young men who worked occasionally, this relief allowance formed one-half or more of the annual income. For aged people living alone, it was the whole income, although gifts of food and clothing from other Indians would make up what was lacking.

b) The sale of fenceposts, which was intermittent, but accounted for between one-half to three-fourths of the income of some families.

c) Manual labor, on an intermittent basis, from ranchers, the highway department, and similar employers. This means of getting income while once very important, had diminished almost to the vanishing point by 1963.

d) Fees from white ranchers who: rented pasture land from the Indians; paid grazing fees for an occasional cow or two; or bought hay from Indian land by combining it and giving the Indians a share. Indians could either use the hay for their own cattle, or sell the hay in town for 50¢ a bale (the latter the more common custom).

e) The sale of cows given to the Indians by the Indian Service. This was strictly illegal: these cattle were inalienable, and were designed to give the Indians a start at ranching. In 1958 the Indians had received fifty-seven head; by 1962 there were only about half this amount.

f) Borrowing and begging money: minor swindling of whites for gasoline or beer money; getting advances on wages or fenceposts and then not following through — and similar illegal or extralegal devices designed to provide pocket money or emergency sums.

g) Occasional trapping of small fur animals, and sale of the pelts. Relatively inconsequential.

Actually, it is extremely difficult to estimate income for any given Indian family, and nearly impossible to do so for the Reserve as a whole. For one thing, Indians were reluctant to report earned wages, since this would jeopardize their receiving full relief payments. Secondly, since many sources of income were illegal — such as the selling of hay, etc. — they tended to conceal these. Finally, it is doubtful if Indians themselves knew with any accuracy what their incomes were. They kept records neither of income nor of expenditures. The latter is of course difficult in the light of Indian tendencies to act "impulsively" and "extravagently" with respect to money, at least from the white man's point of view.

The annual income produced from these various means for an Indian family of two adults and about five children, ranged from roughly $1,000 to $1,500, but fluctuated considerably, depending upon the opportunities in category (c). Income in this category also varied depending upon the desire of the Indian to undertake a job which might require his steady and faithful presence each day for a month or more. By the 1960's the Indian habit of looking for small amounts of cash rather than steady jobs, whenever a specific objective was in view, had become dysfunctional because the jobs were too few in number, and those that turned up required relatively conscientious work, not casual labor. When the growing shortage of casual laboring jobs developed due largely to haying mechanization on Jasper ranches, the Indian Affairs Branch inaugurated the monthly relief check. For Indians, whose culture did not value work as a calling, or in general did not accept the philosophy of a consistent "job" to support a family, this relief check simply became a means of avoiding what jobs there might have been. The Indians referred to the day relief checks arrived as "payday." Jasper whites who had considerable sympathy for or anxiety about the Indian situation, universally condemned the relief allowance as the one measure which had worsened the lot of the Indian — although they were not so articulate about the unwillingness of Jasper employers to take a chance on Indian labor. Their argument was that relief robbed the Indian of initiative and the will to be self-supporting.

In the past many Indian families had resided in shacks on the property of ranchers, working as a family for the enterprise. By the 1960's this practice had almost entirely ceased. Between 1963 and 1965, this was attempted on only two ranches, and in both cases it ended in disaster: the Indian became increasingly unreliable, going into town and drinking up his wages, being prevailed upon by his relatives and friends to share his windfall, and encouraged to steal from the rancher. Ranchers declared that their relations with the Indians had reached an impossible state of affairs, and that they could no longer make these residential arrangements.

The Indian habit of "conning" or swindling whites out of small sums of money was a consistent feature of the interaction pattern and while it did not provide a significant part of the annual income, it was a matter of considerable sociological interest. We found that in numerous cases, the white knew perfectly well he was being swindled: an Indian truck or jalopy would cough to a stop before the ranch or farm gate, and an Indian would walk in, explaining to the rancher that he wanted to borrow some gasoline, or $2 to buy some in town, saying he would pay the man back next week. The rancher would invariably provide the favor, knowing full well that he would never be repaid, and knowing also that the Indians were capable of simply camping in the car in front of his house, saying that there was not enough gas to get further. In a typical but spectacular instance, a rancher agreed to buy a windmill and water pump from the Indians. This sale was illegal, since a permit would have had to be obtained from the Indian agent, whose office was over 200 miles from Jasper. The rancher took the apparatus apart and hauled it home. That same night, a group of Indians crept into the yard, stole several pieces of the equipment, and took them into town and resold them to a junk dealer. None of these instances, petty or imposing, was ever reported by the ranchers to the Mounted Police.

The ranchers and townspeople involved in these curious dealings invariably explained them either by expressing sympathy for the Indians, who needed things and had no security or money to get them, or in a comic-anecdotal bluster, regarded the stories as evidence of the rough old frontier way that has such symbolic power in Jasper. However, in either case the whites regarded the Indian behavior as proof of their childlike qualities: the behaviour was used as evidence that the Indians were incurably childish and irresponsible. "They're not really adult people, you know — just like children, and you have to accept that." This attitude confirmed the white image of the Indians, and thus indirectly sanctioned the discrimination and segregation.

But it did more: it concealed and rationalized the exploitation of the Indians by ranchers whose property surrounded the reserve, and with whom the Indians had the most frequent interactions. These men bought and sold Indian property illegally; made deals with the Indians for pasturing and hay cutting which were to the Indians' disadvantage, and often as outright a swindle as those practiced on them by the Indians themselves. Indians sometimes retaliated with violence: fights between the Indians and these ranchers, both in the Hills and in town, behind the beer parlors, occasionally occurred. These battles also were not reported to the Mounties, who of course knew full well what was going on. The Police routinely arrested Indians for drunkenness or traffic violations, or for major crimes, like a rare shooting, but this was the limit of their concern. The Mounties, too, saw the Indians as irresponsible kids, or as "savages", as one sergeant remarked in an unguarded moment. Actually the Mounted Police attitude towards the Indians was identical to that held by the Police in the early days of the frontier when the Police curbed violence, but followed a policy of ignoring petty infractions and Indian internal disputes.

People in this kind of marginal, impecunious position everywhere tend to have loose social organization with few organized groups and structures. In their place, one finds "personal networks" of influence and manipulation. Most Jasper Indian men had several whites with whom they had a variety of friendly, swindling, and hostile relationships — people on whom he might count for help from time to time, or people whom he could use to some advantage in his struggle to exist and to enjoy life. Indians had these same network-like relationships among themselves: instead of a tightly-organized society on the reserve, there was a loose band of people, with a variety of relationships of mutual aid and mild exploitation: an Indian family who abandoned their house for a month or so would almost always find a group of Indians living in it upon their return; an Indian who wanted money to buy beer would borrow it from another (or a white), and eventually pay it back in the form of a lift to town when his car was running; and so on.

Thus in order to survive, Jasper Indians had to develop ingenious strategies of manipulation of the socio-economic environment. The Indians were neither more nor less skilled in these strategies than other marginal populations, and to some degree they were manipulated and exploited, in their turn, by the ranchers and other whites.

SUMMARY

Through the years since the establishment of the reserve, the Jasper Indians did not develop a "Protestant ethic" of conscientious work and a sustaining economic enterprise. The slender budgets of the Indian Affairs Branch, and its unwillingness to do very much for this undersized and isolated reserve, prevented it from supplying the kind of equipment, funds, or vocational training which would be necessary to accumulate the surplus needed to make the shift from a migratory, live-from-day-to-day way of life, to a sedentary income-and-capital-oriented economy. It was argued by Jasper whites that if the Indians had enjoyed leadership which could have helped them to mobilize and use their own labor and determination as "social capital", they might have done more with their slender resources (developed more pasture, or bred cattle instead of selling them one by one). However, the surviving Cree social organization, with its lack of a clear-cut authority and leadership patterns, its emphasis on sharing and disposing of possessions to people with need for them, lacked the impetus for this kind of organization. Added to this is, of course, the fact that their resources were hopelessly inadequate. When jobs had been frequent, and wood for fenceposts was abundant, and people in town still needed fuel for their wood stoves, these deficiencies in Cree economic behavior were not so critical. And then, too, there was less visible difference between whites and Indians in material possessions. But with the drying up of these sources of income, the Indians were forced back into manipulative strategies in order to get what they wanted and needed, aside from the relief income. It is clear that the Reserve could not support its members by agricultural means alone. And, even the old reliable means of income had become corrupted by the situation: fenceposts were supposed to be dipped in blue vitriol to protect against rot, but since the cost and time investment of this operation was considerable, Indians often bought cheap laundry blueing for the task, thus swindling the unwary buyer; although some buyers knew full well that they were not getting what they paid for — and then found ways of not paying the Indians the full price.

The marginal role of the Indian was illustrated clearly in his participation in rodeos and other local sports and festivals. Jasper people often mildly boasted about the participation of the Indians in the old Greenfields Stampede in the Hills, but in fact the Indian role was confined to bucking horses and steer-riding, the two "rough" sports of the rodeo. These do not necessarily require specialized ranch training, like calf roping and steer decorating, or the elaborate barrel racing and other "show" events. Indian spectators sat over at one side of the arena, where no one else would sit because of the prevailing wind and the dust from the grounds, and it was understood that Indians were not to invade the better spots.

At the same time, some of the values of the Indian male were shared with those of the rancher. Masculinity, taciturness, individualism — these are all values which find an echo in the old Plains Cree social organization. The Indians were aware of their similarity, and so found it possible to identify with the ranching-and-riding culture; their participation in the rodeo was a symbol of this identification. By successfully swindling a white man, particularly a rancher, the Indians manifested their equality in their own eyes, and thereby avoided destructive loss of identity. The white, in turn, found his conception of the Indian as an irresponsible child fully validated.

The Indian population of Jasper is an example of a society which has minimal adaptability to natural resources insofar as development of these resources is concerned. It was also a society lacking a sufficient cash surplus to acquire a stake in the local economy. However, the Indians succeeded fairly well in manipulating the social resources of the white community to obtain a degree of satisfaction and a survival income.

BIBLIOGRAPHIC NOTES

The Indians of the Great Plains were the first to be studied intensively by the first generation of professionally trained ethnologists, since the latter completed their training only shortly after the Indians had been placed on reservations in the West. Some of the more illuminating works from the standpoint of the ecological approach are Clark Wissler, "Influence of the Horse in the Development of Plains Culture," *American Anthropologist*, 16: 1 (1914); George E. Hyde, *Indians of the High Plains*, University of Oklahoma Press, 1959: Symmes C. Oliver, *Ecology and Cultural Continuity as Contributing Factors in the Social Organization of the Plains Indians, University of Publications in American Archeology and Ethnology*, Vol. 48, No. 1 (1962); W. W. Newcome, "A Reexamination of the Causes of Plains Warfare," *American Anthropologist*, 52 (1950), pp. 317-330; Waldo R. Wedel, "Some Aspects of Human Ecology in the Central Plains," *American Anthropologist*, 55 (1953), pp. 499-514.

The definitive study of the role of the bison in Plains and white culture, and a history of the exploitation of these useful animals, is found in Frank G. Roe, *The North American Buffalo*, University of Toronto Press, 1951. A more specialized treatment of the bison herds of the northern Plains and Canada is found in Frank G. Roe, *The North Buffalo*, University of Toronto Press, 1951. See also H. Clyde Wilson, "An Inquiry into the Nature of Plains Indian Cultural Development," *American Anthropologist;* 65 (1963), pp. 355-69. For prehistoric aspects of Indian-bison relationships, see Helen M. Wormington and Richard G. Forbes, "An Introduction to the Archeology of Alberta, Canada," *Proceedings,* Denver Museum of Natural History, Vol. II, Denver, Colorado (1965).

The Cree Indians of Canada were a humble woodland and hunting group and even the bands that entered the Plains and took up bison hunting were unspectacular as compared with the more famous and flamboyant Plains tribes to the south. The standard monograph on the people is David Mandelbaum, *The Plains Cree,* Anthropological Papers, American Museum of Natural History, Vol. 37, Pt. 2 (1940). Another and more recent specialized study is Verne Duesenberry, *The Montana Cree: A Study in Religious Persistence,* Almquist & Wikesell, 1962. A general description of the Cree and their neighbors is found in Douglas Leechman, *Native Tribes of Canada,* Gage, 1956. Material on the Cree migrations described in the chapter can be found in Frank R. Secoy, *Changing Military Patterns on the Great Plains,* Monographs of the American Ethnological Society, No. 21 (1953).

A novelized version of the life of a group of Indians like those of Jasper on a reservation in Montana is provided in Dan Cushman, *Stay Away Joe,* Viking Press, 1953. Some of these people are relatives of the Jasper Indians. A motion picture based on the novel, and starring, of all people, Elvis Presley as "Joe," the Indian who becomes a rodeo star, was released in 1968. A description of the Piapot and Front-man bands and their culture is found in Abel Watetch, *Payepot and His People,* Modern Press, 1959.

The term *Métis* is French patois for "half-breed," and is applied to a variety of populations representing intermarriage between various Indian groups and Scotch, English, and French settlers. Most of these marriages took place during the period when western Canada was under the control of the Hudson's Bay Company. These people are one of the true, "forgotten" populations of North America, and have become objects of interest to social scientists only in the past several years. A good general description is found in Wallace Stegner, *Wolf Willow,* Chap. 4. An available technical study is B. Y. Card and G. K. Hirabayashi, *The Metis in Alberta Society,* University of Alberta Committee for Social Research, 1963. The two rebellions of Metis and Indians led by Louis Riel are described in George F. G. Stanley, *The Birth of Western Canada,* University of Toronto Press, 1960 — which also has much information on the Metis people. Louis Riel is biographized in William McCartney Davison, *Louis Riel: 1844-1885,* Albertan Publishing Co., 1955.

The mutual swindling and hostile interaction between Jasper Indians and whites described in the chapter is treated in greater detail in Niels W. Braroe, "Reciprocal Exploitation in an Indian-White Community," *Southwestern Journal of Anthropology,* Vol. 21 (1963), pp. 166-178. The type of adaptive behavior displayed by the Indians has been found to be typical of economically marginal people the world over. A description for a South-American Negro group is found in Norman Whitten, "Strategies of Adaptive Mobility in the Columbian-Ecuadorian Littoral," *American Anthropologist,* in press.

8

The Kwakiutl:
Indians of British Columbia*

Ronald P. Rohner

Evelyn C. Rohner

The Northwest Pacific Coast Indian group had a rich material culture and an aesthetic sense. The Kwakiutl are commonly identified by their massive artistically carved totem poles. They are linguistically distinct from their Canadian neighbors, the Athapaskan Chipewyan, and the Algonquian Cree. Little remains today, however, linking the Kwakiutl with the cultural vitality of former times.

The traditional Kwakiutl community owed its social cohesion to the potlatch ceremony which established and sanctioned an individual's rank within the community. The destruction of one's own property was a central feature in the potlatch ritual. The white onlooker did not understand this aspect of Kwakiutl culture and consequently the potlatch was first outlawed in 1884.

With the eventual end of the potlatch era, traditional social organization collapsed. The Rohners recount developments since the potlatch period, and note vestiges of the traditional culture which persist today. They are optimistic in thinking that aspects of the former culture pattern may be revitalized and become a part of the present socio-cultural milieu.

Life for most Kwakiutl Indians is confined to a slender strip of coastal water, fiord-like inlets, sounds, and hundreds of densely forested, almost impenetrable islands and outcroppings of rock between the western coast of British Columbia and Vancouver Island. Fifteen southern Kwakiutl bands representing about twenty indigenous tribal groups occupy this territory between Smith Sound and Campbell River. One of these groups is the Gilford Island Band, which is formally com-

*Reprinted from Ronald P. Rohner and Evelyn C. Rohner, *The Kwakiutl Indians of British Columbia.* (New York: Holt, Rinehart and Winston, 1969), with permission of the authors and the publisher.

prised of two closely related Kwakiutl tribal groups, the Koeksotenok and Hahuamis.[1] The residents of Gilford are the people described in this case study.

The Kwakiutl are today as they have always been — even in their mythology — a fishing people. Their self-identity is bound to the sea and to the life-forms within the sea. The great forests are exploited by white men, but only gradually and reluctantly are the Kwakiutl involving themselves in the logging industry. Agricultural enterprises are virtually unknown among the Indians. Some of the younger men take advantage of vocational training courses offered by the Indian Affairs Branch, and a very few go on to higher education. But ultimately many of them return to the sea, reaffirming a style of life that is as old as memory and tradition combined. Thus, even though the Kwakiutl are hardly the same people today as described years ago by the American anthropologist, Franz Boas, important elements of cultural continuity with the past are nonetheless maintained.

The majority of the houses in the village on Gilford Island, as well as the school and teacherage, were acquired from a Canadian Air Force base in 1950. These identical prefabricated houses were transported to Gilford and arrayed on posts two feet off the ground in two neat, parallel rows on a newly bulldozed end of the village. Thus the disposition of houses at Gilford is exceptional among Kwakiutl villages in that their style and arrangement look like the suburb of a Canadian town.

Not all houses in the village . . . have running water. Several families carry pails of water into their homes from one of the faucets protruding from several paths around the settlement. The nine outhouses in the village are shared by various families who normally lock them to keep unauthorized people out and to keep them from being damaged by mischievous children. A number of families use chamber pots for convenience at night.

The population of Gilford (about 100) — as well as most of the other small, isolated Indian villages throughout the region — changes constantly. Individuals and sometimes whole families migrate easily from place to place among the local Reserves throughout the area, although an individual's strongest attachments are usually maintained with his home Reserve. Fluctuation of village size and composition are also influenced by marked seasonal variation. The village is practically deserted during the commercial salmon fishing season in the

---

[1] The Band legally consists of the Koeksotenok tribe, who traditionally occupied the village site, and the Huhuamis tribe. The Tsawatenok, a third Kwakiutl tribe, however, outnumbers either of the other two groups in the village. These three groups along with the Guauaenok form the Four Tribes of Gilford, an informally knit collectivity or confederacy who historically had exceptionally close contacts. Ninety per cent of the residents at Gilford are members of the Tsawatenok, Koeksotenok or Hahuamis tribes. The Guauaenok are unrepresented in the community today.

summer, but it fills again briefly after the summer fishing season ends. The size of the settlement is only moderately reduced in September after the residential school children leave in the fall, but the age composition of the community is radically affected.[2] Population ranks swell again in the winter when members of other Kwakiutl Bands come to dig clams. Most of these visitors leave in early spring when the clam season is over. Finally, the village burgeons for a short time before summer fishing begins and after the residential school children return home.

Even within the village internal household shifts are commonplace. If one family leaves a house a second often moves in, vacating its own home or leaving a host family to itself once again. Not infrequently this leads to conflict because the owners of the abandoned house may be unhappy about this intrusion. Moreover, young people often move or are moved within the village from one household to another where they live for indefinite periods of time.

Despite the residential instability of the villagers, the people spend most of their lives within the perimeter of an easily definable and circumscribed region. The psychologically real options for movement are restricted. The most extensive network of social relations for Gilford Islanders is localized among five other adjacent Indian villages — Kingcome, New Van, Village, Turnour, and the Bay.[3] When a Gilford Islander moves he usually goes to one of these villages.

The only way a person can travel in the region is by boat or pontoon plane; consequently distance is typically reckoned in terms of the length of time required to get from one place to another by gill-net fishing boat, and not in terms of statute or nautical miles.

Alert Bay with its paved roads and automobiles is the major commercial and social center of the entire region and is two hours from Gilford. The population of 1200 people there is evenly divided into about 600 Indians and 600 non-Indians. The Indian Agent's office is at the Bay along with two hotels, shops, beer parlors, fish canning companies, government offices, and the Royal Canadian Mounted Police (RCMP).

Indians and Whites in the Bay sometimes refer to the more remote, isolated villages — such as Gilford — as "the islanders", and they think of the island villages as being collectively depressed and conservative, whereas they view themselves as being progressive. Many Indians feel that living in Alert Bay gives them social and economic advantages not common to the remote villages. The islands are also thought of as being "tough places". Some individuals and families on these island villages share this negative evaluation of their village held by others. This, in part, accounts for the migration of families from the island Reserves to, most typically, Alert Bay. As a result, the isolated villages throughout most of the area are losing their population as families move to larger, more commercial areas. Quite frequently adults explain that they want to give their children a better education than is provided in the day schools situated on the island Reserves. This is often a legitimate reason; rarely, however, is it the only one. Not infrequently certain families complain about their home village, and state emphatically that they are going to leave as soon as possible. Some of these families have been threatening to leave for several years without acting on the decision or desire. Despite their disadvantages these traditional village sites still symbolize fundamental security and identity for many of the villagers. The village also provides for some of the older Indians a firm identification with the fading image of a passing tradition. This is the life space of the Gilford Island Kwakiutl where our account unfolds.

I. THE KWAKIUTL AT WORK

The majority of the village men define fishing — especially salmon fishing — as their most important economic activity. Clam digging is less important for most Indians than fishing, both in their over-all life process and in their self-destruction. This is true even though they spend almost an equal number of days throughout the year doing both. Many men could earn a great deal more money through logging, but they choose not to. None of the men during our year at Gilford could remember exactly how much money he had earned the preceding year in logging, clam digging, crafts or trapping, but many of them could recall quite closely how much money he earned from fishing (mean $1,700; range $400-$3,200). We interpret this as an indication of their close identity with fishing. Furthermore, there were ninety days in which people could dig clams during the 1962-63 season. Given the fact that the diggers produce an average of at least three boxes of clams per tide per person, one could expect their mean personal income from clams that year to approach five hundred dollars. In fact, however, the average (mean) income from clam digging during the 1962-63 season was two hundred dollars, or sixty per cent less than expected. This too reflects the people's more casual attitude toward clamming. With these facts in mind we turn now to the commercial salmon fishing season.

[2] The Indian population of British Columbia was almost wiped out after European contact because of the introduction of diseases such as tuberculosis, measles, and syphilis. Since 1939, however, the population has been burgeoning at an accelerating rate. Consequently, fifty per cent of the Indian population in British Columbia in 1963 was under sixteen and seventy-five per cent was under thirty-two. The same trend holds true of the Gilford Island Kwakiutl: fifty per cent are fifteen or younger and seventy-five per cent are thirty or younger. Thus any alteration of the school age population within the village seriously affects the character of the entire village.

[3] The full name of each village is Kingcome Inlet, New Vancouver, Village Island, Turnour Island and Alert Bay respectively, but we use these shorthand terms because they conform with the standardized usage of the Gilford Islanders.

A. Commercial Salmon Fishing

The Kwakiutl Indians fish on two types of boats — gill netters and purse seiners. The mechanics of gill net fishing are quite different from purse seining. In the first place, gill netting is a one- or two-man operation, whereas seining requires a crew of four to seven men. More importantly the style of fishing is totally different on the two types of boats. Different kinds of nets and other equipment are used. Seiners fish during daylight hours (in the early summer from 4:00 a.m. to 10:00 p.m.) whereas gill netters can fish equally well during the day or night. The process of netting the fish on seiners bears no relation to netting fish on gill netters. In the latter, the gill net (from which this type of fishing takes its name) is managed from a drum anchored toward the stern of the boat. When a fisherman arrives at his chosen fishing grounds he drops his net out into the water through rollers secured off the stern. The boat is positioned down wind from the net so that the craft does not drift back into the net. Once the net is out both the boat and the net are allowed to drift. Fish swim into the net and try to pass through but they cannot because the mesh is too small. Then they try to withdraw and in the process their gill covers become entangled in the net. Periodically the fisherman rolls his net back onto the drum, disentangling the salmon and other fish that have become caught as the net passes over the rollers.

During intervals between net checks, the gill net fisherman sleeps, reads or listens to his radio; if fishing has been very poor he may make one set and leave it until morning. But the men usually sleep very little during the night at Rivers Inlet because of the large number of fish that swim into the net and because of the dangers of drifting into another's net. Men who damage the net of another fisherman are responsible for making reparation. Moreover, a sleeping gill net fisherman runs the risk of having his net or boat drift into a restricted area. Fisheries Department boats and planes carefully patrol the areas and levy a fine against anyone who has allowed his net to cross a restricted boundary.

A packer boat from one of the three fish-packing companies based in Alert Bay usually collects fish from the Gilford fisherman at least once a day. Each boat flies his company flag as identification to the packer. Occasionally, however, depending on the area, the fishermen take their fish to a buyer stationed on a scow near land. The men are expected to sell their fish only to the company for which they work. No money actually passes hands except when a fisherman sells his fish to an independent buyer for cash; independent buyers often pay more for the fish than the fish companies. The men recognize that selling to independents is a risky practice, however, because they are dependent on their fish companies for credit, for financing boats, for nets and other equipment, and for a steady market. The companies extend credit at the beginning of the season for food and supplies, and they perform other services as well. Part of a man's commercial success depends on his reputation with one of the fish-packing companies. A fisherman who is caught selling his fish to an independent buyer may lose favor with his company, and this can create a major hardship.

Most men at Gilford prefer to own or at least operate their own gill netters rather than sign on as crew members of a seiner. One of the village men, Victor Philip, expressed the sentiment of many others when he explained why he prefers having his own gill netter: "I'm my own boss. Some guys on seiners are real haywire and others get stuck doing all the work." Most of the village men, including older adolescents, have worked at one time or another on a seiner, but most of them agree that they can make more money by operating their own gill netter — if they can get one. They catch fewer fish but they also have fewer expenses. Only one person receives the earnings — but he must meet the costs too. None of the men at Gilford skippered his own seiner during the commercial salmon season.

Fishing is a risky venture and it is becoming increasingly uncertain each year as more people enter the industry with more efficient equipment and as the provincial government enforces stricter limitations on the times and places where men can fish. Although commercial salmon fishing is open from May to October, the most productive fishing tends to occur from the end of June through early August. Thus, the effective fishing season for the people of Gilford is about three months. Fishing closures are determined by the Fisheries Department as part of their conservation program. Fairly tight controls must be maintained at the northern end of Vancouver Island where the Kwakiutl live in order to protect the fishing interest of men further south, as well as to assure that enough salmon reach their spawning grounds.

The Fish Commission notifies fishermen of impending closures by radio broadcast. Seiners have a radiotelephone on board, but most gill netters do not. Those people who do not have a radiophone are notified through the informal communication network of other fishermen and fish packers. Many people keep their transistor radios or radiophones tuned to the marine frequencies for fishing information. Listening to marine bands on transistor radios and use of radiotelephones to intercept messages have major implications for communication throughout the area. Radiotelephones are used extensively by the fishermen to exchange information about fishing. Fishermen are often secretive about their location if they are discussing good fish catches because they know others are listening. In fact Indians often speak Kwakwala, the native language of the Kwakiutl, in order to exclude at least non-Indians from this information. The radiotelephones are also vital to notify others of an accident or of a breakdown.

B. Logging

Although some of the ... men ... log for brief periods of time, especially during the low income months of April and May when they have less to do than during any other time of the year, logging is not popular. In fact a few Kwakiutl express fear of working in the woods. Frank Bean, for example, described his work in one of the local camps and concluded that he is afraid of logging but that he needs the job. "I have to pull my share in the work or be a coward," he confided.

Logging in the "gyppo" or "gyp" outfits, as the small logging companies are locally known, is sometimes dangerous, but it is probably no more so than some of the other jobs the Indians regularly perform. Danger is hardly a sufficient reason to explain the reluctance of the men to work in the woods — except that the Kwakiutl more readily perceive the risks there because they are not at ease in the forest. A more important reason for their reserve about working in the lumber industry is that logging often requires them to be away from the village and from their families except on weekends. They are willing to do this for a few months, but seldom for longer. Moreover, the logging camp nearest Gilford is said to be understaffed, thus each man must perform jobs that normally require two or three men in the larger operations. Indians have the reputation among logging employers for being valuable and hard workers, except that they very often do not get to work on time. If they have been drinking, or if some important social event is taking place, they frequently do not show up for work at all. A few of the men have a long history of being fired from jobs because of this.

C. Crafts

Ambrose Cedar is in his early fifties, overweight and has a bad heart so he cannot fish or log anymore. Over the years he has become an extraordinary artist and craftsman. He makes his living largely through carving, but this modest income is supplemented by family allowance and an occasional relief check. Pat, his nephew, has a badly curved spine which Pat attributes to being pushed down a cliff; but it is the opinion of a local doctor that his hunched back is more likely due to tuberculosis as a child. Pat can do no heavy physical labor, and he too relies largely on art for his small income. He has watched his uncle carve all his life and under this tutelage has become a capable and rapidly maturing painter. Jeffrey Hardy, also a brilliant craftsman, is the third village resident who gains most of his livelihood from a commercial craft. A few of the other men in the village also carve during their free time. The work of each of these men follows traditional themes. Ambrose and Jeffrey produce such artifacts as stylized ceremonial masks and hamatsa (cannibal society) whistles belonging to the traditional winter ceremonial dance societies. Pat often depicts dancing figures in their ceremonial costumes and scenes from these winter dances.

Craftsmen usually sell their products to the store owner at Echo Bay, but they sometimes ship them directly to dealers in Vancouver. The price paid for masks carved by different men varies greatly, reflecting not only the difference in quality but also the minimum price that some of the novices will accept. Jeffrey complained to me with annoyance that the "beginners are selling their masks cheap and bringing the price down on good ones."

Some basic changes have taken place in Kwakiutl crafts over time, mainly through the influence of Whites. Carving and painting are being transformed to suit the demands of the commercial market, or at least to match the Indians' perception of such demands.

The people are losing a large part of their traditional technology as they become increasingly dependent on industrially produced goods. At one time they manufactured fishing nets from the fiber of nettles; now they buy nylon nets. They once produced adhesives from the translucent tissues between the skin and flesh of the salmon; they now use glue and tape. They used to utilize natural elements in the environment to produce colored pigments for their oil base paints, but today they buy commercial enamels.

II. BEING A KWAKIUTL

The Kwakiutl are no longer exceptional because of their economic activities, their religious practices and beliefs, their social or ceremonial life, their house style or the food they eat. In most ways, in fact, they live in a style very similar to the White fishermen and loggers who also reside in the area. Therefore the Indians can be viewed as a rural, working-class subcultural variant of the North American class structure, rather than being a distinctive cultural group.

What then makes the Kwakiutl Indian unique today as a culture-bearing population? To be a regularly participating member within the social system at Gilford, in a very broad sense, implies a status with its associated role (s) — as demonstrated by the fact that the villagers maintain a definite set of norms that guide their behaviour and by which they evaluate the behaviour of each other and outsiders. It is these norms and valued behaviour standards that give life within the village at Gilford a large part of its distinctive flavour. Individual decision-making processes are guided by these norms as are interpersonal relations, and aspects of the Indians' world view. These norms and values also give a fair amount of stability and continuity to village life over time. That is, social system survive only insofar as the constituent roles (which imply the maintenance of socially legitimated and recognized normative standards) are performed, and they are performed largely because they satisfy personality needs. Thus, the individual's motivation to continue performing the roles is provided. In this way the requirements of the social system are met in that the social roles continue to be performed, giving appreciable stability and continuity to the system, and simultaneously many personality needs are also satisfied.

From this point of view, the subcultural system at Gilford has a double-edged quality about it insofar as individuals must adjust to the valued behaviour standards if they are to live comfortably within the village, but at the same time, these standards supply the condition for villagers to make a personal adjustment. A sense of security, a reference group for personal identity, and social approval are provided for those who adhere reasonably well to the normative standards. On the other hand, the villagers impose compelling and often subtle negative sanctions on the person who violates norms too extremely or too often. These sanctions are effective, of course, only for those Indians who are motivated to remain within the system.

A. Social Control and Normative Standards

Through at least minimal contact with Whites for over one hundred years, two general acculturative classes have developed among the Kwakiutl. The most prevalent is the *subsisting oriented* class and the second is the *future oriented* class. Subsisting orientation implies a focus on the present — on continued existence or the condition of subsisting at a day-to-day level. A central characteristic of this class is the need to cope with life in its immediacy, as it actually presents itself, rather than to strive to create some new form for an indefinite future. Villagers in the subsisting oriented acculturative category prepare for the predictable, anticipated or known future, but they generally do not plan for the remote or unknown future. Villagers tend to cope with the way things are now rather than attempt to change them. Men gather logs and cut them for firewood; they catch fish which are sometimes canned or dried for use in the winter. These activities are forms of preparation for a predictable future. Rarely do villagers plan, however, if planning is understood as thought and effort given to some long range goals which are considered to be at least potentially realizable. Consequently families rarely save money or other goods for some unknown exigency. Thrift and saving are not included in the value system of people in the subsisting oriented class. Individuals who conform to the same set of characteristics as the subsisting oriented, except that they tend to look to past traditions as being as good as, if not better than, contemporary living, are *past oriented*. This acculturative class is a special case of the subsisting oriented category. Almost invariably these people are fifty years old or more. This attitude is rarely shared by the younger Kwakiutl. With a major exception noted below, the Islanders tend to be characterized as subsisting oriented.

No individual who remains in the subsisting oriented web of interaction within the community can sink too low or rise too high, either economically or socially, because of the patterns of borrowing and sharing. Borrowing and sharing have sharp leveling effects and occur from an interaction between personal choice and social obligation. Items are borrowed (often permanently), given, exchanged and freely taken among members of the community. An individual or family in need may borrow from another who has a surplus. Requests are sometimes refused, but consistent refusal sets an individual apart from the remainder of the community and disrupts normal social relationships. It also directs criticism against the person who refused. An individual who accumulates material wealth and is interested in maintaining close social ties in the community must be prepared to share his wealth. But since they know that they may have to redistribute their wealth — and therefore not be able to enjoy it — the motivation to accumulate more than enough to satisfy short-term desires is weak.

Reciprocity and "non-stinginess" are two important norms guiding interpersonal relations among the members of the subsisting oriented class. Both are related to the people's expectations of sharing and borrowing. Individuals who want to maintain their position within the network of social relations must reciprocate and be generous. A person who drinks someone else's beer but is stingy with it, that is, closely controls its consumption or removes the supply, is open to criticism. John Patch, for example, bought beer at Echo Bay and returned to the village with six of us. He drank the beer that was offered to him on the way back and then took his own beer to Paul Moon's house. He is reputed to have taken one case which did not belong to him. Frank Bean criticized John saying, "He drinks other people's beer, but won't share his own!"[4]

Conflict within the village sometimes gives the impression of being rampant, but effective social controls are nonetheless operating. Serious damage to the body or to property is rarely committed even during periods of the most unrestrained parties and fighting. Windows or furniture may be broken, but houses are not burned; a person may have his nose broken or his face cut with glass, but he is not mortally stabbed. In fact, according to the RCMP, major crimes of all types are infrequent among Indians. Most problems among Whites and Indians are minor offenses against body or property and are associated with drinking; when serious offenses occur, however, they are usually committed by Whites. Crimes committed by Indians are usually not premeditated.

The valued behaviour standards on which the members of the community operate are not always clear to us, but the major forms of

---

[4] The incidence of alcoholism among the Kwakiutl is reported to be very low. We know of no Kwakiutl, in fact, who can be correctly diagnosed as an alcoholic.

social control that are applied when norms are violated are more easily recognized. Among the Kwakiutl the process of interpersonal interaction itself is one of the most powerful mechanisms of social control. As we said above, a sense of security and, not insignificantly, identity among the subsisting oriented group is firmly anchored within the community. Because of it, special or coercive control devices are not usually needed. In the first place, through a long socialization period individuals have internalized most of the normative standards in such a way that they are able to evaluate the behaviour of others and to agree that a norm has been violated, and the offender is aware of the legitimacy of the evaluation against him. For most members of the village the community has become the primary reference group, that is, the group with which they identify themselves and in relation to which they think about themselves. Through this reference group an individual establishes his frames of reference through which perceptions, experiences and ideas about himself are ordered. To this extent members of the village are in a position to give positive social rewards and punitive sanctions. Any threat to one's position within this system — such as the withdrawal of acceptance, favourable recognition or approval — poses a personal threat to the individual. Thus, the withdrawal of favourable recognition and approval, in threat or in fact, is a powerful social control mechanism. It is often communicated to the individual through such media as gossip, indirect criticism and constrained social relations.

B. Death and Religion

Accidents are the principal cause of death among the Kwakiutl and drowning is the greatest single form of accidental death. Drowning often occurs in the contexts of drinking when, for example, a man gets drunk in the Bay, buys more beer and attempts to travel back to his home village. We suspect, however, that some reputedly accidental drownings are not accidents at all. They are probably suicides. The true incidence of suicide among the Kwakiutl is unknown, but threats and attempts are not unusual and often appear in association with drinking. James Jack, a vistor from another village, was drinking and began talking about death. He recounted an episode when Jennie Drake fell overboard and because of her great weight he could not drag her back onto the gill netter. She pleaded with him, "If you can't get me up, let me go! Let me go!" With the help of seven men she was brought safely on board but she wanted to jump back in once rescued. James concluded, "I guess she thought she should have died." He talked about natural death in the hospital and accidental death from such causes as drowning. I asked him which was a better way of dying and he responded indirectly by saying that his father had been drowned as had his father's father and so would he, probably. Continuing, he said that his half brother probably wanted to die at the time of his drowning. The latter had "fallen" overboard five times shortly prior to the final incident.

Religious beliefs among the villagers range from a firm commitment to the doctrine of a particular church, to a nondoctrinal belief in God and the divinity of Christ, to skepticism or questioning of both and finally to outright disbelief. According to Hilda, the White Pentacostal lay-woman in the village, most Kwakiutl have religious feelings, but one would have trouble getting them to express these feelings.

Pentacostals do not believe in drinking, smoking, dancing, attending commercial movies, playing cards, or the use of facial cosmetics. Because of these restrictions, especially on drinking, it is doubtful that many Indians will become true converts to the church, even though many find it attractive for other reasons.

A useful but rough index of the relative influence of and differential attitudes toward each denomination [Pentacostal and Anglican] is found in the unique situation where the two groups held services simultaneously within the village. The Pentacostal service was attended by fifteen people, including eight children; twelve people attended the Anglican service, including four children. The majority of the village attended neither service. Some of the men who were fishing did not attend, as is true of a small group who were drinking.

Several reasons exist why relatively more villagers attend Pentacostal services than Anglican. An Anglican communion service furnishes an example of the difference between the two. It was attended by sixteen villagers, ten of whom took communion. The service, which lasted thirty minutes, was read from the Book of Common Prayer, and two hymns were sung in English which were notably lacking in spontaneity and volume. Members of the village were somewhat uncomfortable during the service because it was highly formalized and replete with symbolism in dress and paraphernalia. Both of the clergymen who officiated were in their clerical frocks. The members of the village were more accustomed to Pentacostal services with their spontaneity and casualness. The fact that a considerable part of the Pentacostal services are in Kwakwala and that audience participation is encouraged make these meetings much more comfortable. The Anglican service, by contrast, is formal, mechanical, subdued and ritualistic, with a minimum of participation by members of the congregation.

The indigenous religious practices and beliefs of the Kwakiutl revolved around the acquisition of and right to supernatural or spirit power. Winter ceremonials were the occasions at which individuals publicly demonstrated their prerogatives in the religious dance "societies", especially in the *ts'eiga*, "red cedar bark dance". The Kwakiutl had no belief in a single supreme being, but rather in many spirit forms, some of which inhabited the body of different animals, and others of which were purely spiritual. They also believed that humans have a spirit which leaves the body at death and goes to the spirit world. Spirits were believed to live in villages similar to those on earth.

III. GROWING UP KWAKIUTL

Gertie and my wife [Evelyn] were drinking coffee in Gertie's kitchen when they heard a fight outside. Gertie opened the door and yelled at two preschool youngsters tussling over a tricycle. She told the neighbor girl to leave the trike alone and to go home if she did not want to get hit by her son; the trike did not belong to the girl anyway. A little while later there were more sounds of children fighting. Gertie got up and yelled at the two children. This time they were both her own and the older boy was beating on his younger brother while the latter feebly tried to take the tricycle. Gertie told the younger boy to leave the trike alone, it was not his and if he did not want to get beaten up by his older brother he should leave things alone that did not belong to him.

The children involved in the dispute over the tricycle that afternoon were two brothers aged three and four, and a four-year-old neighbor girl. No attempt was made to control their aggression; in fact Gertie rewarded the actions of the aggressor-owner. As far as Gertie is concerned, the owner of the tricycle has the right to play with it and he is not expected to share his toys. If a child spoils his sibling's possession, villagers consider it to be the owner's fault for leaving the toy unprotected. The owner is expected to protect his property; if he neglects his possessions and they are spoiled, it is his fault.

Women wanted children; consequently even children who are produced from casual sexual affairs are generally accepted. Four youths within the village who resulted from such unions are accepted by other villagers as well as their parents, although comments are occasionally made about their origin if someone becomes angry. Infants are loved, petted, fondled, and held by everyone who is old enough to do so.

By age nine, or ten, young people begin to identify with sex roles. Girls help around the house; boys are given more freedom to hang around the beach or on the float and occasionally they accompany their fathers fishing. If a man or a group of men go to the store and beer parlor they may take a boy along, but almost never a girl.

Sex role identity is revealed in children's drawings. Girls typically draw pictures of houses and people and sometimes such things as laundry, flowers, and tables with dishes, but they do not draw pictures of boats. Boys at Gilford, on the other hand, most frequently draw pictures of boats and people (men and boys), usually a wharf, sometimes a canoe, fish net or fish and occasionally Indian designs. When the children tell stories about pictures they have created in school each child is able to specify who the people are in the drawings and whose house or boat is represented. None of the stories which accompany the drawings is purely imaginary, and only a few pictures contain fictitious elements, for example, a fence where there is none.

The closest children come to making up stories is in the area of humor, where their stories sometimes take the form of *klikwala*, translated very loosely as "just fooling" (or a "white lie"). Some Whites misunderstand this form of behavior and decry its usage. The mother of a past teacher in the village, for example, was convinced that the children were inveterate and malicious liars.

School represents a discontinuity in the lives of many children since teacher expectations are not reinforced in the home, in the village generally, or by other life experiences. As a result formal education tends to become compartmentalized and disassociated from other life experiences. To the individual it appears to have no basic, immediate relevance for his life at the moment, or for the perceivable future. This has an important bearing on the educational progress of the children and is one set of factors contributing to the high incidence of school dropouts. School experiences tend to controvert some of the basic learning which takes place in preschool years and in nonschool activities. For example, independence and mild aggression are rewarded in nonschool activities but are negatively sanctioned in the school. The child must learn a form of compliance behaviour in the classroom which is not expected out of school; competition with peers rather than aid and cooperation are expected. Concern is about delimitable time units leading to the concept of punctuality is important in the educational system and becomes a moral issue for many teachers.

The most important difference between formal education and the cultural system of the villagers lies in the method of learning. This difference creates an important discontinuity in the enculturation process of the children. A Kwakiutl child learns, fundamentally, by observing, performing and then having his behaviour rewarded, punished or ignored. Unlike middle-class children, however, the Kwakiutl child initiates most of his own action. He neither expects nor waits for verbal or formal didactic instruction. A child learns to operate a boat and set a net largely through observation of others and subsequently by trying it himself, either in play or by helping his father; he learns to ride a bicycle or to Indian-dance in the same way.

In the classroom, on the other hand, Kwakiutl children must peers rather than aid and cooperation are expected. Concern about methods of learning require language skills in English. Language skills are not as important in the native context; a very small part of becoming a fisherman, for example, is learned through verbal or written instruction.

The fact that the life of the children is structured to a very limited extent within the village constitutes another basic discontinuity between the social and cultural background of the children and the expectations of the school. Whereas parents are permissive toward the behavior of their children, school life is authoritarian and formal. This conflicting situation often imposes as much hardship on the teacher as on the pupils. The lack of structure and the degree of permissiveness by parents may explain, in part, why children bicker, swear, throw things, hit each other and generally pay no attention in the classroom.

Moreover the children's experience with formal education has been highly inconsistent. Little continuity has existed in the procedures, demands and expectations of past teachers beyond the formal requirements of the Indian Affairs Branch, and the quality of teaching at Gilford has been inconsistent. Children have not had to meet and conform to a uniform set of demands by past teachers which might have allowed them to standardize their behaviour and expectations for future ones. To this extent older pupils are not in a position to furnish models for the younger ones regarding appropriate classroom behaviour. The inconsistency and discontinuity of educational experiences influence the performance of children. They experience many failures and little pleasure in school activities; as a result some develop a psychological set which predisposes them to anticipate and react to failure in characteristic ways. These include anger, giving up, and, in the extreme, not trying in the first place. Many children have a low frustration tolerance for difficult school assignments. They react with anger, or sometimes cry if they cannot complete their work with relative ease and they often give up and refuse to try.

Frequently we heard from city dwellers that, whereas the Indians may not know much about "Dick and Jane", they certainly know all about their village environment. This is untrue. The younger pupils express amazement that animals once lived in the shells found on the beach. They were surprised to discover that they could make pots from the clay deposit we found near a stream at one end of the village. And none of them had ever looked closely at a snake. One day, for example, I came into the classroom with a small garter snake; the children screamed in fright. Even at the level of the most elementary readers children are exposed to things which they have never seen or about which they have never heard. A few of the children have never seen a horse or the other farm animals which are included in the vocabulary of early readers.

IV. TRADITIONAL SOCIAL ORGANIZATION

During the Potlatch period from about 1849 until almost 1930 the Kwakiutl were, in principal, totally rank stratified: each tribe was ranked in relation to each other tribe; each major tribal subdivision, the *numima*, was ordered in relation to each other numima, and each individual within each numima was ranked in relation to every other individual.[5]

Rank and class were determined primarily by inheritance — the inheritance of socially validated names and "privileges" such as the right to sing certain songs, use certain carvings or designs, wear certain ceremonial masks and perform certain dances. Associated privileges included the right to sit at a particular place during a potlatch, to have one's name called at a certain point in a sequence, and to receive greater or lesser amounts of property dependent on one's overall position in the rank structure.

Kwakiutl social organization has changed radically in the last half century. Today there is no significant tendency to associate only with members of the same class. In fact, the rank and class system has broken down. Older adults in the village remember the social stratum to which they traditionally belonged, but many of the younger do not know where they would be placed. Spontaneous remarks sometimes made by members of the community, however, suggest that the past traditions are not totally ignored; for example, Flora Abel, her son Andy, and several others were drinking. Andy became abusive toward his mother and she ran out of the house into a second where another party was in progress. She asked some of the men to help her but they ignored her request. She cried at a table, repeating over and over, "He can't do that to me. I'm *naqsala* [nobility]! He can't do that..."

We do not know of any children at Gilford today who have validated privileges. This further attests to the major changes in the Kwakiutl social system over the past decades. Over seventy per cent of the men in the twenty to thirty-nine age group do not have any validated privileges, whereas almost ninety per cent of the men who are forty and over do have. A comparable trend exists regarding validated names; only thirty-five per cent of the men from twenty to thirty-nine remember having any, and they have only one each, whereas more than ninety per cent of the men who are forty or older have from one to four names, or more.

A. THE POTLATCH

[Potlaches are the] public display and distribution of property in the context of one individual or group claiming certain hereditary rights or privileges vis-a-vis another group. While this statement suggests the general nature of the potlatch, the actual mechanics of the potlatch are more complicated than that description intimates. Potlatches may be described from an alternative point of view as a congregation of people who are invited to publicly witness and later validate a host's claims to or transmission of hereditary privileges, and to receive in return, each according to his rank, differential amounts of wealth.

[5] Elsewhere, I (1967:27) wrote that the correct term designating the tribal subdivisions of the Kwakiutl is *numimot*. The term actually refers to the members of the tribal subdivision, not to the subdivision itself. The term *numima* correctly identifies the subdivisions, although in practice some Kwakiutl do not distinguish between these terms anymore.

Potlatches were given at critical life events: birth, adoption, puberty, marriage, death. They were given as penalties for "... breaches of ceremonial taboo such as laughing, stumbling or coughing at winter dances." (Barnett, 1968:36). Face-saving potlatches were closely related to penalty potlatches. They were, in Barnett's (1968:36) words, "prompted by some accident or misfortune to one's self or a member of the family. The capsizing of a canoe, a bodily injury and the birth of a deformed child..." were all appropriate occasions for a face-saving potlatch. A third category of potlatch was the competitive, rivalry, or vengence potlatch. These were extravagent, ostentatious, contests with property, each claimant trying to give away or destroy more property than his rival and thus establishing his right to a contested privilege or position.

An essential feature of all types of potlatches was its public nature. The host, with the support of his family, numima or tribe, invited other families, numimas or tribes to act as formal witnesses to his claims.[6] The potlatcher traced his line of descent and his right to the claim. No name, dance, song or other privilege could be used without having it publicly acknowledged and legitimated by the attendants of a potlatch. Since only people of substantial wealth could afford to potlatch lavishly or often, rank and wealth were but counterparts of each other — one implied the other.

The right to membership in the prestige-graded dance societies — the totality of which comprise the winter ceremonial — was inherited in the same way as other rights and privileges, that is, through one's parents or as part of a dowry from one's father-in-law at marriage. The prerogative of claiming a particular place in one of the dance societies was as personal and individualistic as a potlatch name. Dance society membership corresponded closely with the composition of the nobility, but even a nobleman had to assume his right to a position by going through formal initiation. Commoners were excluded from important participation in the ceremonials because they could not be initiated into any of the dance societies.

These dramatic winter ceremonials are no longer produced, but the Kwakiutl still sing the same songs and perform the same types of dances, wearing finely carved, painted masks, button blankets, and red cedar bark neck and head rings. The performances, however, are not embedded in the ritual context of rank stratified system where only certain people have the exclusive right to use particular names, sing specific songs, perform certain dances. The dances today are severely abbreviated versions of what they once were; dramas that originally took an hour or more to complete are now typically performed in a matter of minutes. Currently, anyone who has the skill and knowledge can perform any dance. Dancing is still an important component of potlatches, but the Indians are also beginning to popularize their art during, for example, the summer tourist season in Alert Bay and when a dignitary such as the Lieutenant Governor of British Columbia visits the villages.

Many Kwakiutl are developing a renewed interest in their traditional art forms and other indigenous customs such as carving, painting, dancing and perhaps non-competitive potlatching. Some of this revitalization is due to the enthusiastic response of White consumers. Different aspects of traditional Kwakiutl culture are well enough preserved so that they may be revived and maintained, but with reformulated meaning. The Kwakiutl are unlikely to reproduce their former heritage, but essential elements from the past may be perpetuated in the future as a distinctively *Kwakiutl* life-style.

⁶ Usually a family invited a family; a numima invited a numima, or a tribe invited a tribe. The host group did not receive gifts at a potlatch.

BIBLIOGRAPHY

BARNETT, HOMER G. *The Nature and Function of the Potlatch*. Monograph. Eugene: Department of Anthropology, University of Oregon, 1968.

BOAS, FRANZ. "The social organization and secret societies of Kwakiutl Indians." Washington: Report of the U.S. National Museum, 1895.

———. *Kwakiutl Ethnography*. Chicago: University of Chicago Press, 1966.

CODERE, HELEN. "Fighting with property". *American Ethnological Society, Monograph No. 18*, 1950.

———. "Kwakiutl." In E. H. Spicer ed., *Perspectives in American Indian Culture Change*. Chicago: University of Chicago Press, 1961.

CURTIS, EDWARD S. *The Kwakiutl (The North American Indian, Vol. 10)* Norwood Connecticut, 1915.

DRUCKER, PHILIP. *Cultures of the North Pacific Coast*. San Francisco: Chandler Publishing Company, 1965.

DRUCKER, PHILIP AND HEIZER, ROBERT F. *To Make My Name Good: A Reexamination of the Southern Kwakiutl Potlatch*. Berkeley: University of California Press, 1967.

ROHNER, RONALD P. "The People of Gilford: a Contemporary Kwakiutl Village". *Bulletin 225*, Ottawa: National Museum of Canada, 1967.

WOLCOTT, HARRY F. *A Kwakiutl Village and School*. New York: Holt, Rinehart, and Winston, Inc., 1967.

9

The Unjust Society: The Tragedy of Canada's Indians*

Harold Cardinal

Cardinal is a new Indian, not — in his words — an "Uncle Toma-hawk." As a contemporary Indian leader, Cardinal supports the position that Indians should firmly articulate their own needs and policy preferences within the framework of Indian organizations.

The Canadian Indian leadership which Cardinal represents strongly opposes forced Indian assimilation into white society. As an original Canadian, the Indian does not need to be concerned with becoming a Canadian, but unfortunately he has to be concerned with being accepted as one. Cardinal is militantly seeking the survival and revitalization of the Indian's cultural heritage; he is equally intent upon securing for his people the opportunity to contribute "colourful red tiles" to the Canadian mosaic.

Torrents of words have been spoken and written about Indians since the arrival of the white man on the North American continent. Endless columns of statistics have been compiled. Countless programs have been prepared for Indians by non-Indians. Faced with society's general indifference and a massive accumulation of misdirected, often insincere efforts, the greatest mistake the Indian has made has been to remain so long silent.

It sometimes seems to Indians that Canada shows more interest in preserving its rare whooping cranes than its Indians. And Canada, the Indian notes, does not ask its cranes to become Canada geese. It just wants to preserve them as whooping cranes. Indians hold no grudge against the big, beautiful, nearly extinct birds, but we would like to know how they managed their deal. Whooping cranes can remain whooping cranes, but Indians are to become brown white

*Reprinted, with permission, from Harold Cardinal, *The Unjust Society: The Tragedy of Canada's Indians*. (Edmonton: M.G. Hurtig Ltd., 1969).

men. The contrast in the situation is an insult to our people. Indians have aspirations, hopes and dreams, but becoming white men is not one of them.

The facts are available, dutifully compiled and clucked over by a handful of government civil servants year after year. Over half the Indians of Canada are jobless year after year. Thousands upon thousands of native people live in housing which would be condemned in any advanced society on the globe. Much of the housing has no inside plumbing, no running water, no electricity. A high percentage of the native peoples of Canada never get off welfare. This is the way it is, not in Asia or Africa but here in Canada. The facts are available; a Sunday drive to the nearest reserve will confirm them as shocking reality.

Bigotry? The problem grows worse, not better. A survey by the Canadian Corrections Association, entitled *Indians and the Law*, reveals some of the problems that the native person faces in the area of prejudice and discrimination. The survey reports bluntly: "Underlying all problems associated with Indians and Eskimo in this country are the prejudice and discrimination they meet in the attitudes of non-Indians. The result is a conviction on the part of the Indians and Eskimo that they are not really part of the dominant Canadian society and that their efforts to better themselves will fail because they do not have an even chance."

Probably the most perceptive statement of the report observes: "Few non-Indians will admit to feelings of prejudice against the Indian and Eskimo people because such views are no longer acceptable, but the façade often vanishes when problems arise."

Many Canadians, however, have always claimed and continue to assert that Canada has little racial difficulty. Statements of this nature are just so much uninformed nonsense.

In any area where there is a concentration of native people there exists racial tension. Urban centres with their multiplicity of attractions and opportunities are drawing more and more natives who come in hope and stay in misery. These migrants, with little financial security, all too often with insufficient job training and nearly always with terribly inadequate knowledge of white mores, inevitably jam into ghettos, increasing not only their own problems but those of the city. The people of the city answer with bigotry, wrongly attributing the problem to colour or race rather than to any inadequacy of opportunity and social response.

As Indian people attempt to organize and as Indian leaders become more vocal and articulate, the shades of bigotry which now appear in pastel will show up in more vivid colours. People who are tolerant of a problem which hasn't touched them are put to the test when the problem moves next door.

As an ethnocentric society, the Canadian non-Indian society puts its own peer group at the centre of all things desirable and rates all other cultures accordingly. It is an assumption, quite often becoming a conviction, that the values, the ways of life, the whole culture of one's own group must be superior to those of others. Tell a person long enough and often enough that he is inferior, and likely he will eventually accept the false image you thrust upon him.

We listen when Canadian political leaders talk endlessly about strength in diversity for Canada, but we understand they are talking primarily about the French-Canadian fact in Canada. Canadian Indians feel, along with other minorities, that there is a purpose and a place for us in a Canada which accepts and encourages diversified human resources. We like the idea of a Canada where all cultures are encouraged to develop in harmony with one another, to become part of the great mosaic. We are impatient for the day when other Canadians will accord the Indian the recognition implied in this vision of Canada.

The vast majority of our people are committed to the concept of Canadian unity and to the concept of participation in that unity. The Indians of Canada surely have as great a commitment to Canada, if not a greater one, than even the most patriotic-sounding political leaders. More truly that it can be said of anyone else, it is upon this land that our heritage, our past and our identity originates. Our commitment to Canada exists because of our belief that we have a responsibility to do all we can to ensure that our country is a nation with which we can proudly identify.

To fulfill our dreams for participation in the greatness of Canada, we must be able to contribute to Canada. We invite our white brothers to realize and acknowledge that the Indian in Canada has already made a considerable contribution to the greatness of our country, that the Indian has played a significant role in Canadian history. Our people look on with concern when the Canadian government talks about "the two founding peoples" without giving recognition to the role played by the Indian even before the founding of a nation-state known as Canada.

However, Canada's Indians look to the future as the greatest period for participation. Our contribution will be based upon what we are as a people, upon what, as a culture, Indian society will add to the mosaic and upon what we can accomplish as individuals to add to our country's total potential.

Here there is a lack, glaringly obvious. Our people lack the skills through which we might best contribute as individuals. If the Indian receives no training as a doctor then he cannot add to Canada's potential in medical advances. If he does not acquire the skills of a politician, he cannot hope to advance Canada politically. The Indian people must realize their greatest contributions to Canada's potential through whatever skills they may be able to add to Canada's pool of know-how. This is why Indians include in their aspirations better training in skills at all working levels, from professional to technical, to make it possible for each of us to work with our fellow Canadians so that the sum total of our efforts as Canadians results in the growth and expansion of the land we call our home.

No one realizes better than the Indian that the road ahead is long and hard going. There exist more than two thousand reserves across Canada, situated in every geographical area of our immense country, some actually within the boundaries of major cities (in Vancouver, Winnipeg and Toronto), some deep in the underdeveloped northern wildernesses, many isolated not only from the mainstream of society but from one another. The needs and the problems of Indians living in such diverse circumstances vary widely and, of course, the environment influences greatly their desires and ambitions.

The language barrier has isolated our people as truly as the geographical barrier. There are eleven different major language groups among the Indians of Canada with scores of dialects changing from band to band. Only recently has English become universal enough among Indians to serve as a medium of communication. And, even today, the most articulate (in English) Indian will confess readily that he still feels more at home in his mother tongue.

Nationwide Indian unity represents a dream long held by Indian leaders well aware that the emphasis upon individual bands and tribes is a decisive influence. Only recently, with the growth of strong provincial organizations in turn leading to the creation for the first time of a viable national organization, the National Indian Brotherhood, has this dream shown signs of realization. When our people begin to call themselves Indians instead of Crees or Saulteaux or Mohawks, when intertribal cooperation no longer allows the government to threaten our individual treaties, then we will have the strength of unity, the power to help make some of our other dreams come true.

Canada is an enormous country. Even within a single province such as Alberta, conditions vary so widely from reserve to reserve that common needs, aspirations and goals that can be attributed to the entire Indian people are often difficult to determine.

Perhaps our most persistent dreams stem from our most insistent reality — poverty — the one reality most Indians share. Perhaps because the Indian people face the most difficult and demoralizing situation in Canada, our aspirations are the more intense. We face the greatest challenge and, at the same time, the greatest threat.

Indians gladly accept the challenge — to become participating Canadians, to take a meaningful place in the mainstream of Canadian society. But we remain acutely aware of the threat — the loss of our Indian identity, our place as distinct, identifiable Canadians.

However idealistic some Indian dreams may be, there remain everyday hopes that come right down to earth. Indians are like anyone else. We look around and see a very affluent society. Just like our non-Indian neighbours, we want a share, a new car, a well-built home, television. These represent surface things, but it hurts deeply to see the affluence of our country and not be allowed to benefit from it. We want better education, a better chance for our children and the option to choose our own pathway in life. If we are to be part of the Canadian mosaic, then we want to be colourful red tiles, taking our place where red is both needed and appreciated.

A. DEFINITIONS AND DIVISIONS

Canadians worry about their identity. Are they too English? Are they too American? Are they French Canadians or some other kind of hybrid? Indians worry about their identity, too. For the most part they like to think of themselves as Canadians. But there are towns and cities in Canada, in every province of Canada, where an Indian dares not forget his identity as an Indian. There are towns and cities in Canada where a Canadian Indian simply dares not go.

If that seems a shocking statement to the non-Indian, it shocks Indians even more. There are towns and cities in Canada where simply being an Indian means getting a beating. Indians in such towns and cities have even been dragged out of restaurants into the streets and beaten. In such cases an Indian foolish enough to attempt to bring charges finds *himself* charged with creating a disturbance. No citizen is likely to forget his identity under such circumstances.

For the Canadian Indian the question of identity bears heavily on the kind of life a native may lead. Under Canada's mixed-up legal definition, full-blooded Indians may be classed non-Indian, and full-blooded whites can legally be Indians. The *Indian Act* defines an Indian as "a person who pursuant to this Act is registered as an Indian or is entitled to be registered as an Indian." This simplistic legalism, however eliminates roughly 250,000 native people, who, under the American system, would be recognized as Indian.

This *Indian Act* definition has been and continues to be a divisive force among Canada's natives. If you are legally an Indian, then you and your family can live on reserves and are entitled to certain limited rights. No matter how full-blooded you may be, if you are not a legal Indian, you can forget the reserve. You can't live there.

The whole silly bit about who is an Indian and who isn't came about as a result of the treaties. On the Prairies, the native people were given a choice at the time of signing as to the status they wanted. If they chose to be Indians under treaty, native people were promised certain treaty rights, including land on a reserve, perpetual hunting and fishing rights, along with myriad lesser pledges, but they were denied the right to vote or access to liquor.

The alternative was to choose script, a legal piece of paper proclaiming the victim's citizenship, providing a sum of money (it varied in different treaties) and a piece of land (the area varied). This choice gave access to liquor and the vote, the same privileges accorded any citizen of Canada.

If a man chose to give up his Indian status, he never could reclaim it. But if a native chose to become a registered or treaty Indian, he still retained a sort of horrible option. He could enfranchise. This meant and still means that a treaty or registered or legal Indian still could and still can give up his special status by applying to Ottawa for enfranchisement. This remains a pretty drastic decision for an Indian. He gains full citizenship rights, the vote, liquor (which he now can get as an Indian, anyhow) and, in theory, becomes a Canadian like anyone else. But he renounces his Indianness: he loses all treaty or aboriginal rights; he gives up forever his right to membership on a reserve and all title to his portion of resources or reserve land. He cannot return to the reserve to take up residence where the rest of his family, his relatives and his friends live.

If the parents make this choice or if an entire Indian family enfranchises, then the children of that family and all subsequent grandchildren and direct heirs lose forever the right to claim title to being Indians, at least legally. The only exception to this loss of identity occurs in maternal lineage. If any woman, Indian or non-Indian, marries a treaty or registered Indian, she automatically becomes a legal Indian; no matter whether she is red, white, yellow or black, married to a legal Indian she becomes one, too. However, it doesn't work the other way around. If an Indian woman marries a non-Indian man, she automatically forfeits her claim to be an Indian.

Just to make it more confusing, when a white or non-Indian woman becomes by reason of marriage legally an Indian, this does not mean that her children necessarily will be Indian. Under section 12, subsection (a) 4 of the *Indian Act*, effective in the 1970s, a person whose mother and paternal grandmother are non-Indian (except by right of marriage) also loses his claim to be an Indian.

This legal hocus-pocus has created many problems for the younger generation. In some instances, where full-blooded Indian families have for one reason or another enfranchised, they and their children are, in the eyes of the law, non-Indian, Metis or even white — in theory. At the same time, in the case of a white woman marrying a registered Indian, she and her children suddenly, in the eyes of the law, are Indians. Among the younger generation where pride of race once again is growing, Indians in all but the law have found themselves classed as non-Indian no matter how much they want to be Indians, because parents enfranchised. Many young Indians today are being denied their birthright because someone else decided to renounce his legal claims to being Indian. They have no recourse; they can never legally reclaim their birthright.

Stan Daniels, president of the Metis Association of Alberta, puts the problem this way: "The question of my identity is hard for me to understand; on one hand, when I consider myself an Indian, and I say this, the Indian says, 'Who do you think you are: you are nothing but a white man.' And when I consider myself a white man, talk or act like one, the white man says to me, 'Who in the hell do you think you are? You're nothing but a damned Indian.' I am a man caught in the vacuum of two cultures with neither fully accepting me."

Legalities continue to play a divisive role among Canadian Indians. Even among those who have a legal right to be Indian, further classifications complicate the matter. There is, for example, a distinction between treaty Indians and registered Indians. A treaty Indian is one whose ancestors signed a treaty with the representatives of the queen and ceded some land rights to the crown in return for specified rights. Treaties have been signed with Indians in Ontario, Manitoba, Saskatchewan, Alberta and portions of the Northwest Territories. A registered Indian is one whose ancestors signed no treaties such as Indians in the Maritimes, in Quebec, in portions of the Northwest Territories and in British Columbia, but who did choose under the *Indian Act* to be regarded as legal or registered Indians. Maritimes Indians signed "pacts of friendship" with the representatives of the queen. Many treaty Indians fear that association with Indians from non-treaty areas will jeopardize their claims to their treaty rights, while Indians from the non-treaty areas are concerned that association with treaty Indians will compromise their requests for settlement of aboriginal claims. In some cases, even minor differences between treaties can confuse and worry Indians as to their rights when they intermingle. Treaty Six carries a medicine chest promise, which in present-day usage can be considered the right to paid-up medicare. Treaties Seven and Eight, although the question of medical treatment was promised verbally, never followed through on this issue in writing. A Treaty Six Indian conceivably could lose her claims to medical care by marrying a Treaty Seven man.

Sneakier things than that have come from government offices. In fact, the government, specifically the Department of Indian Affairs and Northern Development, seems to enjoy this divisiveness and even, in many cases, to encourage it. Anything that divides the Indians makes the department stronger. No wonder no Indian in his right mind trusts the department.

Some progress is being made toward unity among Canada's native people, but much work remains to be done to tear down this inner Buckskin Curtain. It is self-definition, not this network of inhuman legalities or the recently proposed alternative of assimilation, that will foster Indian unity. All the legal definitions fail to accomplish one thing — they fail to solve the real human problem of identity. Identity means as much to an Indian as it does to the Québecois in Trois Rivières or the Icelander in Gimli. Obviously this has no meaning for many people. They are the sort who feel that the only future for the Indian lies in assimilation. Such people see all residents of Canada as Canadians, without regard to ethnic background. As far as we are concerned, these melting-pot advocates don't understand the nature of our country, let alone the nature of the native. To all too many, being

Canadian simply means, "white is right," or "be Anglo and you'll be happy," or "be like me and all your problems will vanish."

For a long time many, many Indians accepted the white man's evaluation of them as a race and as individuals. So often were they told openly and brutally that they were no good, that they were nothing, that they came to accept this negative image. "What can we do?" one hears an Indian say. "We are just Indians." Or, "How can we talk of equality? We will always be Indians no matter what we do. The government can't just suddenly rule that we are equal and make it a fact. Will the person who hated us yesterday because we are Indian love us tomorrow because the government says he should?"

Young Indians who went off to residential schools were obviously at a disadvantage. The missionary teachers soon made them aware of it if they didn't know it when they came. It doesn't take many times being called "an ungrateful little savage" to impress your difference upon you. And those who went into the white man's schools to be integrated found their little white friends brought their homes to the classroom: "My father says all Indians are drunks; my mother says Indians are dirty and I can't play with you." Indians who went to the cities to try to make their way found themselves isolated, pointed out, penalized for being Indian. Small wonder many Indians sought to hide their Indianness. They had lost their pride. They had overlooked the one thing they had that no white man had or has or can have — Indianness.

Today the trend is the other way. Young Indians are proud of their heritage and are learning more about it. During and after World War II many of our people crossed the colour line. It was a status thing to do. They had lived in a white world; they had fought as well as the white soldier. They were accepted for the time being, at least. Many married across the colour line. Now social pressure swings the other way with Indians, and is against marrying into white society.

Of course no one can deny there still are many negative factors relating, if not to actual Indian identity, then to the popular image of our identity. Indians are sensitive. We know that we may be turned away from the odd hotel because of our colour. We know that available suites at good highrise locations suddenly are taken when we show up. We are careful about the kind of restaurant we go into. But we also know that more and more Indians are suddenly standing straighter, walking with a firmer step and finding a new pride in being Indian.

The political aspect of our identity causes misunderstanding. In a meeting with the National Indian Brotherhood, Prime Minister Trudeau seemed concerned that a possible growth of separatism might exist among Indians. It is necessary to emphasize that the question of establishing a positive Indian identity does not mean political separatism — not yet, at least, not if the white man will agree to be reasonable — nor does it mean a desire to return to the days of yesteryear.

The fact remains, however, that most Indians firmly believe their identity is tied up with treaty and aboriginal rights. Many Indians believe that until such rights are honoured there can be no Indian identity to take its place with the other cultural identities of Canada.

Our identity, who we are; this is a basic question that must be settled if we are to progress. A native person in Canada cannot describe himself without basically talking about himself as a Canadian. Being Canadian is implied and understood. To an Indian, being Indian in Canada simultaneously and automatically means being Canadian. The German Canadian has a homeland called Germany; the Ukrainian has a homeland; even the French Canadian, although he may have ancestors going back three hundred years in Canadian history, has a homeland called France. The Indian's homeland is called Canada.

The challenge to Indians today is to redefine that identity in contemporary terminology. The challenge to the non-Indian society is to accept such an updated definition.

If I were to accept the bothersome term *Indian problem,* I would have to accept it in light of the fact that our most basic problem is gaining respect, respect on an individual basis that would make possible acceptance for us as an ethnic group. Before this is possible, the dignity, confidence and pride of the Indian people must be restored. No genuine Indian participation in the white world can be expected until the Indian is accepted by himself and by the non-Indian as an Indian person, with an Indian identity.

As long as Indian people are expected to become what they are not — white men — there does not and there will not exist a basis upon which they can participate in Canadian society.

Before we can demand acceptance by the white man, we must earn his respect. Before we can take our place in a larger society, we must regain our own confidence and self-respect. To do this we must be allowed to rebuild our own social institutions, torn down by their white counterparts. We must rebuild our structures of social and political leadership, demoralized and undermined for a hundred years by the Department of Indian Affairs; we must restore our family unit, shaken and shattered by the residential school system; we must rebuild communications between the younger and older generations of our people. We must recognize that the negative images of Indianness are false; the Canadian government must recognize that assimilation, no matter what they call it, will never work. Both Indian and non-Indian must realize that there is a valid, lasting Indian identity.

We are not interested, therefore, in the government's newest definition of who and what an Indian is, or must be. We have ceased to allow our identity to be a paperwork problem for members of the Department of Indian Affairs. Our people are now in the process of discovering what they are in a positive sense; Canadian society must accept us in a positive way before there can be an identification of common purpose and before true citizenship can develop. It is only when men are able to accept their differences as well as their similarities and still relate to each other with respect and dignity that a healthy society exists.

B. CULTURAL RENAISSANCE OR CIVIL DISORDER

The Indian has reached the end of an era. The things that we hold sacred, the things that we believe in have been repudiated by the federal government. But we will not be silenced again, left behind to be absorbed conveniently into the wretched fringes of a society that institutionalizes wretchedness. The Buckskin Curtain is coming down.

The Indian, and with him the larger Canadian society, faces two alternatives — a future in which the Indian may realize his potential through the provision of the essential resources which are rightfully his, or a future where frustrations are deepened by a continued state of deprivation leading to chaos and civil disorder.

Many factors, some of them still beyond his control, will influence the Indian's choice. His choice will not be an answer to the question of who he is; that can never change. Rather, his choice will lie in how he decides to protect and build his sense of identity; his choice hinges upon his definition of the role he will play in modern society.

I will outline the steps I feel are necessary before the Indian can begin to develop his full potential, the action needed to solve the many problems the Indians of Canada face.

Such action can come only through effective strengthening of existing Indian organizations. The first step is the provision of the resources needed to enable the National Indian Brotherhood to become an effective coordinating body, so that it may provide its member organizations with a national voice. The second step is the creation of strong and viable provincial organizations across the land.

Simultaneously, and coordinated with the strengthening of Indian organizations from national to local levels, the Indian must initiate action on four vital fronts: federal government recognition of all Indian rights must be secured; new concepts in education which can bridge the gap between our people and modern society must be found and introduced; restructured social institutions based on the community itself must be fashioned and broadly based economic development, sufficient to free the Indian at last from his subservient role, must be managed.

Within the next five years the Department of Indian Affairs is to be abolished. That is the one welcome aspect of the new government policy, but from a practical point of view, some interim body will have to be created. The duties and responsibilities of the department will be passed on to other federal agencies, and from past Indian experience, we know that all government departments have a tendency to pass the buck from one to another. To meet this prospect, the National Indian Brotherhood can play the role of a human resources authority, coordinating the services offered to the Indian by the many federal departments. This role would save the Indian many headaches and aid him in all his dealings with the federal government. At the same time the brotherhood would be in a position to help the various government agencies establish priorities in relation to the needs of the Indians of Canada.

Because of its political structure, the Indian people are assured of continuing control over the activities of the National Indian Brotherhood. This enables the Indians of Canada to participate in the democratic process and assures them an active role in the broad workings of government. In practical terms, this may be the closest the Indians of Canada can come to achieving Prime Minister Trudeau's concept of participatory democracy.

The tough, pragmatic problem solving must take place at the provincial and local levels, and this is the reason provincial Indian organizations must be made as strong as possible. The nature of these primary organizations necessarily must be political. Auxiliary organizations also can be created to work in close harness with the political bodies, to carry the task of concentrating Indian efforts on economic problems and solutions. Such auxiliary organizations can serve effectively in the fields of research and development, but the major provincial organizations must be political, because only through political vehicles can the Indian people express their needs and create pressure for their programs.

One new role that Indian organizations must play lies in the area of restoring and revitalizing a sense of direction, a sense of purpose and a sense of being. The white man in the last century has effectively killed the sense of worth in the Indian. Many factors, some of which I have dealt with in earlier chapters, have been responsible for the psychological and spiritual crisis of the Indian. The political organization must be the core of an effort to redefine the word *Indian* in such a way that our people can begin to develop a positive sense of identity.

Perhaps over the long term the most important responsibility the local organization must assume is the creation of a new order of leadership. This must be a leadership that will know and be able to relate positively to the traditions of the past, to the culture of our people and at the same time be tuned into life in the twentieth and twenty-first centuries. Above all, this must be a leadership totally committed to the Indian peoples. It must be a leadership that cannot be corrupted or bought off by those who would support the status quo so that they may continue their stagnating and stifling hold on our people.

The Indian must see his provincial organization in a new perspective. There must be a consolidation of all the scattered ineffective local organizations into strong provincial, political bodies. In order for this to happen, present leaders must reassess seriously their positions and their motives in occupying them. They must learn to put the interest of their people above their own personal needs and desires. This is happening, but the process has not yet been completed. Consequently, forces of the federal government in too many instances still are able to divide our people by skillful catering to the psychological needs of some of them. Until all our leaders have learned to subordinate personal ambition to their peoples' wishes, the Indians of Canada will remain weak and divided.

The new generation of Indians looks to its leaders for guidance, for example and for a sense of purpose. No more vital responsibility for the new leadership of our provincial organizations can be imagined.

For the scattered and isolated reserves which can be found in every province, the Indian organizations must work to create a sense of brotherhood to help weld these communities together into dynamic, growing forces that can participate in their twentieth century environment. In the process of creating a new leadership, the provincial organizations must help these divided, forgotten communities find a common identity.

The Indian people of Canada must assume new confidence. There must be a rebirth of the Indian, free, proud, his own man, the equal of his fellow Canadian. Some naïvely believe that true equality will come to the Indian by dispensation from some outside force. It is not within the power of any outside force, be it the prime minister or any minister of the crown, to command equality. In twentieth century Canada, equality comes only from economic strength, political power, good organization and through the pride and confidence of a people.

As long as the Indian does not have a positive image of himself, no Canadian, no human being will have a positive image of him and no one will ever respect him. There can be no equality as long as the dignity of the Indian is not respected. Today, most Canadians are either indifferent to Indians or hate them or pity them. The worst of the three is the man who pities the Indian, for he denies the object of his pity the opportunity to be a man. Canadian society will stop pitying the Indian and respect him only when the Indian has gained economic, political or organizational strength. A man who believes Canadian society will grant equality to the Indian because of its sense of Christian responsibility or its adherence to Christian beliefs or because of its obeisance to any concept of human rights common to all men, believes in myths. The Canadian society, self-righteously proclaiming itself just and civilized, has not extended equality to the Indian over the past century, and there is no reason to believe, expect or hope that it will change its spots over the next century if the Indian stays weak.

As the Indians of Canada are working to 'strengthen their organizations, they must initiate forward movement on other levels.

The Indian must have from the federal government immediate

recognition of all Indian rights for the reestablishment, review and renewal of all existing Indian treaties. The negotiations for this must be undertaken in a new and different spirit by both sides. The treaties must be maintained. The treaties must be reinterpreted in light of needs that exist today. Such interpretation and application of the treaties by the Canadian government will help bring all generations of Indians together with a common sense of positive purpose. This is not a concept that should be strange to the government. The treaties differ little from the way the government deals with corporations or corporate bodies, and for that matter all segments of Canadian society, except Indians and possibly the poor of Canada.

Apparently, the government has been unable or unwilling to understand the importance of this concept to the Indians. The treaties, or the concept of Indian rights, must be respected, for they form a major factor in the question of Indian identity. The Indian simply cannot afford to allow the government to renege on its obligations because, if he does, he commits cultural suicide. This is the reason for the position adopted by the Indian people — that their rights are not and cannot be negotiable.

Almost equally important is the area of education. Here, too, both sides must move forward into new concepts. The institution of education is largely a cultural phenomenon. Since the introduction of formal white education to the Indians of Canada, their own original educational processes have either been shunted completely aside or discouraged. The only purpose in educating the Indian has been to create little brown white men, not what it should have been, to help develop the human being or to equip him for life in a new environment.

A new look must be given, then, to the fundamental purpose of educating the Indian. It is not enough for the government to promise it will change the content of history books more truly to tell the Indian story. In comparison to the real purpose of education, this is an almost frivolous approach. Of course we would like the falsehoods deleted and Indians characterized more truthfully in what the youth of Canada is taught, but Indians are much more interested in and must approach education with completely new ideas. Indian leaders must be given the opportunity to see and study the educational processes of different peoples in different countries. Only in this way can they help to develop a new conceptual framework related to education and to the solving of their own social problems.

I believe that different forms of education are both possible and available. The majority of our people do not have the opportunity to benefit from existing provincial institutions of education, especially those at the postsecondary level. Few of our people have sufficient academic background to make proper use of the technological schools, trade schools, colleges or universities. Even if they did, there would still be a need for some new form of education or institution that would help them develop a living, dynamic culture. For education to mean anything to our people a new kind of institution or process to bridge the gap between where we stand now and the available post-secondary institutions must be created. This means some form of temporary but special mass educational process. Indian initiative, channelled through our own organizations, must develop such institutions to enable our people to benefit from programs now offered by existing educational systems.

These new institutions must be prepared to help Indians develop their sense of identity. The function of such institutions will lie in the areas of social rebuilding, psychological renewal and cultural renaissance. Indian organizations must operate these schools, for only they qualify for the task of identifying teachers and administrators with the resources to meet the cultural needs of Indians.

The white person must come to realize that the Indian cannot be a good Canadian unless he is first a responsible and a good Indian. Few Indians can discover a sense of purpose and direction from the white society. They must find such a sense of identity within themselves as human beings and as Indians before they can begin to work creatively with others. The government must understand this, because it is in this area that Canadian society can form a successful partnership with the Indian, in working together to find ways and means through which the educational process will develop human beings with purpose and direction.

The Indian communities themselves carry the responsibility for solving the social problems faced by Indians. Social development is irrevocably intertwined with leadership development, educational progress and economic advance. To tackle these problems the Indian communities will need extensive resources, both human and economic. The federal government's proposal to transfer all services to provincial governments does not solve anything. This changes nothing; it leaves the Indian in the same bogged-down bureaucratic predicament. Attempts to solve his social problems will still be initiated by people from the outside who know little and understand less of the Indian. It is true that the provincial governments can play a useful role in providing support services to Indian communities, but first there must be created, within the communities, structures that attack the problems at their source. Ideally, most of the services within a community should be provided by the community itself. Before this can happen, huge sums of money must be provided, aimed at community problems. No outside bureaucracy, whether in Ottawa or in a provincial capital, is flexible enough either to meet the problems head-on, or better yet, attack the causes. Before the local communities can take over such responsibility, skilled, highly trained leadership at the local level must be found. Once again, that premises educational institutions geared to the needs of the Indian and controlled by the Indian.

Service and support structures in the social field — recreation, welfare, special education programs, community development and law and order — must be set up in every community. Creation of a provincial Indian police force, trained and equipped to handle problems in any community, should be supervised by provincial organizations. It seems reasonable to think that once an environment of self-reliance and independence exists, activities in which non-Indians can participate will develop naturally. From that foundation could grow cooperative ventures, both social and economic, which could help bring the races together, eliminating or dissipating to a large degree much existing bigotry. Racial cooperation is a two-way street. So far only the Indian has been expected to come the extra mile.

The Indian peoples of Canada are just beginning to be aware of the broad implications of economic development. Any progress to be made must be bolstered by basic sound economic programs. For the first time the Indian peoples are beginning to realize that this means more than isolated, make-do farming, fishing, trapping or lumbering. Huge sums of money are needed to enable Indian groups to take advantage of economic development opportunities on our own reserves.

An economic development corporation, funded by both national and provincial levels of government, should be founded in each province. Qualified Indians must have control of such fund resources to enable them to finance the necessary programs at the community level. Such development corporation funds would initiate research into the economic potential of every reserve, then get the necessary development programs underway.

To handle properly matters like these, Indians must have the resources to hire the best brains in the country as consultants. Voluntary workers are not trained for such work. Indians will gain from the psychological advantage of knowing that such hired consultants are their employees, that they do not come as civil servants who in the process enslave the Indian. The Indian Association of Alberta, in preparing its policy paper in answer to the federal government's white paper, will go into detail in this area. For the purpose of this book it is sufficient to say that the subservient role of the Indian is fast drawing to a close.

I have dealt briefly with four areas in which I believe, given the opportunity, the Indian can more than fulfill his responsibilities to our country. There exists a belief among our people that we were given this country to share with all peoples and to ensure that its natural resources are used for the good of mankind. There exists also among the older generation of our people the feeling that the ancestors of the white people who came to our country came as human beings who were able to accept the Indians as human beings. Our elders believe that the process of time and a changing world has caused the descendants of those first white people to grow less sensitive toward the Indian and, for that matter, less sensitive toward any human being.

Our older people think that it is part of the responsibility of the Indian to help the white man regain his lost sense of humanity. I believe that the Indian people are not afraid of responsibility; in fact, they welcome the chance to play a new role in contemporary times. This can happen only if the rights of the Indian people are honoured, their dignity respected.

I have outlined some of what must happen if the Indian is to realize his potential and take part in today's world. We have seen what frustration, deprivation and misery can lead to in the United States and throughout the world. The young generation that is even now flexing its muscles does not have the patience that older leaders have shown. If the present leadership is unable to come to terms with the non-Indian society, unable to win respect for Indian rights and dignity, then the younger generation will have no reason to believe that the existing democratic political system has much meaning for them. They will not believe that the present system can work to change our situation. They will organize and organize well. But, driven by frustration and hostility, they will organize not to create a better society but to destroy your society, which they feel is destroying our people. This is the choice before the Indian; this is the fork in the road that the government and non-Indian society must recognize.

Controlling our choice of a path — the realization of the full potential of the Indian people, or despair, hostility and destruction — is our belief that the Indian must be an Indian. He cannot realize his potential as a brown white man. Only by being an Indian, by being simply what he is, can he ever be at peace with himself or open to others.

The present course of the federal government drives the Indian daily closer and closer to the second alternative — despair, hostility, destruction.

10
Metis of the Far North*

Richard Slobodin

Metis is the name given those born from the intermarriage of European (primarily French-Canadian) and native people (most usually Cree Indian). The Metis, unlike others of mixed racial ancestry in Canada, once constituted a viable cultural and political force on the Prairies. In the course of attempting to secure political legitimacy for the Metis Nation, their leader, Louis Riel was martyred.

Although Riel since has been exonerated and exalted to the status of a Canadian folk hero, his people are still a stigmatized group. Richard Slobodin reports some change for the better in the status of the Metis in the far North. Here the status of the Metis is higher than in the provinces because the frontier Metis is respected for his skill in coping with his natural environment. As the acculturation process in the North continues, many new Metis will be created. In the words of one Canadian in the North, "it looks like everyone is becoming Metis."

The Metis in the prairie provinces, on the other hand, is the classic example of the "marginal man". He is marginal to both white and native society being accepted fully in neither. The Metis is barred from participation in White Anglo-Saxon Protestant society, but at the same time is denied the protection and benefits to which treaty Indians are entitled. Consequently, Metis communities tend to be socially disorganized and behaviourally deviant from the norms of the larger society.

INTRODUCTION

The word *métis* is a French cognate of the Spanish *mestizo*, "mixed." It is a fact that Metis are for the most part of both aboriginal American and of non-aboriginal ancestry, bearing a culture — or elements of culture — of European and native American derivation. For a

*Excerpts from Chapter VIII, "External Relations" and Chapter IX, "Metis Identity", from *Metis of the Mackenzie District*, by Richard Slobodin. Reprinted by permission of the Canadian Research Centre for Anthropology, 1966). Selected by the author with an Introduction written for this volume.

number of reasons, however, this statement, although true, is a considerable oversimplification. The definitive characteristic of Metis is a distinctive range of statuses not to be found in aboriginal societies or in the central structure of Canadian society. These statuses may be occupied by persons of entirely aboriginal or of European ancestry; it is also true that persons of "mixed" ancestry may be Indian, Eskimo or generalized Canadian in status or culture. In fact it is well known that most North American Indians are of mixed ancestry; this in itself does not make them Metis.

"The Metis might be called the offspring of the Canadian fur trade," W.L. Morton has remarked (1966:53). Although Metis have engaged in a very wide range of occupations, most characteristically they have been employed in the transport aspect of the fur trade, as canoemen, bateaumen, york boat men, dog drivers, trail breakers or "forerunners", and in modern times, as pilots and crew of steam- and motor-driven vessels on the inland waterways. Some are now pilots and mechanics of bush planes. In their most famous manifestation, as members of *la nation métisse* under Riel in the old Northwest, the basis of their economy was the procurement and supply of buffalo meat for the fur trade. Although most Metis have done some hunting and trapping, only a minority have subsisted as commercial trappers.

Whatever their occupation, Metis have characteristically been people of the frontier, and as the frontier has passed, the Metis way of life and identity has declined. The strains induced by this impending decline led to the Northwest Insurrections of 1870 and 1885, followed by a long-standing depression in Metis economy and polity in the northern prairie provinces.

In the Northwest Territories, the recent history of Metis and, therefore, the nature of Metis identity has been different, than it has been in the prairie provinces. There is a marked cultural distinction between the Metis in the southern half of the Mackenzie District, heirs of the Rid River tradition, and the "mixed" population residing north of Fort Simpson, N.W.T., for the most part descendants of recent miscegenation. These people are often called "halfbreeds", a term which is inaccurate and pejorative. In the study excerpted here, they are termed Northern Metis.

The author of this study thinks it likely that another difference between Metis in the provinces and in the Mackenzie District is that for the latter population, the rapid changes in the past quarter-century, marking the all-but final extinction of frontier conditions and frontier society in the District, have not resulted in chronic depression and decline for the Metis. Rather, the Mackenzie Metis are emerging as the core of a regional proletariat, a mass of industrial and semi-industrial workers with a peculiar style of life and outlook, to which are being added on the one hand Eurocanadian immigrant workers, and on the other, partially-urbanized Eskimos and Indians.

There is considerable literature on the Canadian Metis, most of it concerned with the causes and the political effects of the Northwest

Insurrections, Louis Riel (1844-1885) is now regarded by many as the founder of Manitoba, and, with Gabriel Dumont, (1838-1906), as an authentic Canadian hero. Most of the work on Metis focusses upon the significance of this people, or population sector, for Canadian society at large. There is little on Metis history as such, and even less on Metis society and culture, insofar as these have been differentiated from regional Canadian Society. Notable exceptions are the works of Howard (1952) and Giraud (1945), which deal with Red River Metis of the recent and the remoter past. There are also several specialized sociological studies of high quality, such as that of Lagassé and associates for the Metis of Manitoba (1959), and that of Card, Hirabayashi, and French for Alberta (1963).

If there has been little study of Metis as such, there has been almost no work on the "halfbreed" descendants of recent miscegenation. Although ubiquitous in the northern parts of the provinces, the Mackenzie District, N.W.T., and the Yukon Territory, the "mixed" population has been until recently a little-understood people.

I. THE METIS' EXTERNAL RELATIONS

Social Problems

To many observers, the Metis seem to be a plexus of social problems, a collection of "deviants". It is strikingly true that most northern Canadians of indigenous background have graduated — if that is the correct term — from independent marginal subsistence economies to poverty in the terms of our society. Ethnographies describing the present situation of northern peoples are likely to scant such time-honoured rubrics as "Material Culture" and "Ceremonial Life" in favour of "Dependency" and "Drinking Behaviour." It is also true that the Metis have not constituted an independent society — except briefly and partially, as a "nation" in the Old Northwest — but have comprised, rather, a rural, or at any rate a backwoods proletariat. Nevertheless, the most valid basis for an initial study of the Mackenzie District Metis lies within the tradition of social and cultural anthropology: consideration of them as humans who have worked out and are working out some means of living within the limitations and possibilities of their ecology and their culture.

As has been mentioned, the opinions of Metis on their own social problems may differ from those of Eurocanadians, and especially from those of Eurocanadians in positions of responsibility and authority. Thus, few Metis would see as a problem in health and welfare the irregular hours of their children for meals, bedtime, etc., whereas White educators and social workers do see it as such. Most Metis families would like to improve their housing, and many have been doing so, but their tolerance for crowding seems far greater than that of White functionaries. It should be remarked, however, that a majority of Metis homes visited were reasonably clean and orderly; some, very much so. Ramshackle, squalid huts and shacks were in a minority, although at Inuvik this was a rather large minority. Some Metis feel that law enforcement agents discriminate against them, whereas it is the opinion of these agents, and of others, that if there is any discrimination in law enforcement, it is in favour of the natives generally.

On the other hand, District Metis and Eurocanadian authorities would probably form a consensus that Metis are under-employed, relatively insecure in employment, and, in a majority of cases, subsisting on a low standard of living. Most would also agree that many Metis, like other northern natives, have a drinking problem.

Conditions of Life, "Deviance", and Law Violation

Almost every person interviewed, whatever his ethnic or other status, referred to drinking as a serious problem. This was as true of men and women known to be heavy drinkers, as it was of police officers and clergymen.

Here is a sampling of Metis comments:

That — that drinking is a big problem. If they have money, they spend it at the bar. Drinking is worse now than it used to be. Used to be, one big bust a year, and that was it ... [Northern Metis man, born 1912].

It's all liquor! Every one that comes in there [the town jail], *it's all liquor. And that's why I figure there's a reason for it. And some of their stories are — like, they didn't know what to do, they didn't know where to turn to, so they feel that after the drunk, they don't have any more worries ...* [Red River Metis woman, a jail matron, born 1920].

Womans, they're worse than men! You take like when they get their Family Allowance, most of these people around here spend their money on liquor. They don't buy nothing for kids. And some people uptown [the Whites], *same thing* [Red River Metis man, born 1895].

Another thing is booze. Seems to be they lose their minds. They's all weak minds for the liquor. Some guy might be a good guy when he's sober; honest. When he's drunk he's complete loss. He hasn't got a mind at all... That's how the crime, everything, comes. Any man who's done the crime, he's always influence by liquor. That liquor's a good thing, one way, if you use it right. But how many can do it? Even the White, they can't do it. Indians worse [Red River Metis man, born 1885].

The solutions offered were many and various. They included total as well as partial prohibition, adherence to a religious faith (especially the Pentecostal; v. Clairmont 1963), the moving of families or groups into the bush to get away from it all, or conversely, gaining experience outside and learning to handle liquor. There were those, especially among Whites not holding responsible positions, who viewed the situation cynically, offering no solution. They professed wry amusement at the spectacle provided by periodic group treks to the post office for Family Allowances and other governmental assistance cheques, thence to grocery stores to cash these — "but taking care not to go to a store where they owe money" — thence to the liquor store and on to an increasingly erratic social round.

A pertinent set of observations on drinking behaviour in the District, and its implications, were proffered by an officer of the Royal Canadian Mounted Police. These were based upon about ten years' experience and a special study of Police records in a number of District communities. The officer's conclusion was that Mackenzie District natives probably do not drink at any greater rate than Whites in the District, and that their actual rate of law violation — as contrasted with their arrest rate — is probably no higher than that of Whites, except in (1) violations arising from the conditions in which the natives drink, and (2) petty crimes against property which stem directly from deprivation. These conclusions were largely corroborated by other experienced law officials.

The Police officer went on to point out how it frequently happened that living conditions, the contrast between those of native and of Whites, militated against the native in terms of law violation.

> *If you or I, or a White family, decide to have a party or some friends in for a drink, we phone the invitations or we ask people at the office... After they've come they may decide to make it a bigger party, phone other people. Maybe some others bring bottles. Some may get pretty plastered, but if anyone gets boisterous, there are always enough people around who retain a consciousness of the consequences and who cope. There will be someone to take the drunks home in a car.*
>
> *If an Indian or a Metis gets hold of a bottle, maybe he calls out to a friend, or someone wanders into his house in the usual visiting pattern, or they meet on the street and decide to go to one of their homes. Pretty soon they think it would be fine to have Joe join them. But they can't phone Joe, because they have no phone. They can't drive to Joe's house, because they have no car. So they walk over to Joe's. After a while the trio go to someone else's house to get him into the party. After two, three or four such moves, most of them are plastered. If they would stay in someone's house and keep relatively quiet, they would be violating no law and would get into no trouble. But by the nature of the case they will be going from house to house; they will get into the road. They will think less of the consequences, because they are not used to thinking of consequences*

in the same way we do — but that doesn't make them criminals, in itself. Pretty soon some of them are picked up by a patrol car, or on a complaint — 'intoxicated in a public place.'

Liquor violations are by far the most common Police charges in District communities. The records of the Fort Smith Police court show 199 convictions on liquor violation charges in 1962, of which 145 were for being "intoxicated in a public place". Of those convicted on this charge, eighty-one were "White", including Metis, and sixty-four Treaty Indian. Officials estimated that at least eighty per cent of the "Whites", i.e., non-Treaties, so charged were Metis. The approximate ethnic group composition of the Fort Smith population in 1962-63 was: White: 525; Metis: 900; Indian 250. When it is considered that convictions on liquor violation charges run to less than two-thirds of the arrests, the arrest-rate on this type of charge is seen to be high.

The Police officer whose comments on liquor violations have been cited went on to say that arrests on other charges are also related to differences between native and White ways of life.

Take 'breaking-entry-theft': among the natives, visiting informally back and forth, wandering in and out of each other's homes, is taken as a matter of course. Among middle-class Whites this is not done. Anyway, the Indians have no locks on their doors, or don't keep homes locked, as rule. Someone comes in, finds the owners away, and is exposed to temptation, to which, once in a while, someone succumbs. The Whites are not exposed to this kind of temptation. Under law, entering a structure without the owner's or manager's consent, followed by theft, constitutes an offense which carries a heavier penalty than plain theft. . .

Then, part of it is a sheer sort of reaction to poverty and deprivation. Kids steal candy, toys, cigarettes from stores. Girls steal cosmetics. Actually there is less of this than one might expect. But the Whites, not being deprived and having more to lose status-wise from an arrest, seldom do this. . . Occasionally White juveniles do, of course.
Another officer added:

If a police officer comes up to a tipsy-looking White man outside the beer parlour and suggest he go home, the White man will go home without question. A native fellow is as likely as not to say, '———— you, policeman!' or to sneak back into the beer parlour as soon as the policeman's back is turned. . . The first kind of reaction is an expression of his general hostility and frustration, which comes out when he's been drinking. The second is partly because he doesn't want to go to his home. His home may be dreary, miserable place from which he escapes to have some 'fun'.

The Rationalization of Interpersonal Relations

The North has been and remains a region where primary inter-personal relationships are pervasive and widespread. It is also true that since the earliest advent on the northern scene of the agents of Eurocanadian society, the sources of their power and authority, and to a large extent the ultimate ends for which these have been exercised, have been remote from the experience of northern peoples. These two general conditions, of which the former may be said to characterize "personal" relationships and the latter, "impersonal" ones, have not changed markedly. What have changed in the past half-century, and most rapidly in the past two decades, are:

1. the number and the variety of Eurocanadian agents in the North;
2. the rate of personnel turnover among them; and
3. the volume of travel and communication between the North and the Outside.

All of these have increased enormously.

In the mission and monopoly fur trade regime, the northern natives came into contact with Western Civilization along a narrow and rigidly demarcated front. The ramification within Western society of the institutions represented in the North were little understood; even the day-to-day functions of missionary, trader, and later, policeman, were based upon assumptions quite exotic to the northern people. However, a working rationale was developed. As most of these agents remained for many years in a locality, they won acceptance, more or less, as human beings and as embodiments of a superordinate power which came to be taken for granted. Moreover, the exertion of power and influence was by no means uni-directional. The northern communities also had power, on the local level; this was exerted sometimes through leaders, sometimes through diffuse public opinion and the continuing vigour of traditional interaction patterns. In the closing years of "the old days", prior to World War II, it was still possible to observe how veteran Eurocanadian functionaries had adapted attitudes and behaviour to local conditions. Indigenous cultures had affected the Eurocanadians, sometimes in ways of which they were unaware.

As has been pointed out, the Metis were products of Euro-canadian contact with the North, and characteristically were in the employ of Eurocanadian agencies. This employment was in a sense "impersonal"; but there did develop a client-patron relationship between the Metis and the White agents which was in many instances reinforced by bonds of kinship. It is the passing of this "personal" aspect of Metis employment in the older scheme of things that lies behind the bitterness, the sense almost of betrayal, felt by older Metis who in recent years have lost employment or failed of promotion in retail trade.

The three recent changes in the instrumentation of Eurocanadian authority in the North — increase in the number and variety of agents, in their rate of turnover, and in the volume of travel and communication between the District and the south — have all enhanced a "rationalization" of the interaction between northern residents and representatives of the larger society. "Rationalization" in this context means a tendency toward the limitation of interaction to institutional terms of reference: vendor-purchaser, doctor-patient, clergyman-communicant, welfare worker-client, law agent-citizen (or offender). This tendency is, of course, in keeping with that of urban social life, wherein it is far more advanced. No one, native or non-native, who knew the North prior to the recent effect of these changes, fails to deplore the changes. This is how it feels to a Red River Metis, born in 1911:

> *Then you know, there's another thing that bothers a guy. Guys been in the country all their lives, you know, like — sort of built up the country — they're the ones that were here when things were tough — they're being pushed to one side. A fellow don't even feel at home in his own country any more. You know all these other people, they run around like they sort of own it. Makes a man feel like maybe he should move and let them take it over. You know, when things were tough here, why, it was different. They wouldn't have come. They didn't know about it then.*

Another Red River Metis, born in 1915, echoed this sentiment:

> *... This country isn't as good as it used to be. It was more like ours before. Now we feel kind of pushed to the side. It used to be, the White people that did come down here, they had to get here the hard way. There weren't many of them, and they mostly stayed. They became part of the country, too. Now — I don't know who they are. They come and go all the time. . . . Like I say, we feel pushed to the side. It's not a very nice feeling.*

Old-timers among White functionaries complain of what an official of the Anglican Church, long resident in the District, half-humourously called "the curse" of modern communications and travel facilities. "It used to be," this clergyman recalled, "that when the last boat had left, you were left in peace with your people for a year. . . ." A Federal official, also an old-timer in the District, wryly regretted that telephone service had reached his area. Others expressed similar sentiments. These men are quite aware of the neglect suffered by the Northwest Territories in the past. What they now miss is, in part, the security experienced no matter how difficult the physical conditions, in a relatively stable situation, largely under local control and dominated by primary relationships and by considerations apparent and familiar to the people on the spot.

Leadership and Marginality

Developments in the North during recent decades have altered the position of all northern residents in relation to external authority. The position of Metis has changed rather differently from that of Indians and Eskimos. Part of the difference derives directly from legal and administrative organization; i.e., that most Metis are classed as "Other", or "White." It may be more properly said that the legal-administrative classification of most Metis expresses a difference between the status, *vis-à-vis* other ethnic groups, of Metis and that of Indians and Eskimos.

Early in the study it was pointed out that "mixed" populations are generally regarded as socially and culturally marginal, but that any conclusion as to the relevance of this concept for a description of the Mackenzie District Metis should await the evidence. Enough has been presented by now, it is felt, to warrant the observation that in one respect at least, the Mackenzie Metis are marginal. This is, quite, expectably, in the area of their relationship to other ethnic groups and sectors of the general population.

Like other human groups, that of the Metis, in each locality and regionally, has an internal structure. We have noted such systems of alignment as the nuclear family, the extended family, the cluster of families, personal kindreds; and also the communications networks and surname-groups, which might be termed systems of organization, rather than of structure (Firth 1956a: 35-38). Other northern ethnic communities, bands, and population sectors have their more or less distinct internal systems. Human groups must also have external systems, that is, principles for organization of behaviour in terms of the human ecology in which the group exists[1]. Other northern ethnic groups have had distinct external systems. Some still do have; for others, any distinctive external system is now vestigial. It is by no means clear that the Mackenzie Metis have ever had a distinctive external system, although some parts of the Metis population may have had one. At any rate, in recent generations, the Mackenzie Metis seem to have had none, or almost none. This means, among other things, that the external relations of this ethnic group, i.e., its means for dealing with non-Metis, have been through the institutions of the tangential societies. To oversimplify a little, when Metis have dealt with Indians, it has been as Indians; with Whites, as Whites. Since Metis by definition are neither Indians nor Whites, Metis functioning in this area have been marginal Indians and marginal Whites.

The implication of this is that there have been no Mackenzie Metis leaders, as such, confronting the non-Metis world. There have certainly been Metis leaders in other times and places; the names of Riel and Dumont, among others, are part of Canadian history. If the legend of "King" Beaulieu may be credited there were Red River Metis leaders in the Slave drainage a century ago. The existence of these leaders implies that the Metis, or some segment of Metis population, constituted at the time a sufficiently distinct society. This has not been true of the Mackenzie Metis in recent generations; of the Northern Metis, it has never been true.

This does not mean that there has been no leadership within the Metis internal system; there has been and there still is. Nor does it mean that there have been no Metis men of influence, or Metis with leadership potential; but personal qualities of leadership, and the influence which may derive from them, do not in themselves constitute leadership. Leadership is taken here to mean the effective exercise of power through sanctions[2]. Its prerequisite is a source of power, and a means for its channeling, in the independent and distinctive institutions of a group, community, or society. There have been Mackenzie Metis who have exercised leadership in some aspect of an Indian social system. Other Mackenzie Metis have occupied positions of authority and possibly of real leadership in Eurocanadian institutions represented in the District. In so functioning, these men have been on the one hand Indian leaders, on the other hand, Eurocanadian leaders who were Metis. They have not been leaders of the Metis.

To this lack of Metis leadership in external relations there is an instructive exception: the situation at Fort Resolution. This population was unique among Metis of the communities visited for its marked extended-family organization. Strong extended-family loyalties sharply segment the community. With all of the factionalism at Fort Resolution, it is only here, of Mackenzie District communities known to me, that consistent leadership in confrontation with non-Metis can be discerned. Each of the four major extended families has a recognized head, and one of the two minor groups is led by a pair of brothers. These men are the Metis community's leaders. They frequently disagree and quarrel; they compete for authority within the Metis community and for advantage in relation to tangent groups and institutions: the local Indians, the local Whites, the agencies of Federal government and the agencies of the Roman Catholic Church. Nevertheless, they are there. At Fort Resolution, a non-Metis knows precisely with whom to deal when he has to do with Metis. The process of dealing may be, and often is, frustrating

---

[1] The internal and external systems of human groups are discussed by Homans (1950: chapters, 4, 5), Nadal (1953:168 ff), and others. The social psychologist J.F. Brown posited such a dichotomy some years ago (1936:76 ff).

[2] I am indebted to Dr. Rusiate R. Nayacakalou, University of Sydney, for the theoretical discussion in his unpublished doctoral disseration (London School of Economics) on Fijian authority and leadership. Dr. Nayacakalou examines American sociological concepts of leadership, especially as embodied in small-group theory, and is forced to reject such ideas as influence, task and group-orientation, sociometric measures, and personality factors as inadequate to an understanding of leadership. He urges a power-theory. This conforms with and helps to explain my own ethnographic experience.

and exasperating to the non-Metis, but the point relevant here is that the process is different in kind than those involved in relations between Metis and non-Metis at other localities in the District.

In towns other than Fort Resolution, even in those with large Metis populations such as Fort Smith, the terms of such relationships are with Metis as individuals or families. Only in a fugitive, partial, and sporadic sense are these relationships perceived as being with Metis as such. In short, there are in these communities no structured relations between Metis and non-Metis.

At Fort Resolution there exist three conditions relevant to Metis external relations: 1. a majority of the Metis population is organized in semi-corporate kinship groupings; 2. the leaders of these groupings in internal affairs are also leaders in external relations; 3. the Metis sector of the town's population has definite boundaries, an identity as a community within the larger plural community. It is suggested that there is a causal relation between these conditions, in the order stated. None of these conditions prevail in any other District community known to me.

II. METIS IDENTITY

Self-Identification

It was noted that of the 124 known Metis applicants for commercial fishing licenses at Hay River, 1959-63, 109 entered a "racial origin" of Metis, in some form or other, on the applications. Fifteen of the known Metis gave a European "racial origin".

It may be added that some Metis were among the thirty-three applicants with blank or illegible entries under "racial origin." The total of these could not be known, since it was impossible to determine the ethnic affiliation or identity, by criteria other than self-identification, of many applicants from outside the Mackenzie District.

It is hypothesized that a higher proportion of Mackenzie District Metis than of total Metis applicants gave their "origin" as other than Metis. The reasoning is thus; all known or self-identified Metis applicants from outside the District were from the prairie provinces, where there are many centers of Metis activism, Metis social, economic, and political organization. The Metis "Nation" is a meaningful symbol to many. Hence there would be a greater consensus on Metis self-identification in those provinces than in the Mackenzie District, where these conditions obtain not at all or in much smaller degree. Since it was impossible to interview or otherwise obtain personal information on most prairie province applicants, this hypothesis could not be fully verified. However, it was possible to analyse the self-identification of Metis applicants born in the District, and of those resident therein since 1959, as these persons could be identified by other criteria. The results of such analysis in Table 1 are suggestive.

TABLE 1

Self-Identification of Mackenzie Metis Applicants for Commercial Fishing Licenses At Hay River, 1959-63

Entries under "Racial Origin".	Born and presently resident in Mackenzie District.	Resident in Mackenzie District since 1959.	
I. METIS			
"Cree halfbreed"	1	—	
"Halfbreed"	1	2	
"Metis"	3	11	
"Non-treaty Indian"	1	—	
"Native (non-treaty)"	1	—	
Total self-identified as Metis			20
II. OTHER			
"Canadian"	2	5	
"French"	1	3*	
"French-Canadian"	1	—	
"Scotch"	1	—	
Blank entry	3	1	
Total not self-identified as Metis			17
Total known Mackenzie Metis applicants			37

*In one of these cases, "Metis" was entered, crossed out, and "French" written above.

It should be emphasized that prevarication or misrepresentation on the part of Metis fishing license applicants is not an issue. A Metis is justified in identifying himself as of Canadian, or for that matter, of European "racial origin." Moreover, such an entry does not mean that the applicant fails to consider himself a Metis. He may feel that his "racial origin," matter of history, is different from what he is, right now. As a matter of fact every one of the thirty-seven applicants involved in Table 1 considers himself to be a Metis; of this there is evidence either direct: information provided by the applicant; or indirect: information provided by a close kinsman or from long-term observation of the applicant. One of the criteria of Metis identity employed in this study is self-identification as a Metis.

Although all Metis are by definition persons who consider themselves Metis, this does not mean that all Metis call themselves "Metis," or any equivalent thereof, under all circumstances. It is not without significance that seventeen out of thirty-seven, or forty-six per cent of the Mackenzie Metis applicants failed to enter "Metis" or some similar response under this heading.

During extensive conversations, awareness of being a Metis is likely to be expressed at some point. This is relatively easy for a Red River Metis, since he has available the term "Metis", legitimized by a long history, value-neutral at the least, and in some contexts honorific. The Northern Metis is in a more difficult position in self-identification; "Metis" is not common parlance north of Fort Simpson, and 'halfbreed' is a term that Northern Metis avoid. It is interesting that Red River Metis not uncommonly refer to themselves as "breed" and "halfbreed" without apparent strain or pain. Most commonly, a Northern Metis will signalize his self-identification by referring to "the Whites" and "the natives" in contexts where it is clear he is excluding himself. Such contexts do not necessarily occur in daily discourse; hence verbal self-identification as Metis comes less readily from Northern Metis than from Red River people. This difference in facility of verbal self-identification — the fact that the Red River people have an acceptable term for ethnic identification which the Northern Metis lack — is not mere chance. It derives from historical and sociocultural differences between the two sub-groupings.

There are, of course, non-verbal means of signalizing self-identification; e.g., interaction preferences within the community, participation in communication networks. Northern Metis appear to use these as readily as do Red River Metis.

A Metis, Red River or Northern, may speak of "the natives" or "the Indians" or "the Huskies" in tones ranging from cynical scorn to frank admiration.

Nevertheless, Metis do on occasion identify themselves with "natives." Those who do so most readily are people of the Mackenzie Delta and adjacent coastal region and of Sachs Harbor, Banks Island, who are of Eskimo-European and Eskimo-Indian-European ancestry. As might be expected, Metis are most likely to make such identification when confronted by a situation whose foreignness minimizes the contrast between themselves and the Eskimos/Indians and which emphasizes their common allegiances, interests, and understandings. Thus the Northern Metis woman who was moved to remark that "next to Eskimo or White people. I am an Indian". Similarly a youth of European-Eskimo descent, in a discussion of Great Slave Lake Indians and Metis, remarked upon their differences from "us Huskies." A Red River Metis civil servant, trained in a technical school "Outside", described his astonishment at the ignorance concerning the North that he encountered among southern Canadians. "At a party in Calgary, some girls asked me if there were many Indians where I lived. I said to them, 'You're looking at an Indian right now'."

Regional-historical Variation

Some of the older Red River Metis report family traditions deriving from the Metis "Nation". Several told of kinsmen who had taken part in the Northwest Insurrections. There are two Red River Metis men in the Slave drainage, of whom the Metis paternal grandfather of one killed the Irish paternal grandfather of the other, who was with Belcher's force at the battle of Cut Knife. They have discussed the affair together. In his youth, the Irishman's grandson met his grandfather's killer. "He said my grand-dad must have been pretty tough. He had four or five balls in him. But he got one in the heart. That finished him."

Mention has been made of the traditions about eponyms of the Red River surname-groups, especially those concerning "King" Beaulieu. There is also a tradition, related by several people of Beaulieu and Mandeville ancestry, that at some indefinite period in the early nineteenth century these Metis name-groups each constituted a "tribe". As one informant told the story:

These Beaulieus and Mandevilles — there may have been other bunches, but I don't know — they each had a sort of headquarter. The Beaulieus were on the Salt River and the Mandevilles on the south shore of the Lake [Great Slave] near Buffalo River . . . Then they would pack up, the whole bunch, men, women and children, and go on down the Mackenzie and turn up, maybe up the Liard, trading, hunting, on a great big circuit, on into northern B.C. Then over the Athabasca and back down to the Slave . . . No, no, they couldn't do it in one season. They'd be gone for three, four, five years. They lived in the bush, like the Indians; only they kept going more, and they kept trading . . . They were a tribe.

By contrast, the Northern Metis have little tradition appertaining specifically to their Metis status. This is in keeping with the shorter family lines since the original miscegenation, and the shallower genealogies of Northern as compared with Red River Metis in the District. Northern Metis traditions are primarily traditions of the Hudson's Bay Company in the lower Mackenzie. Reference here, as in the discussion of Red River Metis tradition, is to the generations now elderly, or deceased within the past twenty years, and apparently to the generations immediately preceding them. Among the Northern Metis, most persons of this age-range are the offspring of grandchildren of White men who were in Hudson's Bay Company employ during "the Old Days" of the monopoly fur trade. Among Red River Metis there exist attenuated traditions of the warfare between the Hudson's Bay Company and the Northwest Company, in which these Metis played a conspicuous and, at times, semi-independent role.

TABLE 2

Differences Between Red River and Northern Metis

Red River Metis	Northern Metis
Descendants of remote miscegenation.	Descendants of relatively recent miscegenation.
European ancestry: predominantly French (Canadian) or gallicized Scotch or Irish.	European ancestry: predominantly Scotch, secondarily Scandinavian, English.
American ancestry: predominantly Algonkian (Cree, Ojibwa or Saulteaux), Iroquoian (Six Nations), or Athapaskan of the Slave region (Chipewyan, Slave Dogrib).	American ancestry: predominantly Athapaskan of the lower Mackenzie and middle Yukon regions (Bear Lake, Hare, Kutchin, some Dogrib), or Western Eskimo.
Predominantly and traditionally Roman Catholic.	Predominantly and traditionally Anglican (European ancestors often Presbyterian or Lutheran); secondarily Roman Catholic.
Possessing autonomous Metis traditions stemming from (a) old Upper Canada; (b) the Metis "nation" of the old North-West; (c) the voyageur way of life.	Possessing little autonomous Metis tradition. Traditions are those of (a) the Hudson's Bay Company in the northern Mackenzie District; (b) the aboriginal society to which they are related.
Recognizing few European or Indian kin.	Recognizing an appreciable number of Indian, Eskimo, and White kin.
Surname — groups large, diffuse, genealogically deeper than those of Northern Metis.	Surname — groups smaller, more cohesive, genealogically shallower than those of Red River Metis.
In terms of residence and employment, the most mobile sector of the District population.	Less mobile than Red River Metis but more so, on the whole, than Indians, Eskimos, and most Whites.
Although individual employment histories extremely varied, as a group traditionally and still largely associated with transport.	Traditionally associated with fur-trade employ, but not particularly with transport.
Independence and the satisfaction of impulse highly valued. Validation through identification with Metis tradition.	Authority and hierarchy valued. Validation either through (a) identification with White father and Eurocanadian power institutions, or (b) prestige and leadership among aboriginal congeners.

Among Northern Metis, however, there are no historical traditions reaching back in time beyond the Hudson's Bay Company monopoly trade.

Some of the major social and cultural distinctions between the Red River and the Northern Metis in the Mackenzie District are schematically summarized to the left.

Variation of Orientation

The second principal type of variation among Mackenzie Metis as a whole has to do, more directly than does regional-historical variation, with ecology and with tangential cultures, and the influence of these upon life-styles and goals of Metis individuals and families. It has been noted that some Metis live more like Indians and Eskimos, and share Indian or Eskimo attitudes and aspirations more fully than do most of their fellows; while others are closer in these respects to Whites in the North. These distinctions are sometimes seen as evidence of acculturation, sometimes as characterizing social strata or even classes among the Metis.

The Metis are themselves both products and agents of acculturation. They have existed at the frontiers of tangential societies. It is true that some individuals and families have penetrated further into one or another of the societies to which the Metis are marginal, but to view this process as acculturation poses more problems than it helps to clarify. If they are viewed as undergoing acculturation, one may wonder what the cultural base is from which this process has been occurring; for Metis culture, insofar as it is distinctive, is itself a phenomenon of acculturation. As applied to the Mackenzie Metis, the concept of acculturation is too general to serve as an analytical tool. Almost everything about these people is acculturative.

Similarly there is difficulty for this writer with the concept of social stratum as applied to the Mackenzie Metis. By any acceptable definition of social class, no such thing exists among the Mackenzie Metis. Ranking of individuals and families certainly exists, as it did or does in some degree among all aboriginal Mackenzie District peoples. There are, however, no groups or sectors of the Metis population which possess differential prestige, power, or access to limited resources.

There do exist among the Mackenzie Metis differences in lifestyle along a "bush-urban" or "native-White man" axis, but this system of variation cannot be easily applied to Metis realities. Several factors complicate the picture.

1. In the Mackenzie District and much of the western Arctic, "bush" economy and way of life is quite different from aboriginal economies and cultures at the time of Euro-Canadian contact. It would appear that few observers, other than those with a special interest in northern social history, bear in mind that a half-century ago, a date which is certainly "old" to most people talking about the

North, aboriginal conditions had disappeared for most natives of the Arctic and Subarctic. As Diamond Jenness describes it for the Canadian Eskimos:

> By this period — the end of the second decade of the twentieth century — first the whalers, then the traders and the missionaries, had completely shattered the ancient Eskimo culture over most of the Eastern and Western Arctic, and were launching an assault on the still primitive central region . . . The inherited lore of centuries was fading, and the younger generation of natives neither valued the knowledge and skills of their forefathers nor cherished any desire to cling to the old ways . . . What was past was past and could never return. For good or ill their lot was now cast with the white man's . . . So from November until March most Eskimos abandoned the hunting of seals at their breathing-holes on the sea ice, renounced the comfort and support of their relatives and friends and the amenities of village life, and spent their days in the solitude of their individual trapping cabins and tents. It was sheer economic need that drove them into this new occupation, an occupation that was changing the whole pattern of their lives [1964:25]

For Indians of the District, analogous economic and other sociocultural changes had occurred at earlier periods, from the eighteenth century onwards. Even among the Kutchin, a people who experienced the establishment of the mission-fur trade regime much more recently than did the southern District Indians, over a quarter-century ago there were only a few people who had any notion, other than mythological, of conditions and events prior to the advent of the European fur trade. Yet the "old days" — for the eastern Kutchin, the period from 1840 until 1888 — was predicated upon and witnessed significant change ensuing from culture contact[3].

2. It follows from this that the "bush" way of life involves a great deal that is "the White man's, or, to put it more precisely, that is derived from urban industrial and commercial centres. In technology alone, a successful and conscientious trapper may have the latest model firearms, boat engine, and other gear. A town-dwelling northerner, who does not depend upon such equipment for his livelihood, may have older and less efficient gear. During and for a few years after World War II, when fine fur prices were high, several lower Mackenzie Indian, Eskimos, and Metis trappers had substantial bank accounts and extensive dealings with fur auction firms and supply houses in Edmonton, Vancouver, and Seattle. I do not know of any native wage employees with similar financial involvements and interests during the period. Who were the more acculturated? There is no question as to who occupied the higher rank and enjoyed higher prestige; the successful trappers did so.

The concept of orientation, in terms of ideals, goals, and lifestyle, while not without its difficulties of application to the Mackenzie

Metis, appears to be an applicable operational tool. If we may use the terms "bush" and "urban" as convenient shorthand for two poles or orientation, a man like Jock Sutherland is bush-oriented, with all his skill in Eurocanadian technology and business methods. A man such as Paul Menard, an electrician trained at a technical institute, is urban-oriented, with all his interest in Red River Metis traditions and folk music, his zest and skill in minor trapping and in hunting. Sutherland uses his Eurocanadian skills, with others adapted from Indian culture, in order to subsist within the ecology, reaping its renewable resources. His home is the habitat of his maternal ancestors; his working and community relationship with his maternal Indian kin is as close as that of a Northern Metis may be. Menard uses his knowledge of and interest in traditional Red River Metis and also Indian pursuits and pastimes as an embellishment of a life which is essentially that of a skilled workingman, within the peculiar circumstances of a Metis in the North.

A majority of Metis, Northern and Red River, cannot be easily classified in terms of these polar orientations. On a bush-urban axis of orientation, the Mackenzie Metis would fall approximately along a curve of normal distribution. This is illustrated by the relative variety of Metis occupational pursuits, both as individuals and as a population sector. On a scale of the variation in the total northern population, including Eskimos, Indians, and Whites, the majority of Metis are neither strikingly bush-oriented nor strikingly urban-oriented. This majority of Mackenzie Metis evidences another sort of orientation. For convenience it may be called "regional" orientation. The term "regional" is used here in approximately the sense employed in some humanistic, sociological, and geographical studies, wherein a nation may be described in terms of definable regions; there are regional dialects, regional art, regional human ecologies. In this sense, the Western Subarctic, within which most Mackenzie District Metis reside, is a region of Canada; the Mackenzie Metis are and long have been its characteristic people *par excellence*. Members of particular Indian and Eskimo tribes, bands, or local groups have been identified with particular sub-regions far more intimately than have most Metis; some of these areas are quite extensive, but they do not comprise the region as a whole. Although there are widespread uniformities in indigenous cultures, subregional particularisms are much more manifest in them than in the Metis way of life. Insofar as Indians and Eskimos move away from their local and particularistic identities and become relatively indistinguishable from other northern inhabitants, they converge upon the established Metis pattern. The same is true of Whites who, as a result of lengthy residence, type of occupation and social life, including marriage to native women, and other disposing factors, in some degree lose identification with

[3] Slobodin, Richard, "Band Organization of the Peel River Kutchin". *Bulletin 179*, National Museum of Canada. (Ottawa: The Queen's Printer, 1962) .

"Outside" institutions and interests and become, often unwittingly, more closely identified with the North (i.e., the Western Subarctic) than with their regions of origin or with the national life as a whole. They too may be said to have converged upon the Metis pattern, from the other direction, as it were, than that of Indians and Eskimos. The White trappers who flourished in the period from just before World War I until just before World War II were striking exemplars of such convergence, but the process has not ceased with the passing of the old-time White trappers. The White employees of the Engineering Division, NANR, who "have boomed around the North in various jobs are now married to Metis girls and have settled down as property owners". They and their counterparts in other lines of employment show in their domestic lives and manners a good deal of resemblance to the Metis.

More than one White resident of the District to whom the purpose of this study was explained has countered with an observation to the effect that "Hell, everyone is getting to be Metis here." There is truth in such a comment, if "everyone" is taken as excluding the occupational elite among Eurocanadians on the one hand, and the "bush-oriented", "Nunamuit" indigenes on the other. It was remarked earlier that Metis may be seen as constituting from their beginnings a regional proletariat. As other people of various ethnic origins have joined this proletariat, they have taken on in large measure a Metis style of life. At the same times they contribute cultural features, such as work-habits, leisure-time activities and religious preferences which are novel to the region and which are adopted by members of the Metis ethnic group. Whether further convergence will occur between the Metis proper and those who are "getting to be Metis", remains to be seen.

BIBLIOGRAPHY

BROWN, JUNIUS F. *Psychology and The Social Order*. New York: McGraw-Hill, 1936.

CARD, B. Y., G. K. HIRABAYASKI, AND C. L. FRENCH. *The Metis in Alberta Society*. Edmonton: University of Alberta — Committee for Social Research, 1963.

CLAIRMONT, D. H. J. "Deviance Among Indians and Eskimos in Aklavik, N.W.T." *NCRC 63-9*. Northern Co-ordination and Research Centre: Department of Northern Affairs and National Resources, Canada, 1963.

FIRTH, RAYMOND. *Elements of Social Organization*, Second Edition. London: Watts, 1956.

GIRAUD, MARCEL. "Le Metis canadien". *Travaux et Memoires de l'Institut d'Ethnologie, XLIV*. Paris: Institut d'Ethnologie, 1945.

HALLOWELL, A. IRVING. *Culture and Experience*. Philadelphia: University of Pennsylvania Press, 1955.

HOMANS, GEORGE C. *The Human Group*. New York: Harcourt, Brace, 1950.

HOWARD, JOSEPH KINSEY. *Strange Empire*. New York: Morrow, 1952.

JENNESS, DIAMOND. "Eskimo Administration: II. Canada". *Technical Paper No. 14*. Montreal: Arctic Institute of North America, 1964.

LAGASSE, JEAN H. AND ASSOCIATES. *The People of Indian Ancestry in Manitoba*. Winnipeg: Dept. of Agriculture and Immigration, Province of Manitoba, 1959.

MORTON, W. L. "Metis". *Encyclopedia Canadiana, Centennial Edition*. Volume VII. Toronto: Grolier, 1966.

NADEL, S. F. *The Foundations of Social Anthropology*. London: Cohen & West, 1953.

NUTE, GRACE LEE. *The Voyageur*. New York and London: Appleton, 1931.

RALPH, JULIAN. *On Canada's Frontier*. New York: Harper, 1892.

RICH, E. E. ed. *John Rae's Correspondence with the Hudson's Bay Company on Arctic Exploration 1844-1845*. London: The Hudson's Bay Record Society, 1953.

ROSS, ALEXANDER. *The Fur Hunters of the Far West*. 2 Vols., London: Smith, Elder, 1855.

SLOBODIN, RICHARD. "Band Organization of the Peel River Kutchin". *Bulletin 179*, National Museum of Canada. Ottawa: The Queen's Printer, 1960.

SPINDLER, GEORGE D. *Sociocultural and Psychological Processes in Memomini Acculturation*. Publications in Culture and Society, Vol. 5. University of California, 1955.

SPINDLER, LOUISE S. "Menomini Women and Culture Change". *Memoir 91*, American Anthropological Association, 1962.

VALLEE, FRANK. "Sociological Research in The Arctic". *NCRC 62-8*. Northern Co-ordination and Research Centre: Department of Northern Affairs and National Resources, Canada, 1962.

DE RE